THE
SWALLOW'S TALE
— THE EARLY YEARS

Liam O'Conner

BALBOA.
PRESS
A DIVISION OF HAY HOUSE

Balboa Press books may be ordered through booksellers or by contacting:

Balboa Press
A Division of Hay House
1663 Liberty Drive
Bloomington, IN 47403
www.balboapress.com
1 (877) 407-4847

Because of the dynamic nature of the Internet, any web addresses or links contained in this book may have changed since publication and may no longer be valid. The views expressed in this work are solely those of the author and do not necessarily reflect the views of the publisher, and the publisher hereby disclaims any responsibility for them.

The author of this book does not dispense medical advice or prescribe the use of any technique as a form of treatment for physical, emotional, or medical problems without the advice of a physician, either directly or indirectly. The intent of the author is only to offer information of a general nature to help you in your quest for emotional and spiritual well-being. In the event you use any of the information in this book for yourself, which is your constitutional right, the author and the publisher assume no responsibility for your actions.

Any people depicted in stock imagery provided by Thinkstock are models, and such images are being used for illustrative purposes only.
Certain stock imagery © Thinkstock.

Print information available on the last page.

ISBN: 978-1-5043-7054-7 (sc)
ISBN: 978-1-5043-7055-4 (hc)
ISBN: 978-1-5043-7076-9 (e)

Library of Congress Control Number: 2016919727

Balboa Press rev. date: 05/01/2017

Contents

Introduction

Anything, absolutely anything is possible in this life. You imagine it and it can become real and that is how the world has worked from the beginning of time. Prehistoric man would have laughed at you if you told him that one day we would fly the skies and yet this impossible dream started with a thought, an idea and a dream that it could become real. Plans were made and trials failed, new ideas were put forward and some things worked, others didn't. It was not an easy road but the pioneers of flight did not give up. Why? Because it was their passion, it was their belief and it was in the core of their being that they knew this was possible when others laughed at them. These guys had uncluttered minds in that they knew their goal, they knew what the outcome would be and they were not distracted from it. You see, these guys were born with a certain set of talents which was God given and they used it. During the hardest times their passion for what they were doing pulled them through.

The most important thing in this book is to understand that we all have 'genius' within us, we all have our own unique set of talents otherwise we would not be here. The biggest hurdle for most of us is actually identifying that talent, actually realizing what we are passionate about. You would think that would be easy wouldn't you but I am a living example that it is not. I knew I had greatness within me and that is not to sound arrogant or conceited but I have always felt that I had so much to give to the world but I was never sure how, when and by what means. I discovered in my mid-fourties that I was a much more creative and people orientated being than I ever realized. All my life, up until that point I thought I was in a pigeon hole of being just a technical, logical type and that art and creation was beyond my remit this time around. I was wrong because I eventually discovered that I could write and touch people's hearts by being me, talking about my passions, wanting to share with people and make a difference to them and you know what? I created this book. Ten years ago I would have raised a skeptical eyebrow if someone had said I would be an Author. Anything, yes anything is possible.

The biggest thing to stifle our creativity is fear and if we can eliminate fear from our psyche we can uncover what our true potential is in this life, we can unearth our gifts. If we can unearth our gifts and our passions we are half way there to realizing a happy and fulfilled life and we will in turn attract abundance into it. When we make fear based decisions we are at best being safe and sitting on the edge of the river with just our toes dipped in. When we follow our heart and our passion we dive into the river and we flow with it, not against it. We really live and life becomes a glorious Technicolor film where our hearts soar and our head aches with the emotion of crying through happiness. It is as if we have connected ourselves back to source. It is that good; believe me, but the fear that will stifle that freedom must be eliminated. Fear is the huge shadow cast by the tiny statue of reality and when the light of enlightenment shines it quickly disappears.

So my reason for this book is that I want to share my life with you and enable you to realize that no-matter what background you come from, no matter how limited you feel you are as a human being, you can lift your head up, look heavenwards and know that you too can achieve anything, you too can live your dream, you can live in abundant harmony, it is how we were meant to live. Look up and be proud and feel the emotion welling up inside of you when you tell yourself how amazing you are and what an absolutely wonderful gift you are to humanity. I have a story to tell and I wanted to share it with as many people as I could because my life has been an adventure. Initially I was going to write to my family so that in years to come they understood who I was and where they actually came from but It became more than that for me. In my mind it grew into a need to pour out from my heart everything I have learned coming from my working class background in Cardiff to where I am today. The need in my soul was great and I had to get it all down in print before I forgot it. My journey took me from conservative Christian religion as a child and young person to complete disillusion and then by divine intervention on to this wonderful awareness of the spiritual realm and one in which I learn more of each day and continue to do so.

I can honestly say that I have lived such a full life and hopefully I'm only half way through. Like most people, my stories are humorous and also sad but they are sweet and sour too, majestic and farcical, exhilarating and occasionally terrifying. I will talk to you about my life so that you get to share some of the experiences and events that shaped it. I wanted to express myself through 'my story' because it really has been quite a journey and hopefully it might make you think and ponder your own journey. I have gone from being determined and resolute and in survival mode in life to awakening to the possibility that I am allowed to create and that I am allowed to be at peace, to let go and to allow abundance and beauty in to my life.

As I start this book it is February 2014 and one part of me wants to finish as quickly as possible but the other side of me wants to enjoy this journey and for it to never end since this is one of life's many lessons. It's so important to enjoy the journey and not miss out on any of the scenery along the way. This is a story from my heart and a recollection of a spiritual journey that has passed through the deepest valleys and scaled the highest peaks with many plateaus in between. I have learned a lot and I am still learning, in fact the more I learn the more I realize I don't know. The journey of getting to know who you are is not as easy as you might think.

Why the title of this book? Well the swallow is such an amazing bird which has a migration habit of following the summer from the Southern hemisphere to the Northern hemisphere every single year and then back again. In Britain in around spring time we can see these beautiful birds coming back home, with it being a symbolic signal that summer is on its way, winters grip has ceased. In South Africa the same birds will descend in November time bringing equal joy and symbolism to her people that summer has arrived and that it is a time for optimism and that their birds have also come home. The swallow's journey is an amazing one and I draw parallels between my life and that of this iconic bird.

To my beautiful family, I want you to understand me fully and really know where I came from and what makes me the unique me that I am. I will tell a story of my childhood and beyond that really takes you back to that time; it's my version of a time machine but slightly less technical and far less expensive. If you are sitting comfortably I will go and get the kettle on and get a cuppa tea on the go. I've got the digestive biscuits so I'll see you in Chapter 1.

Chapter 1

Before My Time

My Dad, John O'Conner, was born to Sid and Elizabeth O'Conner on 6th July 1945 in Adamsdown, Cardiff. He was the first son of an eventual tribe of eleven brothers and sisters all crammed into a tiny terraced house which was number 8 Augusta Street.

The O'Conner family were part of a poor community but one in which everyone looked after each other in the neighborhood. It was nicknamed 'little Italy' but there was also a heavy Irish influence too. Nana O'Conner, or less affectionately, Elizabeth O'Conner, was originally born in Belfast. She was a red-head, had the temper to match and I can say with hand on heart that she did not take any nonsense. Grampy O'Conner was born in Bristol we understand and he was the more affectionate and placid of the couple.

My Mum, Andrea O'Conner, was born to Trevor and Ceinwen Weldon on 26th April 1946 in Treganna, Cardiff. Mum was the last born of seven children who grew up in the lovely area of Bedw Maes Crescent. Trevor was from Ebbw Vale and Ceinwen from Bryn Mawr in the South Wales valleys.

Mum's upbringing seemed a lot less harsh than Dads because there seemed to be an atmosphere of magic which was created by Dad Trevor and his passion for life. It wasn't always going to be that way though. Dad Trevor was such a talented man and had such a variety of skills but he was to die tragically when my Mum was just seven. He was an excellent carpenter and actually made puppets from wood which were beautifully created. Mum inherited 'Jacks Mother' so I got to look at her and the attention to detail was amazing from the grey hair bun to the lined face. Ceinwen or Cei as she was called was a soft, gentle woman and a real Nanna of which I have the most wonderful comforting memories as a boy.

Dad met Mum in the Treganna ballroom in November 1963 which used to be a local dance hall and meeting place on Cowbridge Road in Treganna. For young people in the area as the name suggests it was a lovely place to come and meet people and dance the night away. Mum was 17, Dad was 18 and they would dance to tracks like 'She Loves You' by The Beatles and of course many other hits of the time. They courted for two years before getting married in October 1965 in St Lukes church opposite Forrest Park. Back then it was common for young, working class couples to go to Blackpool on their honeymoon and this is exactly what they did. So the scene was set, Dad was working at an engineering firm, Mum was working at Williams and Pritchard's Solicitors and their first house was in Gwyneth Street, Cathays.

10th of October 1966, along came my Sister Pauline in a blaze of un-expected red-headed glory. I say 'un-expected' because Mum was blonde and Dad was brown haired but the genes from Elizabeth O'Conner must have had far reaching tentacles. I was soon to find out that Pauline had a similar temper to Nanna O'Conner but as she has just been born let's just allow her to grow up a little before her little, teasing, tormentor came on the scene. Mum and Dad were shortly to move to Bedw Maes Cresent, having bought the family home from Cei. It was the perfect fit and my

Dad at that point was living the most wonderful life. He had just started working for the GPO which now goes by the name of BT and he was a proud and happy man. He had a little family in a beautiful area of the city and his life was about to unfold. Mum was also happy as well but she apparently had a spiritual yearning for more. She needed more meaning in life, more than just comparing how big your house was against your peers, tired of being asked after having just given birth to Pauline, 'Aaah, so when's number two on the way? You can't hang around, so d 'you think you'll get a bigger house after that? '. Mum didn't know it yet but she was about to embark on a journey of knowledge that she is still passionate about and still feeds to this day. Christianity and the teachings in the Bible are Mums passion and we as kids had plenty of guidance and a wealth of understanding of everything related.

I want to put myself in Dads shoes at this point because I can't help but think that he must have thought that he had really made it. When you consider Dads upbringing on the streets of Adamsdown which was basically doing whatever it took to survive and when you think of it, growing up in a tiny house with so many siblings it must have felt like a real success story for him to now be living in a lovely area of Cardiff with a good job and with a lovely wife and a new born daughter. Dad was a restless soul though and things weren't always going to be this blissful for him as his inner demons would invariably rear up and blacken his world.

Dad's upbringing was such that his Mum or Dad would turn a blind eye to stealing and aggression was the way to succeed, dominance was a good trait and the need to take what you can when you can was how you got on. A treat for Dad was to steal a can of beans from the kitchen and eat them upstairs in bed all to himself. In his teenage years he would go down to the local swimming baths, the gloriously named 'Empire Pool' in order to have a shower. Life was hard, survival was a form of success, to battle and fight and scrap against all the odds was the mantra and Dad's blueprint was set.

The O'Conner's are and were the most wonderful and generous people you are ever likely to meet. They were warm and accommodating and very, very protective. They were the type of people who would make sure that you were never at any point hungry and that if they had a slight inkling that you were, they would offer whatever they had. Even after a good 'nosh up' with rice pudding for 'afters' there was always the offer of 'Wan a Maars Baah mate?' said in that broad Cardiff accent. They were good hearted and strong, like a family of closely knit bandits living off the land and it was not advisable to cross them.

Underneath the coarse exterior there was a soft centre though and it is this that so endears the O'Conner's to people. They would help anyone in a pickle and give their all for them. Underlying though was always this sense of danger that could erupt at any given point, for any reason and without warning like an unstable and very disappointed Mafia boss. I remember in my 20's going out clubbing and being aware that my Dad's younger brother, Michael, was also there in the club. He was as gregarious as he was generous and protective but you could sense a steely eyed menace within him, a glint in the eye that would send a shiver down your spine. He was described many moons ago as a 'loveable rogue' which I think says it all because he would never have willingly hurt his family and would have done anything for them.

So there they were, my Mum and Dad; with sideburns, flares and a hairy chest (and that was just Mum) ready to take on the seventies. They had established themselves in their home and jobs and a few years on from Pauline being born they obviously felt it was time for number two to be put in the oven as on the 14th April 1970, just in time for lunch, I was born.

Chapter 2

Creosote, Tarr and a Pedal Car
(Bedw Maes Cresent, Cardiff - 1970 – 1974)

I was born in Glossop Terrace near the Cardiff Royal Infirmary, a stone's throw away from where Dad grew up. It was a case of De Ja Vue for my parents as I was the second 'unexpected' redhead to come off the production line and to be quite honest, I would have been a bit suspicious if I was Dad. 'Too much red die in the system' I was told. So obviously there was some genetic theme going on here and one in which would cause me quite a lot of heartbreak as a child. It seems odd that that would be the case as why would the colour of your hair cause you anxiety? If you're a girl with red hair it is considered racy and dangerous but for a boy it made you a target.

Anyway my first years are naturally difficult to remember as it is with most people but there are things that I recall as my first memories in Bedw Maes Cresent, Treganna. A lot of memories I have are as a result of looking at photographs in my infancy and those images becoming emblazoned in my mind as a memory so sometimes it's hard to distinguish what is a memory and what is a remembering of a tale from a photograph. My first recollection was Mum ironing something on the living room carpet and I'm pretty certain it wasn't the carpet itself, she wasn't that fanatical about having the weave all go in the same direction, I can assure you of that. I can only assume that it was the time before ironing boards were invented because I remember the millisecond delay of shock that occurs from placing a soft bum cheek on a red hot iron and the brain actually realizing that the best thing to do was to scream and then cry your eyes out. I don't actually remember crying but I'm sure I probably did.

Another distinct memory was me scooting around the house in my blue miniature milk float. It was my first set of wheels and even at that age Mum noticed that I had a bit of a daredevil streak in that I would bomb up the kitchen, our narrow little kitchen, and swerve at the last possible second, just missing the table at the far end before careering into the living room and avoiding perilous irons on carpets at all costs. My milk float was one in which an 18 month old could sit on which had a steering wheel straight in front and horizontal to the ground. The engine happened to be my legs that propelled the cart and there were supposed to be plastic milk bottles attached either side of the milk float and between my calves, no not those calves. Unfortunately I wasn't destined to be a milk man because I could not keep the bottles on the cart and alas I was shown the door and introduced to my second set of wheels, my blue, sleek, plastic pedal car.

This pedal car was modeled on the iconic racing cars of the late sixties and early seventies, the type that Jackie Stewart or James Hunt would have driven in their prime. It was low down and had the number seven on the front in white with black border. I was living the dream! By this stage I had been promoted from a milk round inside the house to a race track on the pavement of Bedw Maes Cresent so life could not possibly have been better. I remember going hell for leather up and down the pavement with the smell of black road tar around me and to this day that smell evokes memories of happiness and freedom. I don't fully understand the workings of the brain and the subconscious but I have always been fascinated how smells can take you back in time more effectively than any other method.

Okay, okay, maybe some regression therapists might disagree but for most people it is an amazing way of transporting us back into time. Other smells that would have filtered into my subconscious would have been the smell of a creosoted wooden fence which would have been in our garden and probably the neighbours too. In isolation there is nothing wonderful about the smell to the neutral nose but for me it meant home, security, sunshine, happiness, warmth and stability. Meanwhile, my exploits in my racing car is what I was getting to and my toddler racer reputation was enhanced by my ability to scare the living daylights out of poor old Mrs Jones from up the road. I would race up behind her and swerve at the last moment, missing those American tan clad ankles by millimeters. Bless her, Mrs Jones used to baby-sit me and Pauline when Mum and Dad used to go out and she was a lovely, gentle old lady. I reckon she would have been in her 70's at least when she used to look after us.

So as you will have gathered by now, I was smitten by vehicles of any kind and loved cars of any description, especially the lovely old fashioned ones. I wasn't too keen on the modern makes as I used to think their shapes were boring, unlike the beautiful curves of the vehicles of the 30's, 40's, 50's and 60's. Still to this day, when I see an old car it's like seeing a long lost friend and my heart melts for that bygone era. My favourite Ladybird book of that time was called 'Tootles The Taxi' and each page had a different vehicle, beautifully illustrated but with a character face which made me think that the cars had feelings and a soul. Obviously then, I was in heaven when I used to be playing with my match-box cars or my 'dinkie toys' as Dad used to call them. It was magical as Dad would set up these grey plastic tracks out the back, perfect for little cars to run down and elevated at one end so that the cars would run down by themselves onto the concrete floor in chaotic patterns.

Another memory I had at this time, and this was probably my second memory after the iron, bum cheek encounter was of being chased into the house from the back garden by a giant (well it seemed giant to me) bumble bee. For me it felt like a scene from 'The Battle of Britain' with a furry black and yellow stripped dive bomber pursuing me. That was a very early experience and the only emotion I can recall is one of panic. I think

I eventually outmaneuvered it by running into the kitchen and slamming the door shut after me.

I was the sort of little person who loved his routine and loved being home so when it came to nursery it was a new routine and a new way of life altogether for me. I was a 'home bird' as Mum used to call me and never really wanted to stray too far from the nest. I loved adventure but I still needed my safety line, my umbilical cord back to Mum and Dad, back to source. The nursery school I was to go to was based in Forrest Park near to where the tennis courts are today and I don't recall too much about this time other than that there was plenty of scrambling through plastic castle walls which was thrilling for me. I managed to meet a couple of buddies as well which was the whole point of Mum taking me there in the first place. Jason and Christopher were my two close pals and they also used to live close to us as well, Jason in fact lived in Bedw Maes Crescent too, same as us. It was either Jason or Christopher who told me one day in nursery when we were bungee jumping off the castle wall without a bungee rope (not *that* castle wall) that his Mum was going to be bringing in a 'caravan' each for us after school. Well you know me and vehicles, I was so excited by the prospect of getting a toy after school, and admittedly a bit of a bizarre toy and not one I would have chosen myself but nonetheless a toy. So you can imagine my disappointment when at picking up time I was presented with a bar of chocolate as my 'caravan'. It was a 'caravan bar' you see, that's what my little buddy meant and I think this was my first experience of what we call an anti-climax. Don't get me wrong, I wolfed the chocolate bar down and I very sincerely and hopefully said 'Thank You' to the Mum so it was a partial success but this was to permanently enter me into the chocoholics' anonymous hall of fame and I have to confess that I am still an addict to this day.

Another lovely memory for me was playing at my Auntie Anne's house in Fairways Crescent in Fairwater. Auntie Anne was my Mums older sister and married to uncle Ben who was such a character and still missed by all to this day. The house they lived in was similar to ours in that it was a semi-detached urban house in a lovely area of Cardiff but their house backed onto the woods behind their back garden. We used to go out the back door, up the long garden, past the coal shute on the left and the green house on the right and up to the fence at the back of the garden. At the fence you could see a vast amount of freedom spreading out in front of you. In the foreground was a huge field and at the bottom of the field were woods, dark, atmospheric and exciting woods. We would picnic in summer and walk the woods with wellies on and it was bliss. Children do not need much to keep them happy, just lots of love, lots of fun, plenty of sleep, food and water and you have the perfect recipe. I had all that for which I am grateful. A story relating to Aunt Anne and myself is when we were waiting for a bus in town and she was chewing her Wrigleys Spearmint Gum which used to come in its green wrapper, each one wrapped in foil and green sleeve. It looked so lovely, so classy in my little three year old mind so naturally Aunt Anne asked if I wanted one. I gobbled this minty, never-ending toffee up and since it was my first experience of chewing gum I was taken aback by the fact that a full five minutes later it was still there. I thought maybe I'd got it wrong and that I wasn't chewing it properly so I decided to cheat and just swallow it. I mean, how else was I going to get another one? Well you know how kids are so offensively honest at times, my line on that day has never been forgotten by anyone in the family especially my Mum and Auntie Anne. I said as I looked up at her face looming over me, 'can I have another chewing gum, big nose'. It obviously didn't cause too much offence because I recall there was laughter. Cheeky, but no harm done. A not so interesting fact is that chewing gum is not, as I was lead to believe as a child, made from horses hooves. Okay? Just thought I'd clear that up in case you were wondering the same or was it only ever me who thought that? Turns out it is made from a natural latex from the sap of a sapodilla tree but I am going totally off the point here.

Dad, at this point, working for the GPO (General Post Office) and later to be called British Telecom started to have itchy feet and his head was turned by opportunities for immigration to either New Zealand, Australia or South Africa, all of them beautiful, sun drenched and untamed countries previously of the British Empire and all of them wonderful places to live. I'm not sure if Dad chose South Africa over the other two or South Africa chose Dad but suddenly there were plans afoot. At four years old I wouldn't have been privy to all the planning that must have been involved with this huge move but the amazing thing is that it was all paid for by the South African Post Office. All the shipping of personal effects and the cost of getting out there by ship was to be paid for by them, how amazing and what an opportunity.

One final thing we did was to visit Fishguard in West Wales to visit my Aunt Heather and Uncle Vince before we went. Aunt Heather is my Mums closest sister, she has four sisters including Aunt Anne and Heather, the other members of the clan are Joy and Pearl. Roy and Howard completed the sibling set. Anyway, my best buddy in the entire world was also my cousin Jimmy who was just over a year younger than me. There will be more stories to come containing Jimmy and I but for now I was just getting to know him. We travelled up to Fishguard in a bright orange mini car which we hired for the weekend and I can remember Aunt Heather and Uncle Vince living in a house which seemed precariously perched on the edge of a cliff overlooking a bay. Well that's what it seemed like to me and my fertile imagination, it was probably perfectly safe but it felt as if it was on the edge of the world.

I really bonded with Jimmy on that weekend like no-one else before or since, we were like brothers and indeed to this day, people think we are because we look so much alike. Pauline used to play with Steve who was Jimmy's older brother by a few years. I remember Jimmy and I wrestling a lot and me coming off the worse on a few occasions in the cramped little house. Every time there was an incident I would be running downstairs followed by Jimmy in hot pursuit trying to get his words out to his Mum and Dad before I could by shouting 'Accidentally, accidentally'. I'm not sure it worked as the fearsome Uncle Marv gave Cousin Jimmy a good tongue lashing which to be fair was more often than not deserved. Jimmy, by this stage, had used up his 'Accidentally' quotient for the day because although it was a good get-out-of-jail card, there was only so many times you could pull it. Uncle Marv used to terrify me because of his temper and you could tell the warning signs that Mount Vesuvius was about to erupt as his hairline used to somehow shift upwards as if a toupee was being invisibly pulled backwards. But that aside, it was a wonderful weekend and I got to meet my first real family bosom buddy, Jimmy Hughes.

Not long after we would be packing up our worldly possessions in Bedw Maes Crescent and heading off on an African adventure that was to change all of our lives forever. I can't recall the final days in Cardiff but I certainly remember our journey to Cape Town.

Chapter 3

Safari Suits and Baker Street (Juniper Street, Benoni - 1974 – 1979)

We boarded the Edinburgh Castle in November 1974 from Southampton to embark upon a two week holiday of a lifetime and for the journey to culminate in Cape Town, one of the most beautifully iconic cities in the world. The first memory that drifts in to my head is vaguely of how our 'living quarters' appeared to me as a four year old. There were two bunk beds on each side of our room, a set for Mum and Dad and a set for Pauline and I. We had a porthole which I guess every room had in the ship unless you were in the engine room and this, as a four-year-old was very important. We had incredibly strong tea given to us in the mornings with bourbon biscuits, no expense spared I tell you. Why on earth do I remember this? I don't know is the answer. I was put in an on-board nursery for an hour or so whilst Mum and Dad sunned themselves on deck in preparation for sunny South Africa. In the meantime I recall crawling through a tube the same size as a porthole that linked the nursery with another empty room and this was thrilling for me. Potholing at four years of age!

The evening meals were quite a lavish affair where there was one big dining room with what seemed like endless round tables as far as the eye could see. There was a real holiday atmosphere where sun drenched families and couples would come and relax after a day of unwinding and entertainment. I remember the smells of expensive perfume and aftershave, well I say expensive; they could have been really cheap copies but how was I to know? We would be served our meal by this charming Irish waiter who knew us all by name and it became a common family quote whilst remembering our voyage to just say 'Broccoli Liam?' in a soft Irish accent. Mum and Dad were glowing and happy and this was heaven for us all. There was a pool on board the ship and whilst I couldn't swim, Mum and Dad would happily take both us kids in for a thrilling dip. When we crossed the equator there was a huge party and the captain was covered from head to toe in Angel Delight by his shipmates. There was a fancy dress party which myself and Pauline entered and Mum did all the work in getting our costumes ready. Well when I say costume, the outfit was made from crepe paper which was remarkably resourceful since materials to make costumes wouldn't have been exactly easy to come across on a ship in the middle of the Atlantic Ocean. Pauline and I went as Tinkerbell and Peter Pan and we won first prize. Thanks Mum, not sure I appreciated being dressed up as a fairy though.

Surprisingly I have no recollection of seeing Cape Town for the first time which for Mum and Dad must have been absolutely breathtaking. It truly is such a beautiful sight to see the grand Table Mountain overseeing all that lies beneath her. For anyone who has never seen Table Mountain or Cape Town, put it on your Bucket List of places to visit in this life time, it is so enchantingly beautiful. Our end destination within South Africa was Johannesburg which is where roughly Dad would be starting work. It meant we would be catching a train from coastal Cape Town in the South West to landlocked Jo'burg in the North East, a good day and a half's travel and some 1,600Kms later. I can vaguely recall it being very hot and tedious, especially whilst traversing the great, barren, Karroo desert.

Eventually we arrived in Johannesburg and after a few restless nights in a downtown hotel in Hillbrow we were taken to see our Uncle Freddie and

Auntie Belinda in a lovely little town called Benoni which is to the east of Johannesburg itself. Freddie is Dads younger brother and had been living in South Africa a couple of years already having married Belinda Putney back in Britain. Belinda's family were from the east end of London and the whole family moved out to South Africa, lead by John and Jill the parents. The children that followed them were Terry, Janet, Belinda, Maggie, Leonard and Ben. Quite unusually Terry and Belinda were already married to Georgie and Freddie respectively and Janet old enough to be dating. When I say 'unusual' I don't mean it was unusual for them to be married, rather that it seemed odd to me that in your early twenties, having just married, you would choose to uproot and follow your parents. It all ended up well though as most of the siblings spent many great years happily living there. Terry and Georgie were the first to go back because Georgie felt homesick. Belinda and Freddie were to stay for a couple of decades along with Janet but Maggie, Leonard and Ben would become really close friends, to the point of virtually being family for Pauline and I. It really is testament to the strength of this bond that the O'Conners and Putneys would remain as almost one big family for years. Even living in different parts of the world, there are still strong connections between the two families. To this day we have get-togethers with both sides of the family and it is wonderful.

So we met up with Freddie and Belinda in their lovely home in 10th Avenue Northmead. Upon arrival, Freddie was up on the roof painting the chimney with just shorts on and ladies shower cap. Remember, these were the days before hats were invented, supposedly, so the plastic, frilly cap was of course the natural remedy. Their first born was Justin and something happened to Justin at birth that is unclear but the eventual conclusion drawn by doctors was that he had a slight form of brain damage. He was and still is a special soul who has explored the extremity of his own potential and achieved some remarkable things against all the odds, a bit like a Forrest Gump type of character. I'm not sure how long we stayed at 10th Avenue but before long we had bought a lovely bungalow in an area called Northmead Extension 4.

Chapter 4

Juniper Street was to be our home in Benoni for five sun-soaked years and I have such lovely memories of that house and of that period of my childhood, which spanned from four through to nine, so quite an impressionable time. As I said, we had a typical South African bungalow in a very simple, rectangular style with a corrugated iron roof painted black, which in summer time, when we had hail stone loaded thunder storms, caused one hell of a cacophony. The outer walls were standard white but the guttering and trims were painted bright orange. I have to say it isn't a colour I would have gone for but hey, what did I care at the time. To the right of the house itself was our driveway leading down to our ivy-covered garage. There was plenty of garden area as is the case with most South African urban houses so we could run and play as much as we wanted. We had as much space out the front as we did in the back, but in the back we virtually had a mini orchard. Within this orchard we had a wonderfully large apricot tree which Mum resourcefully made jam from and it became a firm favourite. When apricots become ripe they just get really soft and gravity pulls them earthwards where they end up like wrinkled bald heads. The problem is that if they are not picked off the floor they become a literal 'toe-jam' hazard because if you step on a very ripe one the fermented fruit would squelch up through your toes in a fairly revolting way. Oh and before you ask, most South African children grow up wearing nothing on their feet, just because they can and because the weather permits it. There is no better feeling than walking bare foot through cool, soft grass, unless there are thorns in the grass from fallen trees, and then it becomes slightly different.

So our home was simple and basic but a really special place to grow up, we had more room around us than we were used to because South African gardens are spacious compared to British ones. Dad was up and away into his job with the South African Post Office which back then, and may still possibly be, a very Afrikaans institution with a smattering of Brits. For those of you who are unfamiliar with Afrikaners, let me explain a little about South African demographics. It really is a true 'Rainbow Nation' in that it is young and has so many different ethnicities and cultures. Obviously the main body of the population are the original and indigenous Zulus, Xhosas, Sothos and Tswana tribes who have always been there. But then into the mix we add Indians, Coloured's (a taboo description in some countries but not so in SA) and white Europeans which are further defined into two groups, namely; English speaking Europeans and Afrikaans speaking Europeans. Afrikaans, as a language, is the youngest language in the world and was derived from a mixture mainly of Dutch plus French and German based on the settlers that landed in the 1600's. The language is very direct and guttural and aggressive sounding which reflects the hardy people that they were. They were indeed battle hardened pioneers who fought for every bit of land and they were, and indeed still are, tough people. Against that backdrop, Dad was immersed into the very Afrikaans Post Office life and he no doubt had some banter with them as the Brit. Back in the 70's the most popular unofficial dress code for the Afrikaans working man was the safari suit, made from polyester and with matching shorts, shirt and long socks. There were only three colours available, or so it seemed, and these were light powder blue, beige and insipid light green. Each suit had to have the obligatory fashion accessory of a comb which was inserted into the sock in order that it could be rapidly drawn out in case a blustery wind should go on the offensive. I'd like to say that Dad was too cool for all that but he wasn't, he was in the safari suit cult and could not escape. Indeed it went as far as to have junior safari suits and yes, you guessed it, I had one and it was beige.

Dads pride and joy was his light blue, macho, Ford Cortina 'Big 6'. Big 6 as in six cylinders. In SA you simply had to have a car as everywhere was far away and there was no real public transport to rely on as such. This car was to take us to many a wonderful place in my youth and at great speed as well. Mum would be a bag of nerves in the front saying 'Ooh, slow down John, you'll get us killed, it's not a race love'. Pauline and I would be in the back totally unharnessed as was the case in those days. I think the idea was that at least you had a seat in front of you to break your forward motion. It wasn't very scientific but we managed to survive. I think back then it was only frowned upon if you actually fell out of the car as a child whilst going around a corner with the door slightly ajar. I'm not saying I had personal experience of this but so many of my school buddies did. They used to come to school with friction burns on their elbows and knees and sometimes their face and said, 'Jah, I was frown from ma car going rand a cornah on the weekind'. No big deal really, it was the 70's and we were tough. I never really selected the wisest seat in the car either as I was always diagonally opposite Dad in his driving seat with Pauline, being more street-wize, tucking herself in behind Dad so that she could never be in the arc of Dads huge, meaty handed swipes if we were ever unruly in the back. Whether it was my fault or Paulines, I would normally get the ringing ear and warm sensation on the side of my face after having a 'clap'. In fairness, Pauline used to get them as well but it was Mum dealing these ones out and, bless her, she would give it a go but they didn't have the same impact. With my ear still ringing I would be in a silent sulk for a bit, then my boredom started to rize and I would glance up, fully recovered and notice Pauline would be engrossed in a book, she was ripe for teasing........ again. A quick nudge with my foot on her book in order to startle her and we were off again. On a hot day in SA with no aircon, tensions can get a little frayed in a car and we would have many a lovely holiday or day trip away with the precursor being hot, irritable little passengers. On the other hand though for as long as I live the beautifully haunting and lonely song 'Baker Street' by Gerry Rafferty on the car radio will remind me of a trip to

Pretoria during this time, the amazing uniqueness of this seventies classic and the nostalgia it evokes in me brings me to tears and for some reason it transports me back in time like no other. It always hits me like an arrow in the heart. I would love for more learned souls out there to explain exactly why this is so significant to me.

The time was ripe for me to begin nursery in South Africa and being a home bird I was not keen at all, especially as it was a new country with new rules. I recall Mum walking me to the nursery and breaking down as I was led in to what felt like being taken to the gallows. It was all so strange and unfamiliar, even the milky tea they served was no comfort as it was the alien taste of Rooibos which I have now come to love but with milk it really is quite odd tasting. Like any kids, once Mum has gone, we just got on with it and played to our hearts content, it didn't matter what continent we were on then. One thing which I didn't much fancy though was having to have an afternoon nap when all I wanted to do was play in the sand pit. A bell would ring, we would have a snack of some sort and we would be 'allowed' to lay on these hard, thin mats almost prison style. There would be row upon row of these little mats with little children on them either trying to catch 40 winks or actually sleeping. The thing is, I was so full of energy I didn't want to sleep, I wanted to chase Dion around playing guns and diving under bushes pretending I was a cowboy. I would lie there in the fetal position, eyes pretending to be shut but sleep was a million miles away. Then the bell would ring and it would be hometime and Mum would be waiting for me in the front. My heart would soar with joy at seeing my Mum, my Mum who I was so attached to. You can imagine my despair when Mum said the next day 'let's take you to nursery love'. I didn't say it but I was thinking, 'but I went yesterday Mum?'

Chapter 5

After having got accustomed to nursery it was a swift change and a brand new beginning for me. It was to be my first time at school and although I was filled with dread at the prospect of leaving the nest again, it was to be the most lovely school and I am grateful even now that I was able to attend there. So at six years of age this was it, for me I was going into the big, wide world of school. Well I couldn't have had a better introduction as my first teacher was this lovely, soft, Jewish lady called Mrs Collins who I adored. She was so patient and that's exactly what I needed as I was never a quick learner. I have always absorbed things slowly but surely and she recognized that. Our school was called Arbor Primary and the uniform was deep purple with gold and silver trim. Purple sounds garish but it was actually okay because it was fairly dark, it could have been a lot worse, it could have been orange which would have clashed with my hair. I felt important in my school uniform, like part of a team and we also used to have to take a case to school, it was a standard issue brown miniature hard case with a steel button on the front which if moved to one side would release the catch. It was barely bigger than a large lunch tin but I felt important having it. All our books would have to be covered in standard brown paper, then plastic covering with an identity tag in the top right hand corner which had a blue border. This kept Mum very busy. Once I got into the swing of things I enjoyed my time at school. I loved coming home and couldn't wait for that bell at the end of the day. The school day in SA is a lot shorter than in other countries as the emphasis is more towards play and being outdoors which creates well rounded people. We used to start at 8am and be finished by 1pm ready to play out the back all afternoon with my cars. It was during these early years that I first had the feeling of rejection or of not feeling good enough which could best be described as inferior isolation. The problem, you see, was this ginger mop on top of my head. Yes, ginger, not auburn or delicately described 'strawberry blond' but full on ginger, complete with invisible eyebrows and eyelashes. No, no, there was to be no respite as I had the skin to match and the mere mention of the word 'sun' caused my face to go pink and yes we were living in the land of perpetual sunshine. All of this was fine in reality as I was just a six year old boy wanting to play with cars and run around the back garden but children being as they are used to tease me a lot and I have to say that it hurt me deeply. If I wasn't a sensitive soul I would have been okay but I was and I took it all on board. They used to call me 'rooikop' which is Afrikaans for Red Head or 'rooinek' which means Red Neck but was more a nickname for British people in general, born from the Boer War in South Africa, where the Brits did not have factor fifty sun-cream on their necks and bore the results in spectacular fashion.

All I ever wanted to be back then was 'normal' which meant brown hair, brown eyes and the skin to match but this was not to be. I can recall vividly the feeling of being on the outside and of being different and inferior to everyone else. My shyness was compounded by this feeling of being a bit different from the norm and this hollowness sat within me for years and years. Maybe I should not have been so sensitive, perhaps it was good to toughen me up a bit but I was sensitive then as I am now. On a soul level I would have chosen this path and this seemingly insignificant banter from obliviously innocent children was to become an important hurdle for me to overcome. It is true to say that the teasing, whilst I bear no grudge at all to the children who did it because they were innocently having their fun, did sit within me and has done so all my life. The best way for me to describe seemingly innocuous childhood issues which you don't deal with at the time is that it is like a metaphorical sebaceous cist that forms within you, full of rejection, inferiority and aloneness which was created within my being. A sebaceous cist is not a pleasant phenomenon and readers with a sensitive stomach should look away............. NOW! They are puss filled pockets underneath the skin, with no head and they are caused by a blocked sweat gland normally. They cannot be drained by normal methods and if left, they just get bigger. So instead of immediately getting to the bottom of a childhood issue I allowed my cist to remain and even though I grew out of this inferiority complex and became a confident and brash young man, the cist was still there but covered over by years of living, learning, crying and laughing. The cist, you see, formed part of my blueprint which is created in all of us in those early years. This cist would manifest itself in feelings of just wanting to be safe and normal, not wanting to really dip into my greatness for fear of standing out. It would be decades before I understood this which would end up being the catalyst for change within me.

As a six year old I was achieving great things in my life in order to put on my CV, like learning to ride a bike, going for my first proper haircut and cutting slits into the bottom of our plastic swimming pool, just to see what happened. What happened was that, yes, the water did come out and, yes, Dad was almost speechless with rage. Life was fun and it was the age of space hoppers, yoyos and paddle balls. Mum at some point decided it would be a great idea to get myself and Pauline involved in gymnastics over at the John Barrable Hall and I think it was based on the fact that her gifted dad, Trevor, represented Wales in the discipline. Well I can tell you this much, I wasn't to follow in his footsteps exactly because I didn't quite match his diminutive, athletic frame, I was designed for less flexible pursuits. The club we enrolled into was called 'The Flying Eagles' and all of us were decked out in red shorts, red vests and a yellow sewn on badge showing the flying eagle emblem. All this under the leadership and guidance of the steely blue eyed, bearded phenomenon of a man who went by the name of Jan Steenekamp. He was a very pleasant, athletic, Afrikaans man who nurtured and cajoled us into achieving our tumbling wings which consisted of Arab springs, flick-flacks and cartwheels. I can still remember the smell of the rubberized floor and 'Deep Heat' along with the echoes of exertion in the huge hall. Suffice to say that I did give it my all but I had this overriding fear that I would snap my neck in two if I didn't quite master a flick flack to perfection. This was to become a stumbling block as opposed to being good tumbling stock. The name 'Flying Eagles' painted a picture of strength, grace and agility but my reality was more like a hesitant starfish, biting his bottom lip in concentration. My agility resembled a plank of wood whilst trying not to shatter my vertebrae's as I plunged earthwards towards a slither of foam. Mum was proud of me, nonetheless, but alas my destiny was not to be on a podium, clasping my heart, looking skyward and singing my national anthem having just claimed gold.

A long time before all that we started going to the Duckhams farm on the outskirts of Benoni in a place called Puttfontein. This was a very informal Christian gathering that my Mum was invited to and she was immediately seduced by it all and rightly so as the people we met there were absolutely lovely, trustworthy and genuine people. You see we not only met the Duckhams who were our hosts but also other families, including the Putney clan, and the social side of it was absolute heaven for a little boy. Big farm, a rusting and condemned tractor to play on, plenty of space, lovely food in the form of a barbeque, which in South Africa is called a 'braai', followed by sweet desserts and biscuits. Naturally we were there to learn though and listened to a sermon every week under the watchful eye of Herbie, the head of the Duckham house. He was a fiery and passionate preacher man and although he never really unleashed it, you could sense the bubbling magma of his temper. The Duckhams were to be our first introduction into Christianity and I have to say, that for me, it was a perfect introduction because it was in such an informal setting. There was no church building, we just used to sit in the huge living room with Herbie in his high, winged back chair and everyone else in a circumference of chairs around him, listening to the word of God. Before the main sermon which was attended by everyone, including the children, we would have Bible study with Cassie, Herbie's wife. We were issued with a gold embossed 'Good News' bible which we were allowed to keep and this was quite a thrill for me back then.

The Duckhams were from the mid-west in the USA and I was mesmerized by their accents, they had three children, all older than me and went by the names of Joshua, Sarah and Rachel which gives you that Biblical theme. I must say I don't think I ever encountered a 'Herbie' in the Bible but I could be wrong. Joshua was like my big brother type buddy and although he was much older than me, we would have hours of fun. I really used to look up to him and he had an amazing array of toys, the best of the lot though just had to be his Skalectrix set which had its own huge table. Sarah and Rachel were more Paulines age and they used to really get on well. It all fitted together like a glove and I used to actually look forward to a Sunday, I mean why wouldn't I? The only drawback was that I couldn't really get my head around the sermons and felt that the whole thing was quite tedious but I suppose any young child would have been exactly the same. Mum and Dad, especially Mum, lapped it all up and she took it all in and was a Christian on fire. Sunday consisted of a morning service followed by tea and biscuits or cakes with lots of play time afterwards then there was also an evening service which was another sermon followed by energetic running around outside in the dark playing touch with the other kids until it was time to come home. Just for good measure, and if you felt yourself dipping during the week, there was always the mid-week Bible study class which I was never too enthused about and used to absolutely dread. Sunday school was about all I could digest in one week, but to have all the other lectures and sermons thrown in was almost like feeding a plate sized steak to a new born baby. That aside though, I had fond memories of that time as we used to socialize such a lot and perform plays and pantomimes which every person would be involved with. It's safe to say that my feelings toward Christianity, The Bible and God were pretty healthy and the trickle that was to culminate in my river of spiritual learning had begun. Due to ill health Herbie and his family had to return to the States where they continued their good work. We were to then join a more formal type of church in the heart of Benoni a while later.

In this period of my life I recall so many innocent pleasures that Pauline and I used to get up to and maybe it was just us but I reckon there were a few South African kids out there who would share these memories. One thing we used to do was make our own home-made sherbet which consisted of icing sugar mixed with a brand of fast acting effervescent fruit salts called 'Eno's and we thought it was the best, we were very unspoiled you see. We were living the dream and ripping around the house in a frenzy of flatulence and burping. Picture two balloons with ginger hair being blown up and then being released around the house, that was Pauline and I. Mum used to often get us a little treat after school which consisted of a fizz-pop each which was a sherbet filled lolly pop. There was also the deluxe version which looked the same from the outside but contained bubble gum that kept its flavor for about fourteen seconds before returning to its natural tasteless rubbery state. The ultimate, ultimate treat though and this was reserved for a Friday night, after dinner was to have a huge slab of Cadbury's Milk Chocolate. We would be sitting on the couch watching Charlies Angels or CHIPS and Dad would reverently bring out the purple wrapped slab of heaven. We would all be given a row, whilst Dad would keep the slab on the arm of his chair. It was the closest thing to happiness over the course of one minute to have one of those little blocks melting in your mouth. There was a sense of apprehension when I'd finished my last piece and I would look longingly over to Dad, where he would break off another row and share it out again. It was absolute bliss.

The TV broadcasts in SA were in their infancy and only in the early seventies did the SABC start and back then the TV schedule used to start at 4pm and end at 8pm. There was an alternation between English and Afrikaans so on one night it would be English for the first two hours and Afrikaans second and the next night would be the opposite and so on through the week. Each broadcast would start and end with a message from a biblical man, reading a scripture and the program was called 'From the Book'. Now by this point my scriptural sponge was saturated but I took it all in and listened almost dutifully in anticipation for the programs that were to follow. A huge hit in Britain in the seventies was a police drama called 'The Sweeney' set in inner city London with accompanying hard case Cockney antics and accents. Imagine settling down on a Thursday night to the version dubbed into Afrikaans called 'Blitspatrollie' with Dennis Waterman and John Thaw exchanging unpleasantries with the London underworld in a bizarre, Germanic tone. It was actually hilarious to us on one hand and really frustrating on the other but ultimately it forced you to learn the native tongue which is always important if you want to settle and fit in to a new country. What an ingenious act by the SABC. Thankfully we didn't have to endure JR Ewing from Dallas speaking Afrikaans because surely that would have been soap opera sacrilege.

Chapter 6

Halfway through Dad's initial five year contract we went on holiday back to the UK in the Queens Silver Jubilee year of 1977 and what a lovely time it was. The Airline captain on British Airways made sure we all got replica winged badges for the occasion and Pauline and I thought we were so special. Looking at my life from this perspective I realize that we had it very good, we were by no means affluent but we had wealth. A wealth of love, Dad with a solid income, Mum not needing to work and going on holiday once a year was very special indeed. The one month holiday in Britain was a chance to catch up with family which was mainly Auntie Anne and Uncle Ben with Anne and Amelia, along with Uncle Vince and Auntie Heather with Steve and my trustee strawberry blond side kick Jimmy. By this time Heather and Vince had moved from Fishguard to Caerphilly and again we stayed with them for about a week. In this time I discovered a magical new thing that is quintessentially homely and British and it was the great British digestive biscuit. At Auntie Heathers house there was a cylindrical, brown biscuit tin that I used to raid and I just could not get enough of these brown, semi-sweet discs of malty pleasure.

One evening we went to the Cardiff Tattoo which was a biennial display of military prowess and it made me feel proud and patriotic to see helicopters above with airmen cascading down ropes attached to them, canons being fired into the night sky, the smell of gunpowder, perfectly executed marching lines by the Welsh guards in their blood red tunics and black buzby hats, soldiers performing mock raids and abseiling down the castle keep, the smell of diesel from tanks belching out black smoke, the mighty cracks of rifle fire, it was absolutely thrilling. Dads best mate, Keith and his wife Hilda Lewis were with us and Keith was such a fun person with a down to earth Cardiff humour. He said at one point 'I've got fourteen licorice allsorts in my mouth' because he was getting so carried away by all the action. It really made us laugh and that became O'Conner-code in years to come if something was really thrilling. We stayed at Uncle Neil's house, Dads brother, for a bit and that was special too, although he didn't have any children and my place of rest in the evenings was a folding camping bed which didn't quite lie flat but remained in a semi-upright position, much like a deckchair. It was an evil little contraption made of a thin blue canvass stretched across thin steel poles to give it its shape. The camp bed and I were at war permanently during that stay and the camp bed usually won. The thing is, you see, is that it had this fabulous knack of folding back in on itself if your body weight moved to the middle which resulted in an image of a giant blue, canvass Venus fly trap gorging itself on a wild-eyed, red-headed boy. Better still was that when in the lying position, the cross supports underneath you dug into your back after a while and rumour has it that these beds were used as implements of torture to cause sleep deprivation during the Second World War. We eventually flew home renewed and ready for our life in South Africa.

Shortly after this time it was when one of the greatest musicals of our time graced the movie theatres or Bioscopes as they were called in SA. It was the smash hit 'Grease' with John Revolting and Olivia Newtron Bomb and the girls just absolutely adored this film. Secretly the macho guys also loved it but in the seventies you could never have admitted that as a South African, meat eating, rugby playing, red-blooded, safari suit wearing, lamb-chops-for-side-burns male. In 1978 as an eight year old I was smitten. This was it! This was what the girls in Standard One in my class needed to see. They needed to see Liam O'Conner in a pink shirt, just like Danny Zuko. Surely if I could die my hair black and have a pink shirt I would be made and my self-acceptance and esteem would be complete. What I forgot though is that even if I did die my hair, it still left the problem of albino caterpillars above my eyes and a hot freckled complexion, two hundred billion miles away from the leather jacketed, slick haired, smoldering sex symbol that was Danny Zuko. I remember asking Mum if I could have a pink shirt and Dad was in the vicinity with a very concerned, raised eyebrow and a mild look of horror. Dad, the oldest son of the notorious O'Conner bandits with a son who wanted a pink shirt at the age of eight, 'he's not queer is he Love?' I could imagine Dad asking Mum. That request never made it to the senior management team for approval. But even at eight I loved girls and all they stood for, how gentle they were, how pretty some of them could be, how they could do different things to their hair instead of just a standard 'Playmobil' action figure bowl cut like us simple boys. Like putting bows in their hair or wearing little pink bangles on their wrist that made them feel special, it was an attention to detail I admired and still do. It was these little things that I thought made girls adorable in my innocent way. I would look at girls and want to talk to the ones that I thought were pretty but I just could not bring myself to do it as I was way too shy and I really felt as if I was inferior. I felt like I was on the outside looking into a baker shop window full of cakes but with no money. The glass of the shop window representing all my inadequacies I felt I had. So Danny Zuko had to be temporarily shelved until I was much older and much more confident.

We continued our lovely life in SA and my best buddy at that stage had to be Ben Putney, who was the youngest of the Putney clan and a really good mate to me outside of school. I can remember the thrill of Mum and Dad allowing me to sleep over at Bens house on a Friday or Saturday night and it felt as if I was going on holiday to Hawaii I was that excited. Auntie Jill, you see, was the softest and most lovely of laid back woman and boy was she a good cook and baker. The treats we used to get were out of this world, crunchies, millionaire's shortbread and all manner of cakes and savoury tarts would be made. Their house had such a lovely atmosphere of calmness apart from when Dad John was about as he was a professional drinker or so I thought. All of our family at that time were involved in the Church of Christ, including Auntie Jill but Uncle John would have nothing at all to do with it and openly despised it all. At the time I just thought he was a scary, angry bald man who drank a lot and didn't like church. Bens older brother and sister around his age were Leonard and Maggie and myself and Pauline were so close to them that we considered them as cousins and still do. Family get-togethers and braais were wonderful, sunny, relaxed affairs with no airs or graces, it was just a huge family atmosphere of laughter, games, singing and feasting and I have the deepest, deepest memories of happiness at this time.

A very special time was also when we went to the Kruger National Park and took Maggie who had never been before. Now the Kruger National Park is one of South Africas most wild and beautiful wildlife reserves and it contains everything you could imagine the African bush to contain. Being similar to the size of Northern Ireland in land area you can only imagine the amount of wildlife which includes the 'Big Five' of Lion, Leopard, Elephant, Buffalo and Rhinoceros. Due to the size of the park you were in fact very lucky to spot one of these animals but we were lucky enough to see them all, in fact we saw two of the big five in one scene when we saw a pride of lions eating a buffalo in quite gory but spectacular fashion. It shocked me to see the stark reality of what happens in the wild, there was to be no mercy for that great buffalo. It made me realize that nature was brutal as well as beautiful and we were very fortunate to witness it as it is such a rare event to see Lions feeding in this way. A few days later we were in a convoy of about six vehicles cruising slowly through the veldt when a herd of elephants crossed the path we were going on. They sauntered across in no great hurry, all in single file with the great bull elephant in the front, the big chief. Again, the chances of us stumbling upon elephants moving straight in front of us was a stroke of luck, a minute before or later and we would have missed them or perhaps seen them in our rear view mirror some one hundred meters off. It was a truly amazing sight and we were all in awe in our car, grateful to catch more than a glimpse of this great lumbering beast. Grateful until the car in front decided he wanted to get the 'ultimate' photograph by tooting his horn at the bull to get him to turn his head for that iconic shot. Well the bull turned alright, a sight which I will never forget as his patience snapped. His trunk went into the air as if saluting and a mighty trumpeting blast emanated as he started to move forward towards this noisy metallic box. Six cars in unison were doing the fastest ever three point turn that would have made stunt drivers smile in admiration. It was such a pity that the guy in the front decided to do this because it deprived everyone else the chance to see the little calf elephants at the back, a truly memorable sight.

Meanwhile the spiritual side of our lives took a turn in 1978 when we decided to join a group of Christians in a very new, state-of-the-art building, they were simply called The Benoni Church of Christ and there was another American preacher at the helm by the name of Mal Bourne who was friendly and effervescent by nature but when the mood took him he could be thunderous and brooding with his messages of hell and damnation. I was getting to an age now where I knew the basics of the Bible and appreciated it a lot but was getting fed up of the routine and the constant parrot fashion learning of scriptures. Being a boy who needed to play a lot, as we all do, I was not the best of model students in school and was always grateful for home time and the weekends. You can imagine my dismay then when it came to learning more verses at Sunday school and on top of that, given homework for next week. I used to writhe in silent irritation being pent up in another classroom. It wasn't for me and yet I went along with it, at eight you just do as you're told. After Sunday school we would play for five minutes before going into the main auditorium for the main feature, the preachers' sermon for the week. It was out of the classroom and into the cauldron which was roughly an hour or so of hymns, prayers, sermon and the communion. The communion was a very formal affair where we would eat unleavened bread, which represented the flesh of Jesus and the taking of a red grape juice which was the blood of Christ. I was fascinated by how this was served as it consisted of a round silver tray with two layers of tiny glass cups filled with the red grape juice. The cups each sat in their own recessed hole and each person would take a separate cup, drink it and return it, after which passing the tray to the next person to repeat the process. You could only perform this act if you were baptized and having only had a bowl of cereal before Church my stomach was by now rumbling come 10:30. After the bread and wine was what I initially thought was paying of the bill but in fact turned out to be a collection plate, a donation to the church, to God. I used to marvel at wealthy people in suits and dresses who used to drop neatly folded cheques into the plate, whilst my Mum would be digging around in her purse for the largest coin denomination she dare put in under the watchful eye of Dad. Mum also used to cram a few coins into my hand for me to drop in for me to feel part of the whole thing. Whilst I do not wish to undermine this tradition, it all seemed so formal and so somber.

This is a recollection of my experience in Church and there will be thousands of other people who have the same experience, I'm not by any means mocking the Church or Christianity because it taught me a lot and did a lot more good than harm. The problem I had was with the message and the limitations imposed on how you could live as a 'Christian'. The message was that if I was not baptized and took Jesus as my savior I would spend an eternity in hell and damnation. In one sermon, eternity was described as a bird dropping a feather onto a piece of granite the size of the Empire State building once a year. Eternity ceased once the granite was no more due to erosion from the feather. That was daunting and there was a lot of pressure and motivation for me to get baptized but my time would come. This principle did not sit well with me at all, it didn't seem to make sense but at my age you didn't question it.

Also the popular Sunday school song of 'Jesus loves you' was sang a lot and it was pure and positive and I enjoyed singing it, we were told that this is all we needed to know and accept and that knowing this would be enough. This is a beautiful and true statement and God is always there for us and will always love us but I feel now, not necessarily back then, that the more important truth is that we need to love ourselves first. I mean really love and accept ourselves because by loving ourselves we are only then capable of loving others deeply and truly. We are vessels of love, like a cup, and love is the water that fills that cup and if that cup is full to overflowing we can then genuinely and deeply love others. If we have an abundance of love within our cup, within our being and with self-acceptance we are confident within ourselves. When we are confident we are relaxed and when we relax our true self comes to the fore and it is then that we attract the people we want to ourselves. How do we start to love ourselves though? That was an answer that would take me most of my life to figure out and to accept and that story is for later on.

It used to make me feel a bit panicky and suffocated to think that this was it, you need to go to Church every week and be baptized otherwise you're going to spend a lot of time in misery. I was safe though because only at the age of accountability did this apply, basically when you were a young man. This is what we were told in Church in any case. If you were before the age of accountability and died, you would be saved. Phew, a sigh of relief at eight years. I wondered if God really kept tabs on people's age to see if they were still innocent or not when they had died. It got me wondering on the scenario of a lonely little Bushmen in the middle of the Karroo desert who had not been baptized. If he had never encountered a missionary or indeed Mal Bourne himself, would he go to hell? Was God really this unyielding? I was not convinced.

Again, part of the routine on a Sunday was a double-barreled morning and evening service, with the evening service, thankfully, not including more Sunday school. For good measure there was more Bible study on a Thursday night from 7pm to 9pm, and yes, this time it included more class time plus another lecture afterwards. We were well drilled, professional church goers, there was no room for part-timers and Mum was lapping up all this knowledge. It was a little frowned upon if you missed a service and if for one reason we were to miss one, I could have jumped for silent joy...... a day off. I did learn a lot but it felt oppressive. Church was to be our second home for a short period before we went back to the UK for another chapter of my life. Again, the social aspect of church obliterated all the feelings of suppression I had and we met some wonderful people, some really genuine friends for life.

We would spend lovely summer evenings at friend's houses from the church, having a braai, singing around a fire, playing guitars and laughing until our heads ached. The people were genuine and wonderful and God filled and a lot of them we are still in contact with. I have such warmth and fondness in my heart for those wholesome experiences and we were to do this more often than I can recall in these pages.

Chapter 7

Due to unrest in South Africa, most notably the appalling Soweto riots of 1976, Dad was beginning to feel a little unsettled and the seed was planted that maybe we should go back. Dad was on a five year contract, which started in November 1974, and he was also getting homesick. We were to move from Juniper Street and into a rented house in a less, shall we say, attractive part of Benoni. It was nearer the town and the main motorway and it was a place which felt like exactly what it was, temporary. It was our docking station before we were to leave to go to the UK. It felt more of a harsh place to live and even though there were still wide open roads, grassy pavements and houses that had lots of garden space, it felt different. It felt more industrial with fewer trees and the people seemed more hill-billyish. It was the sort of place where you wouldn't have felt out of place if your hobby was fixing car engines in the front living room. It was a place where you would see proud owners displaying their 1970 Ford Escort in the front garden on bricks whilst they tinkered with the engine. Oil impregnated hands and T-shirts, the big pork chop side burns and mustache the obligatory look. It was functional but it wasn't home and I felt the stomach churning feelings of unsettlement.

We were to have one more magical holiday before going back to Britain. Durban, on South Africa's South East coast, is the holiday destination of choice for most people living in the Highveld region. During the peak of summer, which was also Christmas time, there was usually a mass-exodus from 'Jo'burg' down to the tropical destination of 'Durbs' for a real unwind. Durban in the height of summer is excessively hot and humid to the point of despair so we would usually go in the winter months of June, July and August and even then the weather was warm and welcoming, the sea warm enough to splash about in without giving yourself hypothermia. Even in winter, average temperatures were in the low to mid twenties so it was really beautifully pleasant.

We booked up to go on a long weekend to the Elangeni Hotel on Durbans beach front, Mum and Dad had given me R12 pocket money, which for me was a lot of money considering my average monthly pocket money was R2. To put this in to perspective, in 1979 R2 would have bought you a MatchBox dinkie car. It could also have bought you twenty Fizz Pops or several bars of the hallowed Cadbury's Dairy Milk chocolate. So to have twelve R1 notes thrust into my grubby mitts lovingly by Dad felt like I had arrived. I honestly felt that thrill of power one has when they have more money in their bank account than they are used to. My mindset was not to frivolously squander these riches on chocolate though, I felt I needed to spend it wisely as I didn't know when I was going to ever achieve such affluence again. Well okay maybe one big slab then. You see 'money doesn't grow on trees' and 'you have to work long and hard to get anywhere in life' and 'look after the pennies and the pounds will look after you' were the pearls of wisdom I was accustomed to at that point. That was my financial blueprint and we generally had a collective thinking that 'the meek shall inherit the earth' and 'it is easier for a camel to pass through the eye of a needle than it is for a rich man to enter the kingdom of heaven' and that to want riches was un-Godly and only for the rich and greedy fat cats. Dads view of wealth was that if you were affluent, you had probably 'fleeced' somebody along the way in order to get it or that they were lucky so-and-so's who landed with their arse in the butter. This is not a slight against Mum and Dad as it is just the way that their parents and probably their parents, parents had programmed them, so they passed what they knew of the world on to us, genuinely with love in their heart and of instilling virtues and wisdom. Accepting this wisdom and it becoming part of your sub-conscious attitude towards money is very limiting and prevents the natural flow of abundance to you. You make sub-conscious, fear based decisions around money that never really quite set the heather alight and at best you stay safe and sheltered, leaving those toes dipped only slightly into the rich river of abundance that is our life.

So armed with my life changing amount of money, which I would have put in a silver, bullet proof attaché case if I could have, we were set for our holiday down to the exciting and exotic South Coast. Durban!! Tropical, exciting, palm trees and with the wonderful intoxicating smell of sugar-cane as you cross in to Natal sets the pulse racing, the anticipation of catching a glimpse of that wondrous shimmering greeny, blue ocean is a feeling that used to make my stomach lurch for the love that I have for it. The smell of salt sea air, the feeling of hot sand between your toes massaging your soles back to life, re-invigorating and re-generating your body through mother earth is a feeling that sets my soul free. I love the ocean, I love the sea and I love everything that feeds into it and off of it.

We entered into the hotel reception of the Elangeni hotel and the place immediately oozed affluence and serenity, it was a place of magic. We took the lift up to our room in silent awe of all this splendor, the smells of aftershave and perfume from relaxed, laughing couples as they walked arm in arm laughing down corridors. Our room was really high up, that's all I know, because when looking out of our window and at the street below the cars seemed surreal and like toys, but stunningly detailed and authentic ones. From our window we could see the Indian Ocean in all its shimmering splendor, with huge tankers drifting lazily across the horizon. It was a lovely stay and I remember feeling extremely special eating a chicken and mayo toasted sandwich next to the roof-top pool. It's always the small things folks that kids remember and for me, this sandwich was the best I had ever tasted. When we got out of the hotel I remembered I had R12 to spend and so I spent some time in shops wondering what I could spend this money on, or at least a part of it, bearing in mind that my first and most obvious purchase was to buy the biggest slab of Cadburys Dairy

Milk chocolate available to me. That was tucked away and not destined to last too long. Eventually I decided on a fine golden chain with 'The Saint' character as the centre piece, this being the popular TV series of the 1960's which included the character Simon Templar. The symbol consisted of a stick man in a bit of a camp pose with a halo above his head. I loved it and wore it on the beach bursting with pride. I think Mum and Dad wondered what I was playing at wasting my money on such a thing and I remember the feeling of emptiness that comes with spending all your money and thinking that more is never going to come to you, well not easily anyway.

After a stunning long weekend on Durbans South beach and Dad doing his best to keep his patience with the Indian vendors selling their Samoosas, it was off southwards down to Amanzimtoti, also on the coast but a little bit more wild than Durban. After being totally spoiled by the Elangeni Hotel, the Hotel in 'Toti' was a disappointment, especially when I found my bed already occupied by someone, a cockroach. That though was a minor inconvenience in what was an even better holiday than Durbs. Amanzimtoti boasted wild and wonderful beaches and oceans where the seas were notoriously rough and the waves attacked the sand with relentless ferocity, it was just perfect for a little boy who just wanted to be in the sea. I remember the silent and surreal feeling of being picked up by a huge crashing, dumping wave, like being in a giant washing machine of salty water and then CRASH, onto the beach with a mouthful of salty water and sand underneath your scrotum trapped between your crown jewels and the lining of your swimming trunks. How wonderful, how exhilarating that was. We spent many a sun-soaked day on the beach, eating cheese, pickle and grit sarnies as is customary beach gastronomy. We had a blast and it was time to come home where we stayed with Belinda and Freddie for the last month of October 1979 before returning back to the land of our birth. One amusing last act was for Freddie to buy Pauline a giant, life-sized Panda teddy which raised more than a few eyebrows as we boarded the plane back to Heathrow, it almost needed its own seat. Leaving sunny South Africa was gut wrenching to say the least because we had all settled well there but Dad was a restless soul and a return to murky Great Britain in November was what was decided and this thrust us all into a new chapter in our lives.

Chapter 8

Grifters and Golden Brown (Coedwig Road, Treganna, Cardiff - 1979 – 1982)

After landing at Heathrow we took a train to Cardiff and stayed at Uncle Vince and Auntie Heathers house on one of the busiest arteries in the city, number 333 Cowbridge Road East in Treganna. I'm sure we were all grateful for this help but it was quite a culture shock coming from the wide open sunny suburbs of South Africa to the grey, gloomy and built up city streets of Cardiff. Although this was the place of my birth, I felt lost and alone in this strange black and white land. Where were the trees and the grassy pavements? Where was our apricot tree? The front garden was tiny and about enough room to house a table tennis table, the back garden was almost the same size so running around outside was not really an option if it was raining. It most certainly wasn't all doom and gloom though because I had Jimmy, my cousin and close companion and this was all that really mattered. Heather and Vince were so wonderful to put us up and we were all grateful for their generosity of spirit.

During the first few days Dad had a deep depression and he really felt quite unsettled, which is natural. One morning, laying in a camp bed next to Mum, he looked over and made the motion with his hand of an airplane flying through the skies, a secret suggestion to Mum that maybe we should return and that this was perhaps a mistake. It was all in the moment to be fair to Dad and all emotion based but Mum felt the need to share it with us which obviously unsettled us all. We had a lovely few weeks here at the Hughes residence; well I say lovely, it was lovely for me in any case because it meant I got to have permanent sleepovers with my best buddy ever. Jimmy had the most brilliant array of toys, I was in heaven with all this new gear to play with and even things like stairs were a novelty for me. In SA mostly all houses are on one level without the need for stairs so for me it became a wooden hill to play on and I loved it. Bless her; it must have been exhausting for Auntie Heather having two nine year old boys ripping around the house and she used to shout quite often at Jimmy to stop running in off the street and getting mud on the hall carpet. It's so pure and uncluttered how children are so easily pleased because all I cared about was playing and sampling all these new foods that were uniquely British. Things like Monster Munch, Club biscuits, Mars bars, Salt n Shake crisps, Montego bars and lemon curd on ready sliced thick white bread were delights I had never encountered before and which I thought were a heavenly treat. In SA we were used to what was called a 'government loaf' which was just a brown and largely unappealing uncut loaf, in Britain there were a multitude of different choices of bread and even the thickness of the slices varied between loaves. What luxury.

From Cowbridge Road we went west to Saundersfoot in Pembrokeshire in order to set up camp there and settle. Now this area of Wales is absolutely gorgeous ....in summer. It is an area of natural beauty that nestles on the coast and during summer there is a healthy flow of holidaymakers lapping up the sun there and taking in all the scenic beauty. Winter, however, is an entirely different prospect indeed and resembles a bleak, isolated ghost town. We arrived at a flat we were to rent that overlooked the sea on the Friday and I was introduced to the new school later that day. I was told there were three other Liam's in the school so I was bound to fit in. After an evening of coughing and sneezing, due to an allergic reaction to the blankets on the bottom bunk, we didn't have the best of starts. I can only assume that the landlords used the bottom bunk as a bed for a St Bernard because it stank of wet dog and my chest almost closed up through coughing. It was a horrible introduction. At the same time Dad got a job straight away at a petrol station and came back to us a bit flat and tired. It was too much too soon for all of us and just a wee bit strange having just emigrated back home. We lasted just one bizarre weekend before heading back to Cardiff and back to Cowbridge Road.

Now those of you who have never lived in Britain, apart from January, November is one of the most bleak months because it is simply grey and wet and you know that the largest stretch of winter is still about to enfold. I remember walking to school up Cowbridge Road with Mum to my first day at school in Landsdowne Junior School. I had an overwhelming feeling of hollowness and apprehension because not only was it a new school and I was the new kid again but the place seemed cold and hard and lacking in any greenery. It felt like the concrete walls were closing in on me and I longed for free sunny, summer days of playing in a huge back garden. This seemed so far from all of that because as I trudged up that road to school with Mum I had a lump in my throat and was desperately fighting back the tears. I wanted to hold onto Mum and never let go but I knew I had to be brave.

I started in Standard 3P, where the P stood for Mr Peters who was a tall, spindly old man who wore a dark green suit with paisley jumper underneath. His accent was very English and he had a gaunt looking, bulgy eyed face with an Adams apple that had a life of its own. We were escorted up to the classroom by the school secretary where Mum introduced me to my new teacher. 'This is Liam O'Conner and we've just come over from South Africa…..' 'AFRICA!!?' Mr Peters blurted out, 'Good lord! Well have a seat, please sit down Liam'. I gave Mum a watery eyed wave and I was put next to the grubbiest urchin I had ever laid eyes on, Dwayne Simmons. He was pure Cardiffian toughness through and through and spoke with a typical street-wize way as if he literally lived on the streets, which it turned out later, he actually did. It was a tough baptism and having got the most difficult day out of the way things were destined to become easier as they always do after the first day at school.

Naturally, we were to join the Cardiff equivalent of the Benoni Church of Christ which was based in Moira Terrace in Adamsdown, literally around the corner from where Dad was born. The area was inner city, harsh and run down and it all made us feel quite depressed, especially Mum who was used to the bright, sunny surrounds and spacious grounds of the church in Benoni. Now we all know that church is not all about the building but this particular one was Dickensian and totally lacking in any soul. We all felt like fish out of water and even some of the stragglers were tramps off the street needing a place for shelter and a bit of food rather than people looking for the truth via the gospel. In retrospect though, the cause for looking after lost souls in such a fashion is more Godly than repeat sermons to the already converted. It was a harsh and unforgiving place and it did not feel as if you were escaping from the madding crowd in order to be closer to God, it felt more like another dreary trudge into another grey building. I didn't like it, none of us really liked it but we endured it.

The best comparison I can make going from the vibrant, bright and sunny congregation in Benoni to the dark and foreboding presence of Moira Terrace was as if we were happy football supporters in a huge and packed stadium watching a winning team which was Benoni to a struggling, amateur outfit barely attracting enough people to keep afloat in Cardiff. The church attendance was barren to say the least with a few diligent souls dotted around the auditorium on a Sunday morning. The dynamics of our role within church in general quickly changed from being happy passengers to being proactive 'fishers of men'. Fishers of men meaning to go out and spread the word to not only save the souls of the condemned man but to boost the bums on seats ratio within the church itself. Bill Hercombe was the first preacher we experienced and I can just about remember his very passionate sermons, spitting and frothing with enthusiasm in his very typical Welsh valleys accent. He was a lovely man as we were to find out but his preaching style was of the hell and damnation sort. Bill took a back seat due to ill health and was replaced by an American missionary in Terry Williamson who was of Red Indian heritage. He was here on a mission from God and while he was a wonderful man and a brilliant preacher, he just could not penetrate the brick wall of apathy that was the spiritual landscape of inner city Cardiff. He did his best but left soon afterwards.

Next up was a man who I would come to respect and love because he was so down-to-earth and so hard working and normal. His name was Jack Williams and he was born in Manchester but having lived in the US for many years he had picked up the accent entirely. He was married to a beautiful woman called Val who was from Liverpool and we immediately took to them as people. There was to be no teacher, student relationship as is often the case with preachers and their flock. Jack was a builder by trade and he had the big rough hands to prove it along with a typically rotund and jolly appearance. His heart was soft though and he brought the place to life, he breathed energy and soul and colour into that church with his wit, humour and work ethic. I shall never forget him or his lovely family as Mum and Val became good friends. They had children our age too, Nicky, who was Paulines age, Brandi, who was slightly older than me and Jason the youngest. Let me tell you, as a ten year old boy I had the biggest crush you could ever imagine on Brandi, she was pretty with dark hair and eyes, smelled lovely and to top it off, had this American accent that enchanted me. She was really lovely but I never dared show my feelings too much, well at least not that I thought I did. She made church do-able and I actually looked forward to going because of her.

It was around that time I started wearing deodorant, not that I really needed it but if I was running around playing 'it' after Sunday school and still wanted to impress Brandi, I needed something extra. At the same point in time we had managed to snare the Hughes family into the fold which illustrates the point of being 'fishers of men'. No-one was beyond our reach. This meant going to church with my best pal Jimmy and he too developed a bit of a crush on Brandi, along with Brother Steve, however Steve's threat as a rival turned out to be a red herring as we were to find out in later years. He seemed to get on extremely well with Brandi and found it easy to laugh and interact with her and it was during this time that I had real feelings of inadequacy and jealousy toward people who were more confident than I. Jimmy was also in the mix and his tactic was similar to mine but far more robust and confident, he used to douse his little red cheeked face in aftershave to the point of making people within ten metres of him cough and splutter due to excessive fume inhalation. I would spend many moments in silent admiration for Brandi but never plucked up the courage to do anything for the terror of being rejected or laughed at.

Chapter 9

Before all that though, Mum and Dad also soon bought a house in Coedwig Road, Treganna, right next to Forrest Park and whilst the street was average to decent, the house itself was anything but. I think Mum and Dad paid £12 000 for number 78, a masochistic, handy-man's dream. It was cheap and it needed lots and lots of work which almost drove Dad to the brink of despair. Whilst knocking the sitting room and front room into one, as was the trend in the seventies and eighties, a swinging girder manhandled by Dad and his brother Neil smashed the front living room window which brought fits of laughter from Neil but less of a response from Dad. Dad was ashen with worry, frustration and stress and we all thought he was going to have a nervous breakdown but with the help of a Jack, he managed to pull through. Jack was like a knight in shining armour as he swept into the house and erected one long internal wall within our living room with speed and vigour, it was the fashion of the time to have an internal wall, about a metre high running the length of the two rooms and included a fire opening.

In fairness to Dad, he worked like a Trojan making the house a much better place to live and it was transformed entirely with the kitchen and rear adjoining scullery being knocked into one to make a larger kitchen. It was Mum and us kids job to overhaul the garden from what can only be described as a rubbish dump into what became a beautiful little patch of greenery bordered by pretty flowers. The stuff we found in that garden simply gave me the creeps, eyeless baby dolls with mud-caked sockets, a huge glass bottle of orangey, brown excrement, weird and wonderful bits of rubbish, old furniture and I'm positive there were human sized bones, it was enough to give me the heeby jeebies and I was convinced this place was of a bad energy or some voodoo had been practiced here but I was too young to voice this and not confident enough to think I was right.

In those early days of standard three, because our house was basically the one which needed the most work on in the street, with the peeling orange framed wooden doors and window frames on the outside, I was ashamed of our house. You see the doorbell wasn't a lavish sounding diiiiiing, dooooong that echoed through the halls of our abode, it sounded more like a shallow sounding toy bell, like a dingk, dik and it was just plain embarrassing. For a nine year old that was an important aspect and one day after school I was walking home and behind me, some twenty meteres back was a female classmate, also walking home. Instead of turning into my gate and ringing the bell, I walked on by and turned down another street until she had passed my house. In time, Dad transformed our doer-upper into a lovely place to live and this was testament to his determination that he achieved this so quickly and thoroughly.

My room was decorated in 'The Perishers' wallpaper, which I loved, and was the little box room before the bathroom which, when my door was open, looked up into the hall and the ceiling hatch. This particular hatch used to terrify me as I was convinced there was something behind it looking down on me. It was an irrational fear and I genuinely used to be in a bath of sweat in my bed staring up at the hatch, praying that nothing would come out of it. Every night, for many months I would be in a state of real and genuine fear and I did not know why. I told Mum and she knew it was unusual for me to be behaving in a way that you would if you were three years old and scared of the boogey man but at ten years old she was at a loss to know what to do or think. Years later Mum admitted that she also had weird dreams about the house but she didn't want to heap further angst upon me. There was certainly something very amiss about the place which we never really got to the bottom of. I was fine if Pauline was upstairs in her room but if she wasn't I would be frozen in my bed, heart pounding, dry mouth, eyes fixed to the ceiling hatch. Since all the houses were joined in the street in that Victorian manner, otherwise known as terraced housing, technically someone could actually go in one attic at the end of the street and climb through all of the attics until he reached our house. I would imagine this person hovering menacingly over our hatch until I was asleep, upon which he would invade my dreams or worse still, kill me. Well this is what was in my head at least and I would spend many a night praying that I would be alright. If Pauline was in the room next door, I felt safe. Eventually and after a lot of hard work during the summer of 1980 our house was eventually looking lovely and I was proud of our house and proud of my Dad. We even had a front doorbell that went diiiiing, dooooohng in a rather lavish manner.

Meanwhile, I was chugging along in school and far more interested in the outdoors, sport and playing than Math's, English and Geography but I do remember writing a poem explaining my loathing for maths lessons. I still have it in fact and the words 'loathsome' and 'hateful' feature quite prominently since my mental blueprint was that I was hopeless at the subject. I will talk a lot about a 'mental blueprint' during the course of this book so get used to it but it represents the subliminal and sub-conscious belief patterns we are programmed with in our first seven years. In much later years and after a bout of soul searching it turned out to be entirely the opposite that I was hopeless at maths but that is another story and in another chapter of my life. Confidence is a wonderful thing and can be the difference between average and brilliant in much the same way that if you were to bake a cake, one fundamental ingredient is baking powder. It might only be a tiny percentage of the cakes ingredients but without it that cake is flat and average. With that ingredient it rises and becomes everything it can be. I unfortunately did not have this missing ingredient and although I had the support of my Mum and Dad in a verbal sense I didn't really feel it. Mum would try and cajole me into homework and she would do her best but it was a mental block and I buried my head in the sand. It was not so much the lack of support from Mum, because she was absolutely there for me, but more the feeling I had that I was not bright, not a quick learner, an average plodder at best. Somehow, from somewhere, later in my life I developed confidence and this allowed me to truly soar like an eagle, it unlocked my treasure chest of potential but that was to be nearer the end of my school days.

A typical day for me would be to walk to school which was less than half a mile away, do the bare minimum in lessons I wasn't keen on and to coast along as much as I could. If average was enough to get me through, then that would be my aim but there were exceptions when I just used to thrive without much effort and that was English and drawing. I used to love those subjects but drawing was not too big a part of the school syllabus back then, not the drawing I liked anyway. We did art of course, lots of it, plenty of wonderful paints and colours but I was more into precision and pencil drawings and I had a good eye for detail. I would walk home for lunch time, make myself a sarnie if Mum was working, feed the cat and walk back to school clutching a 10p piece which would buy me a quarter pound of bon bons from the sweet shop on Cowbridge Road opposite Pidgeons the funeral home. My favourites were the plain white powdered toffee bon bons but of course there were lemon, strawberry and chocolate too. Sherbet lemons, pineapple chunks, cola chunks and wham bars were to be my crutch in junior school along with Star Bars and Mars Bars. I would love playing football and 'tag' in the school playground and try to irritate the dinner ladies as much as possible, these dragons in pink pinafores patrolling the playground. 3:15pm was for me the most wonderful time of day as it signaled the end of the school day and a chance to play. If it was in the winter months and rainy, I would trudge home and have a cup of tea by the fire and tell Mum about my day, in the summer months we would go home and shortly afterwards come back out into the street and play 'Mob' with all the other kids in the street. Mob was a combination of 'tag' and 'hide and seek'.

During the time between arriving home and when Dad got home was always lovely because it felt free and fun. When Dad came home though he used to carry with him an atmosphere like a heavy aura. His presence, whether in good or bad mood was large. When in a darker mood, the atmosphere in the house could be heavy, dark and oppressive and I was scared of Dad, scared of his volatile temper, as much as I loved him. My heart used to be in my throat at times around the dinner table with an angry silence brewing, the red face and sighs of exasperation that there was no brown sauce or that there was no bread on the table with dinner. I used to feel sorry for Mum because she was always doing her best and Dad, at times, especially when he was hungry used to be like a caged lion and could be incredibly hard on Mum. People in general, but especially the O'Conner's, are renowned for being ferocious if hungry and if ever you encounter one in the wild and you have an inkling that it has not eaten, walk away, walk away as fast as you can and get food, any food. You tend to see a magical transformation from cold hard 'lion eyes' to happy puppy dog eyes after a simple sandwich. Mum couldn't win at times as in anticipation of his mood walking through the door she would make sure dinner was on the table to counter the 'WHERE'S DINNER!!' rant. However, Dad, being contrary, on the other hand used to say 'Don't throw my dinner at me as soon as I walk through the door Woman' so Mum didn't know which way to turn, bless her. That feeling at the dinner table used to travel from my throat down to my stomach and while I loved Dad with all my heart, I was scared of him in general and just wanted to please him. Unless Dad was worried by something on a deeper level, straight after dinner he would be absolutely fine, joking around and smiling like nothing had happened. Whilst Mum was trying to gather her mood it was tough for her to just flick the switch and become happy too. Dad could often blow up in rage and five minutes later be smiling and very apologetic, very soft and remorseful but the damage had already been done. It's just the way it was and we knew no different. Dad was by no means a bad person, in fact he is a wonderful, generous, warm and giving father who would do absolutely anything for you to protect you but his temper was his black side.

Being a rough and tumble sort of toughie that had grown up in SA and having ginger hair made me a target, a target that boys quickly realized was not to be messed with if provoked. On one occasion one of my classmates, who happened to be cocky and a bit loud and arrogant, the opposite of me, decided he was going to tease me. Previous to this, at lunch time, I had sliced my thumb open whilst attempting to pull the razor sharp lid of a can of corned beef open which should really have needed stitches but Mum patched me up and I was good to go back to school. During playtime the incident occurred because I was telling my classmates how this injury happened so they started calling me a big girl, Mummy's boy and the rest of it. Well I pounced on Mr Nottingham Forrest shirt, Mr Bravado, Mr Popular and found myself punching him repeatedly on his back whilst he tried to escape, with the same hand that had a plaster on the thumb. Well he ran off to the headmaster, Mr Davies, with blood from my hand on his shirt and I was quickly summoned to the office. Now Mr Davies to me was a fearsome character and I was terrified of him, especially his quiff that used to retreat backwards when he was losing his temper. 'Now listen here young man, we don't tolerate any of this savage behavior you have in Africa, DO YOU UNDERSTAND ME!!?' My head was swimming, my stomach was in a knot and I felt scared and ashamed of myself. I found myself in tears blurting out 'But I'm a Christian, I'm not a bad person' and after a chat with Mum, the issue was over. It was a short sharp wrap across the knuckles and whilst I still didn't take any nonsense from any of my peers, I tried to keep a lower profile, it was a lesson learned, temporarily.

Mums best friend in Cardiff from school days was Deborah Hopkins and she very kindly gave me a bike because although Dad was working and Mum was doing some part time work as well, the budget was not at the point where we could start buying new bikes. As grateful as I was to have my own set of wheels, and I really mean that with all my heart, it was still a girl's bike. It was red and had thin little wheels the size of a frizbee with white tyres but essentially it had a cross bar that sloped downwards which meant 'for girls only'. It was a tiny little thing but I was happy enough on it, at least I could get places quicker. My buddy across the street from us, Andrew, had the latest ten speed, Raleigh racer bike in bright cobalt blue and I would race him up and down Coedwig Road in a determined effort to beat him on my little red contraption and you know what? I did! I was so determined to succeed that Andrew couldn't actually keep up with me,

I used to take pride in coming back from the dead and succeeding against all the odds. My heart would soar with pride and determination when I won things of a physical nature, that was my strength, my forte and that feeling of rising up and being victorious against all the odds was a part of my DNA now. Dad had instilled it into us never to give up, keep fighting until your last breath and I would pride myself on this for the rest of my life. As noble and admirable as this quality is, it does have a down side in that sub-consciously you always expect a battle, a fight for anything that is to become yours. Invariably you would get what you expected as well, struggle. In order for true abundance to be attracted into my life, I would have to address this mindset but only after a lifetime of learning.

<u>Chapter 10</u>

The mind in my very simple terms is like an ice-berg with the conscious mind being the part that is visible or the bit that is above the ocean. The sub-conscious mind is therefore the 95% of what is below the ocean. We can repeat positive affirmations, we can read and understand the 'law of attraction' which is logical and true, we can be positive and take the positive from any situation in our conscious state but that has comparatively very little impact upon our natural state of seeking abundance. The greatest and most profound results come from addressing our sub-conscious beliefs and when we do this, we really do open ourselves up to becoming the greatest that we can become. When we live to our true potential and when we live our passion and dharma having addressed 'lack of' mindset we can really take flight. If you think of it logically, it is common sense to fix the thing that affects the 95% portion rather than the 5% portion. Fixing our blueprint, our DNA, our sub-conscious is a separate practice that anyone can do and is something I will share with you in later chapters in the hope that it helps others. Having practiced this technique has enabled me to write this book.

In school we were to undergo a cycling proficiency test which was to test our skills on our bike and also to ensure our bike was road-worthy. I could not wait for this, a chance to take your bike to school and show what you could do. It was brilliant; the school yard was full of children on their bikes eagerly looking to pit their wits against the cones and obstacle courses and there was a general hubbub of excitement and activity. I was up for this and I was going to prove how brilliant I was to everyone. Everyone else had their brand new 10 speed racers, Choppers, Tomohawks or Grifters. I had my red girl's bike that was a bit rusty and with brakes that did eventually stop you at some point. I didn't give a hoot, I was going to lick this test and show everyone what a biker I was. Well we all did the practical test of weaving through cones, pedaling in a straight line, braking at a safe distance and various other tests which I flew through. Some people struggled on their lovely new bikes, I didn't. I breezed through the theory and was ready for the next stage, the roadworthy test.

At this point the bespectacled, mustached examiner in tweed suit and clip board beckoned me to come forth with my little red bike. He was the type of person who had a charisma bypass and took his job a little too seriously in my rebellious opinion. I presented my rusty pride and joy to him and he looked at the bike with an arched eyebrow of alarm and disdain. Mr Clipboard could barely bring himself to touch this beastly contraption and kept the bike balanced with the tip of his forefinger on the end of the handlebar in case he got contaminated with the rust virus. After a few seconds of crosses put on his clipboard he pronounced that my bike was not roadworthy and that I had failed overall because of this and that I could go home if I wanted to. I was crestfallen, frustrated and angry all at the same time. Why could they not have just told me that to begin with instead of making me go through all that testing? I went home and told Mum with a lump in my throat, struggling to fight away the tears and she was typical Mum, soft and sympathetic and full of love and understanding. She made a cup of tea. That was always the remedy in the O'Conner household, if in doubt make a cuppa tea. I was to recover from this setback in my biking career, I was to live to fight another day.

Dad, being what he was, committed to right this wrong by buying me a metallic blue, three geared Raleigh Grifter. We got it second hand from a posh house on Caerphilly Road and I thought I had died and gone to heaven. I could not possibly have been any happier with life, this was it, and this was my purpose for being alive. I was meant to ride a bike around the streets for hours and hours. I remember the feeling of power surging through me as I shifted through the gears and mounted a curb as if I were riding over a lolly stick. I really did love this bike and I would spend a good many hours roaming the streets of Treganna, irritating park keepers by playing my play police, ambulance and fire siren which I got as a birthday present. One park keeper in Thompsons Park was so irate with me that he chased me with his litter stick which had a very sharp end and if he'd caught me, I might have ended up looking like a tripod.

I was getting to an age now where I was interested in music, not that I wasn't before but now I preferred to spend pocket money on records rather than cars. We had grown up with music in the house all the time and I am very grateful that I had parents who loved the Beatles, in my opinion the greatest group of musicians ever. They were kings in our house, everyone adored them and we knew every word of every song. There were always tracks being played from their albums and it was like listening to gold. Dad loved the Rolling Stones as well but they weren't as popular with everyone else in the house. Another favourite was Neil Diamond which at the time I couldn't stand but now I love. Dad would often put his headphones on and connect it up to our 'Steinberg' stereo system and stand in front of it rocking back and forth in a Stevie Wonder style. He was in complete enjoyment singing at the top of his voice, not realizing how loud and out of tune he was and belting out 'Sweet Caroline!!! Dah, duh, duh'. My first single was surprisingly classy as a song and it was Golden Brown by The Stranglers which I used to play over and over again. Jimmy and myself used to go down to a record store in Treganna and pore through what we thought were the latest cool releases. Pauline and Steve, being older, were a little more streetwise and probably bought a better style of music especially considering that my next single was 'Speed It Up' by Eurovision song contest winners, Bucks Fizz. At the time I thought it was astonishingly good and no wonder they won. I think of it a little differently now. One that I took pride and joy in and still think it was a great buy to this day is 'Joan Of Arc' by OMD which probably put paid to our needle on the record player. It was THAT good.

The 8th December 1980 is a date and time I will never forget as it was when John Lennon was shot dead in cold blood in New York. I remember exactly where I was when the news broke, Mum and I in the kitchen in Coedwig Road, Mum says it was similar to when JFK was assassinated; it was a horrible moment of surrealistic disbelief. We were both in tears and I couldn't fully comprehend that he would no longer be making music, it was such a low point, I just couldn't understand it, couldn't understand why someone would need to take his life as an avid fan. I must admit that I still don't understand that.

Around about this time Dad took me to rugby matches to watch Cardiff play merit table fixtures against the likes of Bridgend, Pontypridd, Cross Keys and Neath and I loved it. It was a fantastic atmosphere and I loved the boys in Blue and Black hoops. At ten I wasn't tactically aware of the games finer points but I knew what a good try was and Cardiff scored plenty of them. On a cold, grey January day there is little to really stimulate the senses apart from jarringly cold intakes of air but at a rugby or football ground there is always so much to take in, the noises of fans, some drunken, some not, the indecipherable announcements over a tannoy system, smells of cigar smoke, the green turf, floodlights, the scoreboard and just the thrill of being somewhere different. I was hooked. So much so that I managed to get a Cardiff rugby top which I proudly wore everywhere. Around about this time, 1980, it was Welsh Rugby's centenary celebration season so a friendly match was arranged between a Wales/England XV against an Ireland/Scotland XV. This was a literal once in a lifetime game bearing in mind that tickets were like gold dust and we certainly did not expect to see the game, it was a sellout. There were throngs upon throngs of red and white scarves, blue and green ones too, the atmosphere was electric, the streets were packed with happy, drunken revelers. I just felt privileged to be a part of the street parade so what happened next took me totally by surprise. Dad and I just so happened to be wandering past the Hotel Elang in Westgate Street when a tall, looming police officer walked towards us and looked at me and said, 'Have you got tickets for the game son?' to which I replied 'erm…no' thinking I was in trouble. He thrust two tickets into my hand for Dad and myself to get into the game which turned out to be an absolutely fabulous game of hard, committed, running rugby with the likes of Gareth Davies, Bill Beumont, Andy Irvine and Tony Ward playing. What a thrilling game this was as Wales/England won by 37-34, truly a memorable day and such a stroke of luck to have got tickets. I remember feeling awestruck as I watched a giant Irishman running with the ball in one hand and it has forever stayed in my memory.

This gave me a taste for rugby and since I was to move up from primary school to high school in the summer of 1981 I would get my chance to play since rugby or football was not played at our school in any organized format at Lansdowne Junior School back then. I was apprehensive and also exited at the prospect of going from primary school to high school but not before I had made friends with a boy in my street by the name of Matt Trillby who was two or three years older than me. He introduced me to all manner of military paraphernalia such as model airplanes, toy soldiers and second hand army gear from the local Army and Navy stores. He also had a Second World War air raid shelter still in his back garden which for me was possibly the coolest den a ten year old could have. I really got on well with Matt and we shared so many interests together. We'd go to Forrest Park on our bikes dressed in army gear and pretend we were fighting in the jungle by commando crawling through the flower beds that bordered the park, like no-one would notice. He introduced me to the wonderfully therapeutic world of model making which took my mind off into another direction. It started off with simple airplanes such as Spitfires, Corssairs and Hurricanes but developed into much more complicated builds such as intricate real life plastic gun builds which if the parts were made from steel, they would basically have been a real gun. It was great fun and introduced a logic and method to my mind that school couldn't teach me. I loved the fact that it was hands on creation coupled with logic. I think this was the first seed planted in my mind around the fascination of assembly and how much satisfaction it gave me.

My life was beginning to settle and I had really grown roots again. I had my cousins, Jimmy and Amelia and in school I was friendly with a few lads but not close enough to want to go to their house to play. Back then we all just used to play in the street, between parked cars, playing football or tennis if Wimbledon was on, playing mob and generally being free. Matt was a really good street buddy though and I thought a lot of him, I'm not sure Mum and Dad approved though as he was slightly older and totally not into church stuff.

Meanwhile, back in the parallel universe of churchgoing, we were still in the same habits of attending twice on a Sunday and one evening during the week for Bible study. I have to admit that the church was becoming more and more vibrant with new carpeting, new painted walls and new pews, it was really looking lovely. More significantly though were the additions of lots of young people and families into the congregation which really breathed new life into what was previously a slumbering and depressing place to be. With lots of youth bought lots of fun and we would often have days in the sun out in the countryside with not a Bible in sight. It was a good healthy youth club that taught good morals in a sea of otherwise ill-discipline, violence and rebellion against authority at that time in working class Britain. Against this backdrop of positivity in the church I wanted to be more involved and so took the decision to get baptized much to Mum's joy. In Christian terms this is a huge moment in your life as was the case for me, it is akin to a rebirth, hence the term 'Born again Christian'.

It was a transformational time and when I was dipped into the waters at the front of the church in front of the whole congregation I felt a tingle all over my body, it was an amazing feeling and honestly not what I was expecting. I had had my eleven year old sins washed away and I felt renewed. This allowed me not only to take communion on a Sunday morning, which was the hallowed red grape juice and crackers but also to serve it. I was getting to an age now where girls were more in the foreground of my thoughts than the background and meant that I could get up and be as cool as possible in the front of the church next to the preacher as one of the two servers. I thought this might make me stand out and for the girls to think I was irresistible as a strong silent server of grape juice. I was of course wrong because they were also eleven and even if they did think I was like Danny Zuko, they were not going to show it, I was not about to be pelted with underwear by girls in the congregation now was I. Bear in mind though that at eleven you are more a little boy still than a young teenager wannabee and I would still have giggling fits in the front of the church, mainly because cousin Jimmy was the other side of the preacher as the second server of communion and he simply made me laugh. I remember on one occasion, whilst prayers were being said, there was a moment of contemplative silence and I got the giggles having caught Jimmy's eye on my left. There was nothing to actually laugh about, just the silence and the attention on us was enough. I put my head down and tried to stifle the snort that came from my nose, the reddening of my face and neck a dead giveaway and the more I looked at people with somber, serious faces, the funnier it became. I just could not stop myself laughing, my head was aching and my body was shaking as I sat there in a room full of silence. I barely managed to gather myself and got through the process of serving communion in the end. I can't really remember Mums reaction at the time but in truth, I'm sure she didn't really mind at all, she was just proud I even wanted to be involved to that extent. Although I look back on those times in church as being dull, grey and uninspiring there were actually some wonderful times had, some beautiful people met and lasting friendships made. The biggest issue I always had was with the message or sermon as this did not usually inspire and normally made me feel guilty for being me. There were occasions where it would be positive and funny and even a little upbeat but they were sparse. I didn't really like coming away from church feeling brow beaten and that confused me a little. I was still far too young and embroiled in it all to question anything as the Bible was the alpha and the omega, the oracle and that was that.

At the beginning of 1981 Pauline was fully immersed in Britain and sporting a 'new romantic' style fringed haircut with her maroon long, padded coat and looking like one of the girls from 'The Human League'. She had a few close friends, most notably Lindy Elan, who she was very close to. Pauline and I were always really close and used to look after eachother in a big way, always very protective of eachother even though we used to tease one another mercilessly. During this time Mum and Dad announced that they were expecting child number three, which initially was quite a shock to us both but after a while we got used to it and then really started to get excited. I was eleven by then and the gap between myself and my 'to be' sibling would be quite big. Big enough for me to want to look after her like a second father or at least a very big older brother. That summer was the wedding of Charles and Dianna and in Britain it was quite an occasion with the whole street decked out in Union Jacks and pictures of the happy couple. It was an amazingly atmospheric period with hot weather, a buzz of anticipation for what was to be and especially wonderful because we had Dad's brother and his wife, Freddie and Belinda over from South Africa on holiday. I would play soldiers endlessly with Justin and Richard out the back and over Forrest Park and it was just a lovely time with some stunning memories. We were all to have a wonderful street party on the day of the Royal wedding with some fantastic tunes and some not so fantastic tunes being played on a huge speaker. Who can forget that song by Joe Dolce called 'Shaddap Your Face' which for me was in the latter category. 'Stand and Deliver' by Adam and the Ants, 'Making Your Mind Up' by Bucks Fizz and 'Tainted Love' by Soft Cell were all classics in my mind back then.

Then shortly after Freddie and Belinda went back, my little sister was born on the 20th August 1981 in the same hospital Pauline was born in. Unusually, the first person on the scene was Paulines mate, Lindy much to the irritation of Mum. It must have just been a coincidence that she happened to be there visiting in her warm and friendly way when Mum went into labour. She only lived around the corner from the hospital so it was understandable. It was so exciting to be dragged out of bed in the middle of the night by Dad and heading off to the hospital to welcome another little red-head into the family. This gorgeous, little red, chubby-cheeked girl who Mum and Dad decided to call Cei was such a wonderful blessing to us all. Ceinwen being the name of Mum's Mum, our Nana. She was such a lovely little thing and I immediately felt protective and that I needed to look after this little bundle. She turned out to be an absolute handful of a baby for Mum at the age of 35, she was *so* active and was constantly on the move. She had the O'Conner trait of needing to rock back and forth to give herself comfort and she used to exhaust Mum but we all adored her, this 'little plum' that I ended up calling her.

Chapter 11

So being newly baptized, with a new little sister and with Standard 4 under my belt I felt as if I was entering a new and more mature stage in my life. Having spent my second year in Lansdowne under the tuition of a bearded, baseball mad, tobacco smelling Mr James, I was ready for the new world of high school, or so I thought. As was par for the course with me in school, I did just enough to be average but not in a way that wanted to deliberately underachieve through burned out rebellion but more so because I was not motivated for school in any way. Back in the early eighties in working class, inner city Britain there was a sense of total disregard for school or authority and the kids seemed harder, tougher than I was used to in an emotional sense. The hit song at the time by Pink Floyd 'Another Brick in the Wall' was very typical of the generation. I was a tough little boy physically but emotionally I was soft to the core, I still am. Kids were more streetwise than they were in sunny, well disciplined South Africa. Ambition seemed to be camouflaged in the greyness of the streets but it was all I knew and accepted and I was excited to be starting high school, excited to be wearing a uniform and totally accepting that this was to be my path and my life.

Coming from apartheid run South Africa and starting school in the demographic melting pot of Fitzalan High School in inner city Cardiff was a literal culture shock. I simply was not used to all the different ethnicities, not that I held any racist views but it was an incredible sight to see so many turbans walking to school. Our uniform was grey trousers, grey shirt and grey jersey with a lonely splash of colour in that we had a green tie with thin white and black diagonal stripes. I really felt grown up and man-of-the-world-like going to school until I actually got there. We were all to start in Form 1 and there was already a healthy rivalry between boys from different areas of the west side of the city and docks area, where my Dad came from. Boys from the docks and Grangetown carried an air of invincibility and had a scant regard for authority. The boys from Ely, that huge urban council estate sprawl, were their rivals. I wasn't too interested in any of that gang culture and was just too caught up in football, rugby, model making and all things military to be bothered by it. However, as much as I didn't want trouble, trouble came to me in the form of the stocky little 'hard man' Leroy Jeffries from the docks. He used to strut around with chest out, a grimace of permanent disdain, tie loosened with a curly afro. At 11 he was already starting to grow a mustache and he wanted to make his mark, he wanted to show everyone who was boss. On his first day in school he picked on one of my classmates, 'Tabby', the pair having had an altercation in a primary school sports event. He grabbed Tabby by the tie and proceeded to lay down the law with him and told him what he was going to do to him if he didn't toe the line.

A few days later he tried it on with me and challenged me to an arm wrestle since he had beaten everyone else in the form. Now I can honestly say that I wasn't too interested and genuinely wanted to mind my own business but he challenged me so I had to respond in front of a goading set of classmates. With Leroy 'king of form 1' everyone wanted to be his friend and so when I was challenged, I became everyone's cannon fodder as easy prey. Well I have always come out fighting if my back was to the wall and this time they thought I was going to be another notch on the king's belt. To tell me I'm beaten is the easiest way to motivate me and as I lay on the concrete floor with Leroy, face to face, I was ready. I was not going to give in and this cocky little upstart had awoken the lion in me. We grasped eachothers hands in arm wrestling pose and started the contest. Little did he know that Jimmy and I were always having arm wrestling contests so I knew what to do, I was seasoned. As I lay there, my bicep felt like a rock as I bit my bottom lip in concentration, Leroy was perspiring, he had never had such resistance before, he had usually won by now, but not today. I could see in his eyes he was getting exasperated and frustrated and I knew he was gone. I feigned to be weakening, to start giving way before shocking him with an almighty push downwards and a crash of his hand onto the floor. He looked at me with a grimace and said, 'you're quite strong O'Conner' and just walked away. He was still a tyrant in class but he never bothered me after that.

Fitzalan was quite an eye opening school and it was different and thrilling for me to be going to different classrooms for each subject, in primary school the same teacher took you for all the lessons in the same room. Now we were doing subjects like biology, music, metalwork, woodwork, French, science, math's, English, history and geography. Some subjects I loved, like metalwork, woodwork and English but the rest I just couldn't be bothered with. P.E. was great, I loved that but I'm not sure you got graded for that. Since there was no incentive to do well, such as failing the year if your grades weren't good enough, I naturally just coasted along. In South African schools, if your grades weren't up to scratch you were kept back a year and not many people did for the simple reason of the stigma of it and also because you wanted to continue upwards through the grades with your buddies. I was so disinterested in school that I didn't really bother revising much for exams. In one biology exam in Form 1 the question paper asked 'Explain the term cold blooded with respect to animals?' My answer was 'A cold blooded animal kills without feeling'. I'm pretty certain Mr Davies, our teacher, must have had a wry smile at that one.

A wonderful thing was to happen to me in this year though and I took great pride in joining the school rugby team. This is what I lived for; this was what I loved, in the thick of the action and being physical. I remember being picked for the first team after some trials across the rugby pitch with Mr. Evans and we were drilled by running up and down the length of the pitch throwing the ball in one big line from one to the other making sure it never went forward. Mr Evans said to us in his Welsh accent, 'Boys, the most beautiful thing you will ever see is a try scored right in the corner'. He was right of course, but we were novices of the game and had a lot to learn, even about the basics, let alone the finer points. I lapped it all up though and threw myself into it with everything I had. I relished the physical contact of it all, the chance to dump someone on the floor and I was absolutely in my element. We started the season against Kings College on a bitingly cold day with rain, hail and sleet thrown into the mix. The worse the conditions the more I relished it as I knew that no-one else would be enjoying it. I was crunching into tackle after tackle and hell bent on crossing that line. I was like a boy possessed. With one of the lads going off the pitch with freezing cold hands it made me more determined than ever. I managed to score a close range try and we won the game 8-4, bear in mind that these were the days when a try was worth four points. I was absolutely ecstatic and so proud, so proud that Dad had watched me as well. In the hot showers afterwards I felt I was in bliss and that life did not get any better than this. The rest of the season was not to prove as successful as we were to lose more than we won against generally more experienced teams but in every single game I gave absolutely everything and never, ever gave up. In one match we were 26-0 down and I was distraught and angry but still kept plugging away, still kept tackling anything that moved. We did eventually score in a 26-6 defeat but I held my head up high. Mr Evans was very proud of me, not for my beautiful running rugby technique but for my attitude towards the game, my doggedness to tackle anything and just the general attitude of never saying die. I loved every minute of it; I loved pulling on those green socks, black shorts and green top with a black and white band across the middle. Sheer pride was what it was. At the end of the season Mr Evans, my hero, named me player of the year and I was swelling with pride. It was announced in class that we were to have an evening ceremony in front of the entire school plus all parents so that the trophies could be presented to each winner of each different sporting discipline and of course, each year. The date was announced as the 9th June 1982, starting at 6pm and I just could not wait to go up on stage and receive my trophy. We even invited our cousins the Hughes family to attend and we would pick them all up in the Church mini bus that Dad used to drive, in order that we could all go together.

Meanwhile, school continued and I ambled along from lesson to lesson, feeling thrilled and revolted all at the same time to be cutting into a severed bulls eye in science. That's what you call kill or cure for any potential surgeons. My favourite subjects at this point were art, woodwork and metalwork and when I think back now, I should have listened to my inner voice and thrown myself into these subjects because to this day, these would be my subjects of choice if I was a forty-something year old in the body of a twelve year old. I wasn't overly committed though but still did pretty well in attaining B's and C's, math's however was to be my Achilles heel and my living hell. I had such a huge mental block for the subject that it almost paralyzed me with fear. I simply thought I couldn't do it, I just thought my brain was not wired to accept this foreign language and when they started algebra, I thought I was living in a parallel universe that had gone mad. I used to feel totally exasperated when being asked to add 'a + a', I honestly thought the concept was utterly pointless and because I didn't buy in to it, I didn't bother to learn it. However, what I lacked in confidence, I made up for in cunning so I would sit next to the cleverest girl in class. The teacher would go around the room in a predictable pattern going through the times tables and just before it got to me with a particularly challenging one I would whisper to my girl, boffin, neighbour 'I bet you don't know what 6x7 is?' to which she would haughtily reply, in a tone that said 'Duh, of course I know it's 42, idiot'. My reply would be to whisper 'Correct!' to her with a look of smugness and a raised eyebrow, then when the teacher got to me and asked, I was ready for her. '42 Miss' I said with a queasy smile. Easy, this maths lark.

I didn't fair too much better with languages either, obtaining a lofty 14% for a French oral exam and faring slightly better with Welsh, at least I managed to pass that, it being the tongue of my forefathers after all. School was winding down now for summer and I quickly realized that we would be going to be put into 'streams' depending on our grades attained. The top 'A'grade students would go into A band, the average ones into B band, the below average ones into C band and then the rest of the academic imbeciles were to be put into the 'Remedial' stream which had a separate school building all of its own, a virtual leper colony so as not to contaminate the rest of the school. The school year wasn't quite over but my grades were forecast for me to be in the C band which caused me to sit up and take note, and to start panicking. At the same time though, there was talk in the family of a move back to South Africa as Dad thought the education system there was much better and Mum and Pauline still missed the place. I, by comparison, had settled and grown roots and made friends. I was loving rugby most of all and I really thought I was on to something and eventually the 9th June loomed where I was to receive my trophy, at last a chance to show the world that I was good at something. I recall we picked up Steve and Jimmy on that evening in the minibus and proceeded to the Fitzalan car park, having gone to the corner shop to buy a bag of sweets for the event. With Dads 'Jube-Jubes' in a bag, which is O'Conner or Cardiff slang for jelly sweets, we entered the school with anticipation and butterflies in the stomach. We were to be greeted with a dark, empty and locked car park with not one soul about. My heart sank, my head was swimming and I realized that I had got the date wrong. What an anti-climax! I looked sheepishly at the eager faces in the minibus as I wrung the back of my neck with my hand, writhing in embarrassment as I said 'Erm, I think we're a month early'. You see, not for the first time and certainly not for the last, I managed to totally get the dates wrong and we were a month early. Mum checked the invite in the minibus and saw it was the 9th of July, not June that the ceremony took place. 'Aawh Liam, love you' which was my Mum's soft and gently way of saying 'You bloody idiot'. The return trip, however, was to be a success and not surprisingly, Steve and Jimmy gave this one a miss as I don't think they were up to another sweetless, fruitless journey back into an empty car park. The nerves I had sitting with Mum and Dad were awful but the feeling of being up on that stage and shaking the hand of Mr Hoole the headmaster was absolutely brilliant. 'And Rugby player of the year for Form 1........Liam O'Conner' which triggered lots of applause as I stared out into a sea of faces in the darkness. Standing next to me was the brilliant footballer of that form who won the accolade for 'Footballer of the year', his name 'Leroy Jeffries'. We were not buddies but had a mutual respect for eachother.

Dad broke the news to us in the early summer of 1982 that we were heading back to South Africa after months of rumbling discontent and the news was not welcome to me. I felt happy and established in Cardiff and I had grown roots, my rugby was burgeoning but my school work left a lot to be desired as my end of year grades for Form 1 had meant that I would be in the C-Band, one band up from the duffers of society. On one hand I was immensely relieved that I didn't have to face up to my failure and lack of work ethic by simply jumping ship and going to a new country but on the other I was devastated to be leaving my rugby world, the exciting city streets of Cardiff where I had so many friends, most of all, Jimmy my cousin. I was secretly in despair for not having managed to strike up a good relationship with Brandi from the church and I knew I probably wouldn't see her again. As an eleven year old I didn't know what to expect but I just knew I had missed an opportunity and felt cowardly that I could not banish my demons of shyness and just speak to this lovely girl.

Having sold the house for £17 500, a lot more than we paid for it, we then stayed with Dad's brother Neil and his wife Janet for a couple of months prior to leaving. They stayed in a very lovely area of Cardiff in a street called Pum Erw Road which was in the Heath area. This was a very unsettling time for me because Dad wasn't sure if we were doing the right thing in going back and even though we were staying in this lovely temporary accommodation, it was not home. Mum and Dad were even looking at houses to see if any grabbed at their heart and in fairness, there was one that did for all of us and it was in the same street as Auntie Anne lived, it backed onto a river and was in a lovely street, the price was also just perfect. Dad decided not to though and even after looking at two more houses he eventually decided that we were to have our next chapter back in Benoni, South Africa.

One final memory of Britain 1982 was watching the world cup which was hosted in Spain that year. Prior to watching this tournament football was something I loved playing and watching but I wasn't totally embroiled in it. I remember watching England versus Germany in a thrilling 0-0 draw which England needed to win to progress but Kevin Keegan was not on top form and so they couldn't score that vital goal. I remember watching also that infamous semi-final between France and Germany that had absolutely everything as a game, 1-1 after normal time, France leading 3-1 in extra time only for those mentally tough Germans to come bouncing back to

3-3 and an eventual penalty shoot out win. I was hooked, this was thrilling and as much as I wanted to play rugby, football was tugging at my shirt sleeves and vying for my attention.

Eventually Jack Williams from the church was kind enough to give us a lift to Heathrow airport and my mood was somber indeed. I did not want to be going, I was happy and I felt my roots had been pulled up again but Jack in his wonderful down-to-earth way lightened the mood when we stopped for a snack on the M4 at a service station. We were choosing foods to eat from a buffet area and Jack spied the quiche. He looked up at Mum and Dad and said in a quizzical tone 'Quiche!?? Why that's just bacon and egg pie'

Chapter 12

Hey, You Free, Yes Bouf of You (Boksburg to Benoni – 1982 – 1987)

We arrived on a clear and crisp Johannesburg morning in July and at that time of the year it is mid-winter and cold in the evenings and mornings. Although a typical winter's day in South Africa is nothing compared to a European winters day, it still gets mighty chilly, with some places actually reaching minus figures in the night. A typical Highveld winters day is clear and blue without a single cloud in the sky so this enables the temperature to rise to the mid to late teens during the middle of the day. I still maintain that this climate is the most beautiful on earth as the winters are only four months of the year and the summers don't get overbearingly hot.

Yet again we were staying with Belinda and Freddie in their lovely home of 25 Tenth Avenue before we got into our new home. Bear in mind that houses in SA do not generally have central heating and this particular one was a huge, airy house with very high ceilings and rooms that did not hold any heat at all. I remember waking up one morning inside a sleeping bag which in turn was inside the bed and seeing my breath in the room it was that cold. We were to stay a couple of months before Dad got us into a brand new home in the area of Parkrand in Boksburg and these houses were owned by the South African Post Office which Dad was working for once more. Parkrand was completely different to us and although we had a lovely little place in which to live, we were still a 25 minute drive from where all our previous family and friends were in Benoni. Since the area was intended as cheap rental accommodation for basically British Post Office workers there was an atmosphere similar to a council estate and although I just got on with it, I didn't really feel like making the effort of forging friendships.

Now in Britain the school year starts in September and finishes in mid July with six weeks off for summer holidays. The South African school term, on the other hand, runs from mid January to early December equally with a nice long summer break at the end. We arrived in the country in late July so effectively I had missed half the year's syllabus which I could ill afford to do given my academic lethargy. I could either work like a demon and catch up feverishly, like Pauline did, or I could coast along and hope I did enough to just get by. You guessed it, I chose the latter option and it didn't pan out as I expected. To compound matters, I had just completed my first year of high school in Cardiff and when I say 'completed' I mean I was vaguely present when lessons were being taught. So picture this; in Britain I was 'man-of-the-world' and in high school having just picked up my rugby trophy, yes I felt a bit special. Unfortunately, for my pride and ego, the South African schooling system was structured so that there was an extra year of primary school (Standard 5) which was the equivalent of my British Form 1. Picture the scenario then when I had to go from wearing long trousers, uniform and tie in Fitzalan High back to primary school shorts and the white short sleeved shirt of Arbor Primary. My twelve year old ego had taken a knock but worse was to follow and it was my entire fault.

During the final year end exams it was announced that we were to have a Hawaiian Standard 5 farewell party on the last day of school which I thought was thrilling. The invitation was hand written on a piece of lined paper and subsequently photo-copied several times and given out to all the pupils of that year. Now by some ridiculous twist of fate, I mistook the time of 17:00 as 12:00 due to the figure seven looking like a two with me thinking the line on the paper was actually the crucial line of the bottom of the figure two. By the way, my brain was the only one in the entire standard to see it this way but I was obliviously happy and a tad curious as to why we would have a party half way through the school day. 'At twelve o'clock?' I said to Mum in light hearted concern, 'but hey, whatever, it's the last day, it'll be great', I couldn't wait.

The big day came, it was the last day of school but we still had two exams to get through, one English exam in the morning which I may have even revised for and one in the afternoon. Quite how this party was going to happen confused me a little as our exam was scheduled to end just after it started but I didn't care, that wasn't my problem, all I had to do was get dressed in my finest red and orange Hawaiian shirt with flowery lei, white Bermuda shorts and flip flops. I was like Tom Selleck except without the mustache, dark hair and smouldering good looks, I was the freckly faced ginger version. Now bear in mind that we lived a 25 minute drive away so having been dropped off by Mum in somewhat of a rush, I was all alone as I shyly went through the school gates, heart pounding in anticipation for being totally out of my comfort zone in wearing all this outlandish gear. 'I wonder how all the others are looking' I nervously smiled to myself as I walked, leaden footed over the concrete hall entrance. I looked around the school and all I could see were smartly dressed pupils, diligently in their school uniform, I mean EVERYONE! My mouth went dry and my heart sank with embarrassment as I realized that I was the only person in the entire school dressed up like an extra from a Hawaii 5-0. Had it not been the fact that I had an exam I probably would have hidden in an adjacent street somewhere to save me from ridicule. I didn't though, I had to face up to my teacher and break the news of my latest feat of ineptitude. When our year teacher Mr Treurnicht saw me he raised an amused eyebrow and simply told me to sit down as normal, he wasn't angry at all even though he was a strict Afrikaans disciplinarian who looked liked he'd just arrived off an Ox-Wagan from the Great Trek. I remember him just shaking his head in amused disbelief. Boys in class were asking 'Hey O'Conner, what are you playing at Boet?' as if this were some form of rebellion. I wrote my exam with the odd snigger behind me and with my back ablaze with colour, I was the centre of attention and I could not have been more uncomfortable. All I ever wanted was to blend in and I just wasn't doing a good job of it. Now so far in this book, everything has been true up until this point, you see I didn't actually wear anything Hawaiian but I did wear civvies cloths instead because I didn't actually have anything Hawaiian to wear. This is a blatant embellishment for effect but as long as it made you smile it was worth it. Needless to say, my embarrassment level was the same, Hawaiian or not. I was not amused.

I was even less amused when I got my grades at the end of the school year in Standard 5 as things were to get a lot worse with my ego losing 6-0, 6-0, 6-0. I had not put the required effort in, I had not been motivated enough to get up to the required level and I had failed miserably. There was to be no second chance, no soft option of just going up to the next year and going into the 'C Band' whilst disappearing off into juvenile delinquency. South Africa was no-nonsense, you either worked hard and passed your exams or you stayed back and spent a year with the little guys you had looked down on the previous year. Shape up or ship out! It was black and white, sink or swim, your choice, no safety net. I didn't think it at the time but this was the kick up the back side I needed. I distinctly remember the feeling of abject failure and depression as I trudged home in the hot sun, walking through the dry veld, clutching my useless report with a knot in my stomach. I remember thinking that I really wished I had put more effort in. I had to tell Mum and Dad the bad news, I had to tell them I would be staying back another year. They read the report with mild horror but were generally supportive and understanding and challenged me to do better, to really try my best. I felt daunted because I thought I was a below average student and that my best wouldn't be good enough. I was to prove myself wrong though because by being driven and challenged and hungry, I would end up achieving fantastic results.

Chapter 13

We weren't in Parkrand for long, we had spent Christmas 1982 there and moved in February or March to the most wonderful home I can remember from my entire childhood. This was to be my true home and the closest I have ever been in my life to feeling like I belonged somewhere, somewhere permanent, somewhere with roots. It was 63 12th Avenue in Northmead, Benoni and what a wonderful house it was. Northmead is one of the better areas of Benoni and you always thought you were surrounded by a decent standard of people, it was unpretentious yet refined. I find it difficult to fully give a description of my emotions when I think of my time there but suffice to say it felt settled, safe, warm and good for the soul. You can feel my emotion by closing your eyes and imagining having a golden warming sun on your face, not too hot, just perfect. Hear the sounds of a distant lawn mower humming in the background of your mind, of cooing pigeons in the trees in a way that is distinctly African and of happy laughter from children splashing in their pool on a warm, sunny, summer afternoon. Inhale the smell of cut grass and of the wonderfully aromatic smell of meat braaing. Picture wide open gardens with lush green turf and scatterings of trees. This was my special place, a place in which my soul belonged. Again the streets were wide and expansive with large grassy verges, low walls surrounding each spacious bungalow house. The area was quiet and the landscape was extremely flat with the streets, roads and avenues mainly in a grid system. 12th Avenue was by no means perfect and had a bit of work to do before it was in a condition that would match our taste but it was immediately inhabitable and we all loved it from the start.

South Africa in the eighties was still an apartheid governed country but as children it felt normal, we knew no different. Being immersed into a culture where the white man was separate from the black man felt normal. By saying this, I am by no means endorsing apartheid as a correct way of running a country as morally it is wrong, it is incredible that in a modern era it was able to exist formally. As I say though, to see signs saying 'Whites Only' at a bus station or toilet was not something I would consider wrong as a child because we had no reference to that being wrong. The social circles of black and white families simply did not mix but from our perspective it didn't feel like we were being racists, it just felt like they were other people living in a kind of parallel universe but in the same country. Because of our roots though we were unaccustomed to the typical local attitude towards the black community and as a family we treated any black people that we did encounter with the dignity and respect that any human being deserves, any stranger, black or white deserves. In fact Dad always went out of his way to make sure the guys that used to work with him were well looked after and they used to love working for 'Boss John' as they used to call him. Dad was direct but fair, always playing practical jokes and treating them as they should be treated, on the same level. There were of course many people in the land that chose to treat black people as less than animals and as a family, our moral compass never let us act in this way. In South Africa there is a generation of good people who have never been remotely racist and yet they have an inherited 'blueprint' of guilt for what their forefathers did, in a similar way to relatives of Nazi's after the second world war. It's not their fault and yet they feel a distant guilt and a responsibility for making amends.

Unfortunately in modern day South Africa there is a culture where a lot of white people are paying for the sins of their forefathers over and over again and some might say that this is fair enough and that the wrongs need to be righted but the reality is that if the country continues to re-dress the balance as it currently is it will simply do more harm to the collective people. There are some white South Africans with the purest of hearts who are angry and frustrated at the lack of opportunities they have, because of the colour of their skin. A comment once from a very laid back 20-something year old white man to a bitter government official went something like this 'bro, it's not my fault that my forefathers buggered things up'. This is a typical indication of how the average person feels. South Africa has always been a dynamic and wild melting pot of cultures and that is why it is called the rainbow nation. At best the different ethnicities have got along with each other but it must never be forgotten that it is a young country and it still has a long way to go before there is harmony. We all hope that people can embrace Nelson Mandelas exceptional attitude of forgiveness despite the life he endured. Has there ever been a better ambassador for the human race? I don't think anyone wishes to dilute any heritage that a Zulu man, an Indian man, a proud Boer or a Xhosa man has but the wish is that they see past the colour of skin. We will always, as a human race, acknowledge that we are all different in appearance but it is our moral obligation to understand and accept each others culture and celebrate the wonderful differences we all have. The more we know the more accepting we become. I see South Africa and its people in the same way I see a plate of food, a plate of food that is healthy and balanced. A good balanced diet consists of proteins, carbohydrates, vegetables, fruit and plenty of water. I am not saying they all have to be blended up into a non descript smoothie but that they all complement each other.

In this diet saturated fats must be avoided, along with refined sugar products. Now I'm not going to have the argument as to who represents the protein and who represents the carbs in South Africa's delicious poitjie pot (stew pot in Afrikaans) but suffice to say that the saturated fats and refined sugar so far have to represent the government officials in power but that is a discussion I do not wish to get into. South Africa has the ingredients for greatness. She has great people, wonderful mineral wealth, the most wonderful climate and geographical beauty everywhere you look. As a people they are strong, colourful and vibrant and they are full of energy with a 'can do' attitude. As a collective country they can achieve anything but I pray with all my heart that the leaders of this beautiful land have the wisdom of God. We are all facets of source, of God, we are all connected and a part of this amazing tapestry but there is a generation that have lost their way and need to tap into the wisdom that is theirs, they need to eliminate ego and get back to leading this amazing country to where it belongs.

Ego is like a mushroom that breeds in the dark, that dark being fear. Ego feeds from fear in that it always needs to be richer, bigger and better. It is insatiable and never ending in its demands. It's that fear of failure and the fear of not being richer and bigger that allows the ego to prosper. As we already know, fear based decisions are not constructive. Consider this; a little black boy of 10 years old being brought up in Soweto at the time of the 1976 riots, his blueprint is of never having enough, always being hungry in a metaphorical and literal sense. This little boy grows up, joins the ANC and becomes influential. He has such power and drive and influence that he becomes President. Sub-consciously he still has his 'lack of' blueprint no matter how wealthy he is so he goes about ensuring that he and his family can never want for anything again, ever in their lives. It means he builds palaces and claims land for himself in the way that some leaders are allowed to get away with and all at the expense of his people who still go hungry. The sub-conscious blueprint needs to change and indeed can be changed. I didn't think we could re-program ourselves in this way but I learned, only recently, that we indeed can. This for me is a miraculous and powerful revelation that breaks the mold you thought you came from.

Meanwhile Church was still huge in our lives and naturally, almost before the cases were unpacked we were in the Benoni Church of Christ once more with its futuristic looking buildings and wonderfully sunny disposition. Despite the dread I used to have for church, I still look back on that time fondly. This time though I made a really good friendship with Christian Botham, whose Mum and Dad were close friends of my parents, he was to be my absolute football mad mate for years to come and we would spend hours and hours discussing football, playing football, watching old clips of previous games on the TV. However, with me being 13 now and really starting to take an interest in girls it made church quite a fun place to be as there were lots of pretty girls to ogle. Apart from my Hawaiian episode I was becoming a bit more self conscious about what I wore and in 1983 for me it was all about looking as British as possible. This was the epitome of coolness for me. What did 'looking British' mean though back then? It meant a lot of things to a lot of different people but for me it meant having a Phil Oakey style, massive-fringed side path with polo shirt done right up to the top button and stovvies or drain pipe denims. Winkle picker shoes were also the vogue for this look. The polo shirt done up to the top was not too bad, I could get away with that. But since my hair used to grow like a dandelion clock in much the same way as Leo Sayers afro I couldn't quite master that sultry and sweeping, moody hair flick that Phil Oakey possessed. The drain pipes proved to be a losing battle as well because I had huge calves, they were like Henry the 8ths swashbuckling thunder calves and I struggled to pour myself into that style of trousers.

Once on a particularly embarrassing church youth night out at a 10-Pin bowling alley I decided to wear my drain pipe jeans. Previously I had decided it would be a good idea to modify my perfectly decent, but way too sensible, denim jeans into a homemade skin tight version around the calves. I measured, cut and sewed the jeans with precision, so much so that the jeans were a little difficult to actually get on. I was toying with the idea of Vaseline on my legs and jumping into them from a great height, alah Wallace and Grommit, but eventually managed to wrestle them on in the conventional manner. I was a man in leggings and I was ready to face the world.

So off I went to ten-pin bowling in my skin tight jeans, feeling confident but maybe a tad self-conscious in that I stood out. In fairness to me I did look like that huge bull-dog from Tom & Jerry with the comparatively tiny legs, almost like a triangle. All was great to begin with as I strutted around hoping that the girls found me utterly irresistible. I did reasonably okay in the bowling and was giving my team the customary high fives after getting a strike when disaster struck. I was shuffling down the alley, bowling ball gripped in three fingers as I pouted in concentration, determined to obliterate those pins and further impress my adoring throng of female admirers when I heard a rip and the horrible feeling of air entering around the back of my knee. My handy sewing work had come undone, the little seams could not hold out against the bulging might of my calves and when I looked down I saw holes all the way down the seam with pale flesh and blond hairs pocking through. I looked around in embarrassment and tried to pretend that nothing had happened as I inched back to my seat near all the balls. This was the death knell for my image and there was nothing more I could do than slink off and down a Fanta Grape to drown my sorrows. 'Another one for the diary', I thought miserably. Wendy Murray was not to be mine.

There were to be other church events too and we had a fancy dress evening at one of the parents houses where I went as 'Night Rider' which consisted of me dressing up in my pyjamas, my uncle Freddies riding boots, crop and riding helmet. It was innocent and fun and I enjoyed it, church was actually pretty cool apart from sermons and Bible study. It really was a wonderful social gathering of young and old, my learning of the 'good book' was becoming more and more intense as my knowledge deepened. I was developing a mindset that would not allow me to question the Bible or anything in it, there were always stories of us Christians putting this Jehovahs Witness or another Roman Catholic in their place by outwitting them and proving to them that they were wrong in their belief. You always felt that they had to be converted to 'our' way and that they were lost and needed to be gathered into the fold. This side of religion has never sat well with me and still doesn't to this day. 'We shouldn't judge others' it says in the Bible and yet it's own scholars were doing precisely that against other denominations and other beliefs. There was no concept of acceptance of differences and love being the common ground. It was all quite confusing for me to process but since all my peers were mostly in church, I didn't question it, I just thought it was normal and how a good Christian should be.

All of a sudden it was the start of a new year and me repeating Standard 5 again. Now for me, going back to school on the first day after a long holiday was possibly the lowest I could imagine feeling as a little boy.

The night before was a stomach churning dread for what lay ahead but of course, once the first day was under my belt it was as if I had never been away. You can imagine how I felt then when I had to start the year with little lads and lasses who were younger than me; I became the Standard 5 veteran. A wonderful thing was to happen though, I was to make friends with a boy who would become such a good friend to me and his name was Drew Healy. I got on with him from the start as he was from Leiceister in England and had a really witty way about him. He loved football, he loved joking around as much as I did but the crucial difference was that he was a diligent and hard worker in school, and he got really good grades. We were buddies, we were close and we were competitive against each other in almost everything, even school. I had a point to prove anyway, to say to my teachers 'I'm really not as stupid as you look'. Not only did I have this point to prove but also I wanted to beat Drew which in itself was a mighty task. I ripped through Standard 5 and got much, much improved results. There was even a time when I was disappointed that I got 18 out of 20 in a Geography exam because Drew had got 19 out of 20. I guess this was what I needed; Drew was so good for me in so many ways. I sailed through Standard 5, never to look back, I had the bit between my teeth and I was raring to go.

Thirteen is an odd age though for a boy because on one hand your hormones are going through the roof and you are noticing girls more and more, but on the other hand you still want to be playing with model cars and enacting war games. Before school I just wanted to play football with all the boys on the pitch so my deodorant had to be of the highest quality. After school I would read football magazines and just soak my being in everything football. You may find it strange that I went from Rugby player of the year in Fitzalan to being football mad but there is a very specific reason for this. In Benoni at that time, the English speaking schools played football and only football, the Afrikaans schools played Rugby, exclusively. I was not about to go to an Afrikaans speaking school so that was that, football it was. My uncle Freddie suggested I start playing football for Old Bens, one of three club sides in the area and at first I felt unsure of myself and questioned if I was good enough. One huge bonus was that Christian already played for them so I had a friend there already which made it a lot easier for me to settle in. I was again really proud to be associated with a group of individuals that had a common purpose and the feeling of pulling on an Old Bens golden shirt with black shorts and golden socks thrilled me to bits. For a young boy it is a wonderful experience to be a part of a club and wear the kit of your team, it empowers you and gives you purpose. This is the way I felt and as I started my first game I was so nervous and yet I threw myself into the game with everything in me. We played Benoni FC and beat them 10-3, with me getting a hat-trick which was the most amazing feeling. Those who have played the game will understand what a precious and unique feeling it is to score a goal, there is something magical about hearing the ball hit the net, it is absolutely satisfying. What a start, things could not possibly have gone any better and I firmly embedded myself into the team and then into the fibre of the club. I was an Old Bens boy and always would be from now on.

The time had come and it was finally the end of primary school, I had done very well and was to be promoted to Standard 6 and on to Benoni High School. Before graduating I must add that I did in fact attend a farewell party at one of our class mates house and we had a most wonderful pool party with lots of good food on the braai and lots of fun in the sun. There was to be no Hawaiian shirts or flowers this time, just pure good South African fun. I also went to the school party for all the Standard 5 pupils in the main hall where we had the customary disco. There was no way on this planet that I would even have contemplated asking a girl to dance so the evening slipped by quietly as I tried to act as cool as possible, hoping that some girl would feel compelled to come up to me and pry me out of my shell. It didn't happen of course and I left feeling a little empty and frustrated that I didn't have the confidence to speak to girls. It really was a huge fear for me and I had a mental block about it. This was to unfortunately be my mindset for many years to come.

Benoni High was quite a daunting prospect because it had a reputation of excellence and, granted it wasn't Harvard, it was not a formality to be allowed to enroll into the school. There were conditions of being in the right catchment area for the school and also the fact that there needed to be meetings between the principle and the parents, almost like an interview.

It was, and still is in fact, a government funded school and one of the top ten schools in the province. It had a lot going for it and it really was a place where you didn't put a foot out of line or you paid the consequences. Discipline was strict and virtually regimented, the headmaster, Mr Lotter, was the sort of character you would have seen in 'Goodbye Mr Chips', sporting a black teacher's gown and mortar board. He was a fearsomely impressive figure, immaculately dressed and charismatic. His face was large and ruddy with a presence of a Roman emperor. He was a very tall man with wide shoulders and a slender frame and basically he struck fear into all of us just by his presence alone. His aura was huge and it was as if he used to float around the school with his black gown billowing out behind him. Although he was South African he talked with a very English accent and his pronunciation was crisp and clear. He was the alpha male, the boss of the school, lord of the manner and every single student knew it.

So for me on my first day of high school it was honestly exciting but on the other hand it felt like I was being enrolled into the army. Mr Lotter stood in the central square of the school up on one of the corridors looking down on his centurions below, the new band of ill disciplined rabble had descended into his domain and it would take him 10 minutes to impress on us what would be expected from us and how we were to act. We were left in no uncertain terms as to what we were getting ourselves into by being Benoni High School pupils. The school had a reputation and a tradition and it was as if we carried that responsibility wherever we went, even outside of school. Our uniform consisted of grey trousers, white shirts and black blazer with gold and silver pin stripes. The tie was mainly black with also the same colours diagonally across and the motto was Quam Optime, Latin for 'Better than the best'. The school actually lived up to its motto well, it was certainly not false advertizing. It excelled in sport, especially football and athletics, it had a first class pipe band and academically they were second to none in the area of the East Rand. The pressure was great and you had the feeling that failure was not an option here.

On the first day I immediately struck up a relationship with Robert Hair, a Scottish lad who was to turn out to be less than a good influence on me, not that I was by any means innocent. It was like attracting like. In a way it was unfortunate that I was split up from Drew Healy because he was still my mate but since we went into different classes, we kind of drifted apart. Drew would continue his academic rise where as I would go back to my lazy, ill-disciplined ways of doing the bare minimum to get through. I was immediately taken in by his brazen attitude and scant regard for authority. He was a rebel and although he had decent academic credentials he was not a lad to be messed with in any way. He had anger within him and a continual point to prove against anything or anyone. I liked him though and he was really funny, we gelled together well and he became my firm friend. He was a hard case though and would always be fighting against somebody or other. That first year in school though was just about settling in and getting used to what was expected. I certainly didn't want to rock the boat myself, I just wanted to pass Standard 6 and play football.

I started playing for the school football team, under 15s seconds and after a few performances for them I was promoted to the firsts. I felt so proud to be a part of this, we would go to other schools in the area, on their patch and normally win, usually handsomely, and occasionally by a low score but very rarely did we lose. I felt that I was part of an invincible machine that wasn't only the team itself but it felt as if the whole school ethos carried us wherever we went. It used to lift us up and sometimes it felt as if some opposition were already beaten before they played us. Our reputation preceded us and we felt like an all conquering Roman army. Mr Lotter would walk around, wrists on hips with palms outwards, chest thrust out in pride, purveyor of all around him. There was only one occasion when one team *was* better than us and it was Sunward Park from Boksburg who beat us 4-2 and it was a shock to the system. We weren't used to losing and it was a wake-up call for us. Sunward Park though turned out to form the nucleus of the mighty Boksburg team that Old Bens would have tussles with in the coming years. Naturally the Old Bens (Old Benonians) team consisted mainly of Benoni High School pupils. I felt real identity at this time of my life, a real part of something special in school and also within the school football team and Old Bens. It was all so wonderful, we were black and gold and we were proud. It felt traditional and deep rooted and I was really grateful and happy that I was involved. Deep down in my psyche though I was not 100% confident in myself or my ability and I think this was down to issues not addressed earlier in my childhood. It felt like an inherited self-doubt and lack of confidence and in sport everyone knows that to reach the pinnacle you need mental strength, talent as well as confidence in your ability. I had two out of the three. I was a good footballer but I could have been even better with the right motivation externally and also internally within the halls of my own mind.

At home I would practice football over and over by devising different games I could play by myself such as chipping the ball into a big oil drum from 20 metres to perfect my passing game or doing kick ups with a tennis ball, even a squash ball at times. I used to see how many kick ups I could do with as small a ball I could find and my record was something in the high twenties with a squash ball. I even made myself a miniature goal and net so I could practice shooting with a small ball into a small goal. I further developed this into a miniature stand behind this goal; I had created my fantasy world of playing in a stadium albeit on a small scale. Our back garden was my football pitch and at the wall closest to the road my football stand stood proud. Behind the goal I dug out a pit so that me or Christian could sit in it and control a little wooden goalkeeper I made which was basically a plank of wood with a round handle attached at a right angle. I was absolutely lost in my own passion and the only dream I had was that I could play the game professionally. Christian and I shared this passion and would spend hour after hour playing anything that involved football. It was freedom and like being lost in a forest of football wonderland. We would devour football magazines and know each player of each club, we would know every football result from the weekends English leagues. It was heaven and we both loved it. To this day I still don't understand why I didn't mix more with Christian in school, instead opting to hang out with Robert more. Christian was a much better and more wholesome influence when I think back now. Robert was trouble and he loved that reputation, he loved confrontation and aggression and I followed suit. In class I was focused but not as much as in Standard 5 where I wanted to compete. The work was straightforward enough if you applied yourself but the big word for me was that magic 'if'. I remember Dad used to comment 'if you spent as much time studying your school books as much as you do those football magazines you'd be top of the class'. He was probably right but at the same instant didn't really understand my passion for the game I loved.

At home I was settled and enjoying life, we went on holiday once a year to the south coast and had plenty of weekend trips to faraway places. When we went on holiday we usually took friends. We took Christian a couple of times and before that Drew. Pauline would have brought her friends as well and on one occasion she invited Wendy Tonkin with us on Natal's south coast. I had such a crush on Wendy it was unbelievable. I cringe at some of the things I did on that holiday in order to get her attention but needless to say it didn't work. Well it may have, but not in the way that I was thinking of. She was a lovely girl who had the best legs I had ever seen up until that point in my short life, my little fourteen year old eyes were fixed to them and Drew also concurred with my opinion. One of those cringeful moments came when she was chatting to a would be suitor up at the entertainment area. I was quite jealous but couldn't really object as I was four years younger and not in her league. I was still smarting though and when I asked her who this 'Coonie' was when she had put 'Coonie + Wendy' inside the outline of a heart. She told me it was the name of her pet dog which I was immediately skeptical about. In protest, the next morning on the beach, when I knew the girls would be up in the chalet overlooking the beach, I wrote in the sand in huge letters 'Liam + Tabitha' surrounded by a big heart. This was my puny attempt at revenge against an innocent girl wanting to have some fun. She was probably oblivious and when she started paying more attention to Drew than me, I went into a serious strop. It's really quite funny looking back on it and must have seemed quite obvious to everyone but I thought it was just my little secret crush.

We were never very well off but always seemed to have lots of fun. The fact that we went on holiday once a year was a lot to do with having access to very cheap accommodation via Post Office owned holiday chalets. No complaints here though as they were perfectly functional and at least had stunning sea views which in itself was priceless. A favourite bay for us on the coast was Mtwalume which was relatively quiet and unspoiled. We would spend entire mornings on the beach to the point of wind-swept, sandy faced exhaustion and hunger. When Dad started getting irritable through lack of food we knew it was time to go back to the chalet for a bite to eat. An afternoon playing football, tennis, badminton or pool was all we needed to keep ourselves amused. We would usually have a braai in the early evening overlooking the blue and foamy ocean with the waves still dutifully crashing their way onto the cooling sand. Dad would have a can of Castle lager in his hand turning the meat with a look of pure unadulterated pleasure. It just could not get much better for all of us. We were sun-kissed and exhausted and as much as we wanted to watch some TV in the evening, it was usually just too hot to contemplate being indoors and we were usually too tired, a nice spent sort of tired though. Another particularly wonderful place was Margate which was an idyllic little town nestling on the south coast. It was just the right size for being convenient but without being overly commercial, well that was the case back then, it might have changed now. The beach though, will always be beautiful and with the water slide and Wimpy Bar that was there we had everything we needed.

Overall this was the most memorable and happy time of my childhood as it was settled and I felt like I really belonged. Church was church and although I wasn't keen on going three times a week, at least I had Christian as my church and football buddy. Christians Mum Mary and my Mum were good friends and still are really close to this day. Also for me, church was more like a social event where you could spy out the girls and try and impress some with the clothes you were wearing. In all fairness it was a bit of a fashion parade with everyone wearing their 'Sunday best' and we were no different. I had crushes on most of Pauline's friends growing up and my area of interest wasn't limited just to school, it was most certainly in the Sunday pews as well.

In school I safely progressed to Standard 7 having negotiated Standard 6 fairly comfortably with above average results but not quite setting the academic world ablaze. At fourteen I was about to enter the most difficult and rebellious stage of my life. They weren't quite the rapids of my river of life but they were certainly a tumultuous section of it. As we know, at this age the young boy or girl starts to push back against authority and starts to question it. In a similar way that two year old children have tantrums due to their brain growing at a different rate to their cranium, so it is at a similar point when we are fourteen or thereabouts that we start becoming irrational again. This was the case for me, like any other child, and most notably in school where I was autonomous and my own 'man'. At home I wore a different mask though, I was still the little boy that Mum and Dad knew and loved. They knew I wasn't an angel and that I had a devilish prankster's streak but they didn't know the troubled 'action hero' that terrorized the teachers and students of Standard 7. I think I particularly didn't want to disappoint my Mum too much for fear of letting her down in a Christian sense. I had two masks, one for home and church life and one for school and football. I didn't really wish for the two to mix and perhaps on a subconscious level that is the reason I didn't mix with Christian in school. This was the Yin to my Yang.

Chapter 14

Around this time in about 1985 I started an unexpected love affair which has lasted my whole life. It would have been nice but no, it wasn't a girl, it was my Cardiff City Football Club, my Bluebirds. Up until that point I had always followed the entire Division 1 fixtures but felt I needed to nail the colours of my local team to my mast. I needed identity and uniqueness and felt the core of my being needed to be attached to the boys in blue. This was where I was born, this was where my heart was and I wanted with all my heart to be a part of my club. It's correct to assume that The Bluebirds back in the mid-eighties were not setting the football world alight, in fact they were on the verge of relegation to the bottom tier of the English league. They were in a dire financial predicament and the stadium had seen better days, but you know what? I loved them even more because of it. I loved the fact that there were others out there like me, not *many* others mind you, but others. I didn't care that they weren't winning the league, I was just happy to be associated with them, I just wanted to be there and support them as a team but that was difficult living six thousand miles away and before the time of internet. I used to listen to the football results at 7pm on a Saturday evening, delivered by the BBC world service. There would be baited breath and butterflies in my stomach as the wonderfully measured English accent read out the football results as if every syllable was made of pure gold. 'English League Division 1, Arsenal 1 West Bromwich Albion 0'. It was thrilling and excruciating at the same time, I loved hearing all those results but I desperately wanted to find out how my boys had done. In fact, I would write every single one of them down as they were being called out, as did Christian, and memorize them. Eventually he would make his way down the divisions until he got to 'English League Division 3' and 'Brentford 1 Leyton Orient 1', my heart would honestly be racing now for anticipation of the result, not long now and this wait will be over. At last! 'Notts County 0 Cardiff City 2'….. ecstasy, exhilaration and overwhelming joy coursed through my veins as I would jump up off the chair in delight and run around the house shouting 'Cammon!' It was special. The opposite could be said when they lost, I was inconsolable and depressed and wondered why I did this to myself, only to be back next week for more. It felt like a dagger to my heart when they lost and for me there was so much emotion involved with it that it seemed more than just a game. I honestly felt like my castle had been breached by the enemy if we lost a game at home, my feelings were that passionate and strong. Mum used to try to console me by saying typically Mum things when it comes to sport, like 'Aah, love they can't always win' or 'Just imagine how the players feel love?' Needless to say I would not be consoled by Mums attempts. The love affair would continue my whole life, through thin and thin and my loyalty would never waiver.

Now in school back in the eighties there was still such a thing as capital punishment where the headmaster or various senior teachers could administer the cane on a boy's back-side or girls's hand. This form of punishment was called getting 'Jacks' and for a mild infringement such as not doing homework on a regular basis you would get two jacks. For back chatting a teacher, being sent out of class or having hair too long it was three and for more serious offences such as fighting you would get four. The most you could get was the proverbial 'six of the best' and this figure was reserved for the 'crème de la crème' of crimes such as cheating in exams or bunking off school. In a similar way that World War 2 fighter pilots notched their kills by painting symbols on their engine cowlings, at

Benoni High we would mark the inner lapel of our blazer jacket with a pen mark every time we got the cane. Since the inner lapel had a thin vertical white line going down it, it almost lent itself to being a blank canvass for marking our adolescent crimes.

O'Conner and Hair became the Benoni High version of 'Butch Cassidy and the Sundance Kid' such was our reputation for being naughty bad boys. There was also our buddy from Newcastle called Ronnie Adams who was also part of our group but he was far softer and a lot more sensible than myself and Robert. It was Scotland's Hair, Wales's O'Conner and England's Adams as an invincible triumvirate patrolling the school and spreading terror to our teachers. All we were missing was an Irishman to complete the British Lions set. To get an idea of what Robert looked like, picture 'Begsby' from 'Trainspotting' and you are with me in my time capsule, shaven-headed and menacing looking. When it came to choosing subjects for the forthcoming Standard eight year, which meant pruning back from about ten subjects down to six, for me it was a case of which teachers would actually accept me into their class. For some unknown reason I decided on Accountancy, which leaves me stone cold to even think about doing. At the time I randomly selected it as being something fairly straightforward, however Mrs Curtain, our Accountancy teacher, flatly refused to teach Mr Hair and I. And I don't blame her. You could say the curtains were drawn on my intent of being a book keeper. I had to choose something else, somewhere where they would take me and my troublesome ways. We simply had no choice but to take the compulsory subjects of English and Afrikaans but it was highly recommended that boys take subjects such as Maths, Science, Biology and Business Economics to give them a good grounding for University. At that age I was conscious of making the right choices but felt ill equipped, unmotivated and confused about my future. Rather than select my chosen path with vigour and direction, I let myself stumble into whatever opening was available to me. In the end I was taking the two compulsory ones plus Art, Business Economics, Geography and Biology. They were not strong subjects such as Maths or Science but if you had a passion for them, there could be a place for you in certain tertiary institutions. The problem was I wasn't passionate about any of them apart from maybe Geography which pricked my curiosity a bit. Art was also a very much more relaxed environment where I prospered but painting flowers and apples didn't appeal to me. When we were told 'draw what you want' I was totally blank and I simply felt like I didn't fit into school.

One of our subjects in Standard 7 was 'YP' short for 'Youth Preparedness' and consisted of various disciplines such as shooting a rifle, marching and other aspects needed to prepare you for the army upon turning eighteen. Back then after leaving school it was compulsory to undergo two years National Service which made men of boys. YP was a taster to what we were to expect and the teacher who used to put us through our marching paces was a very hardy Afrikaans ex-army veteran by the name of Mr Kruger, pronounced 'Kreear' in Afrikaans. He was tough and took no nonsense from us 'lighties' but spoke in a very broken accent. His grasp of English was not great but it was way better than my grasp of Afrikaans. One day whilst the British triumvirate was walking across the playing field for a double lesson in YP, under the watchful eye of Meneer Kruger, we were summoned. Now for YP we were expected to look smart, tuck our shirts in, have short clipped hair but 'no exaggerated styles, such as skin heads or afros' and also needed to tuck our ties into the gap between the second and third buttons of our shirts. As O'Conner, Hair and Adams ambled across the football-pitch-come-parade-ground with shirts un-tucked and ties half mast, we heard a booming voice at the top of the steps looking down onto the pitch……..'HEY YOU FREE, YIS BOWF ORF YOU, KAHM YARH' (For the benefit of non South African readers the English translation is as follows: Hey you three, yes both of you, come here). Well we walked sullenly up to Field Marshall Kruger with trepidation but stifling the need to burst into laughter. He looked us in the eyes with menacing intent and said 'You free tuck your blerry shirts in ow kay!'. My head was bursting trying to keep the laughter at bay but I respected Mr Kruger too much not to.

Through school I had the occasional fight but never a full on brawl, Robert was more accustomed to the one on one action. There was totally no need for it and looking back now I think he really had some sort of disorder but of course it was all about teenage egos and testosterone kicking in.

We were outside a maths lesson one day, waiting to go in when I picked a piece of hard broken putty from the classroom window and threw it at one of the lads without him looking, as a practical joke, but not necessarily venomous. It hit my good friend from Old Bens, Neil Jones, full on in the eye and he thought it was Robert. Now Neil, with Scouse and Welsh blood in him, was not one to take any nonsense so the pair started wading into eachother before a prefect broke up the contest. They were marched off to the office for interrogation by Mr Lotter and it was my entire fault. I was subsequently summoned in for questioning and Mr Lotter asked me how big this bit of putty was that I threw. Now me being me, I always tried to diffuse a situation with humour as I could feel the crackling tension within the confines of his office. I responded by putting my hands into the shape of a football as if I had thrown a huge boulder but in fact I had thrown a piece the size of a penny. Mr Lotters wrinkled brow arched back in alarm before I said I was only joking and that it was 'this' size (que the index finger and thumb making a little '0'). He almost grinned before sending me on my way. I had got off scot free whilst Robert and Neil had four Jacks each. Myself, Neil and Robert were leading the charts of those who had the most 'Jacks' in Standard 7.

A most notable occasion where I got four of the best was in Mrs Curtains Accountancy class, prior to us choosing our subjects for Standard 8, where I had yet again forgotten to do my homework. Her patience with this budding adolescent accounts clerk snapped and she kicked me out of class for the entire lesson. Trust me; this is not as cool as it first sounds. The problem with the accountancy class was that it was right opposite the Headmasters office. Mr Orsen was the school principal with Mr Lotter being the vice-principal and it was Mr Orsen who noticed me outside of a lesson. There was a large oak tree in a fairly small triangle of turf between the classroom and his office so when I was first kicked out I positioned myself behind the tree and out of sight of Obergruppenfuhrer Orsen. It didn't work though as he had seen me through his blinds as I left the classroom. He had watched me trying to blend in with the tree in an act of futility. I heard the reception door swing open and as I wasn't aware he knew I was there I started edging around the tree in the hope that he didn't spot me. I thought I was doing a sterling job of circumnavigating the old oak tree as I couldn't see him and therefore assumed he couldn't see me. The problem was that he could actually see me quite easily and it reminded me of something out of a Laurel and Hardy sketch, I can just hear that comical piano in the background. This tomfoolery exasperated him even more as he bellowed 'O'CONNER, get to my office NOW!!' The end result was that I was able to put another four stripes on my blazer so not all was lost.

It was a common occurrence to have an announcement over the tannoy system in school with Mr Lotter menacingly requesting 'O'Conner and Hair, please report to the office'. I would be getting in trouble for anything and everything and once in YP I got pulled out of a line for having hair a bit too long so off to the office it was for more jacks and more stripes on bum and blazer. This was to be the theme all the way through Standard 7 and it's a wonder I actually passed the year but I did and quite comfortably as well.

There was one act of teenage rebellion during Standard 7 that seriously got us both in trouble and I look back with amusement but also with a great amount of sheepishness. Robert and I decided to bunk off school for the first and only time and go to the sprawling metropolis of Johannesburg for an adventure. It was quite a daring thing to do and if our parents had known they would have been absolutely worried sick. The only safe way we could get there was by train which was an hour's journey from Benoni to Johannesburg. We planned the day by making sure we had civvies clothes to change into after leaving for school so as not to arouse suspicion from our parents. I kept a stash of my favourite indigo 'Depeche Mode' trousers and a plain white T-Shirt in a plastic bag hidden in a little coal bunker in a lane behind the house. Taking the plastic bag en route, I left in the morning in full school uniform and met Robert at Checkers in Webb Street before getting changed in the public toilets there. We left after we knew all the teachers and students would be in school and I could have vomited I was so nervous. This really felt as if we were on the run, it almost felt like crime. We walked from Webb Street into Benoni train station which took us roughly an hour, waited on the train platform for about 40 minutes and boarded a train to the big City. The train journey was long, slow and boring but we loved it. It felt as if we were stowaways, prison breakers on an escapade into oblivion. We whiled away the time on the train by talking about classmates and girls we fancied, who we thought were cool teachers and who weren't. Robert was smoking his pack of Chesterfields, looking thuggish and blowing smoke rings and it was pretty awesome to be this free. Free from school pressure, free from any expectations. We arrived about an hour and a half later, around midday, and into the hustle and bustle of the city streets. It was exciting and overwhelming, there were just SO many people brushing past us and in a hurry. I remember the smell of tobacco, diesel and pies as we made our way to a taxi rank to get to the Carlton centre. We didn't exactly have a plan as to what to do when we were there; it was just the fact that we were there by ourselves that made it thrilling. When we did eventually get to the Carlton centre we played arcade video games outside a shop for about half an hour before going to a record shop and thumbing through the latest British releases. We couldn't have spent more than an hour and a half in Jo'burg before having to leave to make sure we made our train home.

So three hours to get to Jo'burg only to play video games for an hour and then repeat the whole trip over again in the opposite direction. When we got back to Benoni we decided to walk past school in our civvies for some inexplicably brainless reason. By this time on a Friday, school had finished but there were still teachers milling around and I can only assume one of the teachers spotted us. The amusing part of this story is that we both were off on the same day. 'O'Conner and Hair' both sick on the same day? Hmm, that's not at all suspicious now is it? And why we chose to walk past school, even after school hours is a mystery to me. Maybe we thought we were untouchable after school hours but we were wrong. It's fair to say that with all that travelling, we were both exhausted so any more afternoon shenanigans were to be short lived as we both trouped off home in the late afternoon.

In school on the Monday we were both separately called to the office for supposedly cheating in a Biology exam where we both got 14%. We definitely didn't cheat, especially given those marks, but we felt like our Headmasters needed to punish us for having bunked off but couldn't quite prove it. The end result was six of the best for both of us from Mr Orsen and my backside had never smarted so much. At the end of the school year we tallied up the jacks on our blazers and I emerged victorious by collecting 47. I wouldn't put it down on my CV but with a blossoming career as a juvenile delinquent I was pretty proud of that achievement.

<u>Chapter 15</u>

When I think of the eighties I can't help but think of all the wonderful music that I grew up listening to. It was an era that was not held in great esteem at the time due to the quality of music that went before it but I think that so many tunes have stood the test of time. It was in fact just as good an era as the seventies in my opinion. During early high school years the tune that defined that time for me was 'Blue Monday' by New Order. It was new and totally different and it epitomized the mood of that time. There were of course other amazing songs of that time but that one stood out the most for me. Frankie Goes To Hollywood with 'Two Tribes' was a classic tune but the group of lads I loved due to my Sister Paulines influence was Depeche Mode. Their music was again innovative and distinctive and we both loved them. Ironically there is one song that Christian and I used to listen to in his Mums car in the Church car park while the sermon was going on and that was called 'Blasphemous Rumours' and it contained quite controversial lyrics about God having a sick sense of humour. It felt wild and rebellious to even be listening to it and I felt guilty to the core. My first album was by OMD called 'Junk Culture' and I played the cassette over and over again. Back then there was of course no internet and we relied on TV to find out the latest tunes, poring over every music video that came out of the UK. It was thrilling to watch the latest hits played out on the SABC at peak time on a Tuesday evening, we used to record the program on our 180 minute VHS video recorder and watch Bronski Beat, U2, Talk Talk and Level 42 over and over. We also used to watch a popular German made pop program called Der Muzikladen which was a few months late by the time South African audiences saw it but we didn't care, we loved it.

The three streams that made up my life then were football, church and school and the first of the three was by far my most favourite pastime. I was by now playing firsts for Old Bens in the under 16s team, playing firsts in the school team and also playing for Benoni Church of Christ in a 'Church League' where I saw more fighting and swearing than in normal leagues ironically. I was loving playing and at times I was playing three times a week; midweek for school, Saturday morning for Old Bens and then on a Saturday afternoon for the Church. It was exhausting and wonderful and I was very fit. In Church I had reached a plateau in my understanding of the scriptures and my rebellion in school was the same in church but very much more diluted.

Standard 8 came and went without much controversy and my exploits of the previous year proved to be the pinnacle of my adolescent buffoonery. I got a little more serious in Standard 8, but not by much. I knew that what lay ahead in Standards 9 and Metric would shape me for the rest of my life and it was time to start taking things a bit more seriously. Everyone else was knuckling down quite seriously, even Robert; so I followed suit even though my heart wasn't really in it. Biology I found to be difficult and learning about photosynthesis and spirogyra didn't rev my motor too much. Pistils and stamens were not the reproductive organs I was really interested in to be honest. I was still in the immigrant Afrikaans class as well which was reserved for those whose understanding of the language was limited due to being foreign. By the time Standard 9 came around you were expected to be strong in normal, standard grade Afrikaans, let alone straggling behind attempting to string basic sentences together. At the time, I have to admit; I despised the language because I simply had no interest in speaking it and never intended to speak it in my normal life. Much later I was to change my attitude towards it quite a lot. Geography and Art were pretty decent and I enjoyed them but without setting the world alight. Business Economics was hard work and extremely dry in substance. I would sooner have thrown sand in my own eyes than to study 'capital gains' and the history of why 'PTY (LTD)' was written as PTY (LTD). Do you want to know? Exactly, neither did I. English was one subject though that I did enjoy but didn't like being made to read certain books and dissecting them at length.

So when Standard 8 finished, I realized that the same subjects in Standard 9 would be a lot, lot harder. Standard 9 was seen as the preparation year for matric and it was perceived as harder as well. There was to be a lot more content and upon seeing Pauline's art books, folders and text books I soon realized that I couldn't do my bare minimum trick this time. I had to be 100% percent committed just to pass and I wasn't sure I was up to it. My fire wasn't there; I had the intelligence but not the drive and will to do it. Mr Lotter had previously requested a meeting with Mum where he explained that I had great potential and great intelligence but that I was drifting along. He said that I was certainly university material but that perhaps I should pursue this in a different school or college. He suggested perhaps a technical college would be better suited to me. At the same moment in time Roberts Mum was also having the same conversation with Mr Lotter and we both felt excited at the prospect of a move away from conventional academic school and into a more technical and practical environment. I suppose Mr Lotter would have said anything to rid his school of Butch and Sundance. College was a place where you were treated like an adult and were allowed to wear civvies not uniform and that really appealed to me. I was really keen to start but I was to complete the first term of Standard 9 first before I finally decided that this was going to be the right route in life for me. I really took it to heart leaving school in Standard 9, I felt like a failure and an outcast, I hadn't quite measured up. I was excited at the prospect of going to Benoni Technical College but I felt that I left with a reputation as being a bad boy who wasn't very clever in school. I had a point to prove and fire in my belly as a result.

Football was now on the wane at Old Bens as I was out of favour and my position as a winger was almost over. In years to come my more natural position due to my size and speed was to become a defender rather than a speedy little winger but at this point in my life I was dismayed at my lack of progress within the team. I saw other less gifted players getting the nod before me and it really got to me and I didn't have the emotional maturity to see it for what it was and just battle back for my place. I took it personally and interpreted it as being snubbed and left out in the cold and I felt hard done by. I should have had someone to mentor me through this and put me back on track but Dad took the more defensive style he was accustomed to growing up. I remember Dad saying 'Oh, the coaches are probably picking their blue eyed boys I suppose are they?' Rather than give me an encouraging pep talk and be told 'Don't give up son, you are a brilliant player, you just need to play to your strengths and persevere and the rewards will come to you' Dad would rather lay the blame elsewhere. Dad's angle was that it was their problem and to jack it in if they were going to be like that. I don't blame Dad at all because he was probably regurgitating what was passed on to him.

I am very proud of my Dad for showing me so much in life and for being a huge influence to me but there are ways that he used to act that left me feeling scared and uncomfortable. It's no secret that Dad had a flammable temper and it wasn't that it was hair trigger but more so that it was inconsistent and very volcanic. Dad could erupt within seconds and have a real expulsion of vitriol from his system that would leave us all shaken and covered in the ash of his volcano. The moods could be extremely heavy and tense as Dad would stride around the house emitting irritated sighs. His presence was all pervading and when he was in a mood, it was as if there was a blanket of tension in the house. He emitted waves of irritation like no other but minutes later, usually after some food or even after a soothing chat with Mum, he would be remorseful and loving as if nothing had ever happened, he was a real Jeckyl and Hyde type character. By then the damage had been done and we would still be a bit raw with nerves on edge, grateful that the outburst was over but fearful for when the next one would be.

Although Dad has mellowed a lot in later years, in the current day I am uncomfortable in a room with a domineering man and it either makes me want to leave the room or be on my guard in anticipation of an unwelcome outburst. I have grown to use my self defence mechanism of humour to see me through those sorts of situations which usually works quite well but I didn't always have the emotional maturity to deal with it back then, certainly not in my teenage years in any case. Today Dad is mellow and I love him but back then he had a temper that scarred me. I started repeating this pattern with my beautiful children and every time I did so I would feel such deep remorse. I would feel guilt for my own temper as Dad probably did and then his mother and so on. When I was feeling tired or scared and vulnerable or even hungry I could lash out like a wounded demon and really hurt people with my words. It was not pretty I can assure you. My nature is generally really placid and easy going but I was not well practiced in dealing with problems in a rational and logical manner. Fortunately I was able to really turn this around as I grew older and asked for God to share his wisdom with me. He did and I realized that it is okay to feel angry, it is okay to feel scared and it is okay to feel absolutely anything that you feel. We are human and we have these God given emotions, you are allowed to have them. It is how you choose to act on them that determine your destiny. What I learned was that it was not wize for them to control you, but for you to be in control of your thoughts. That is easier said than done if you have been 'programmed' to think in a certain way but we can absolutely change the way we think and if we do that we can change our lives. By this I don't mean changing who we are but just eradicating those little ticks and idiosyncrasies that hold us back or cause us harm.

And so here I was, I had just finished the first term of Standard 9 and I was saying goodbye to Benoni High and hello to Benoni Technical College in the heart of the town centre. I immediately felt liberation and purpose and a steely determination to succeed, more so than at any point so far in my young life. I was to start Pre-National Technical Certificate Part 1 otherwise known as Pre N1 which in terms of course content was the equivalent of Standard 6, but it was only a three month course so it was fairly intense but if you committed to it, youcould get through it quickly. I needed to address my fear of maths, my nemesis. I did have a real loathing for the subject but I was so determined to prove people wrong that I did everything in my power to understand every single mathematical principle fully and thoroughly with absolutely no stone unturned. If we were asked to complete 10 math's questions out of a possible 20 for homework for the next day I would complete all of them that were in the text book. I wanted to succeed and I wanted to test myself to see how good I really was. I actually started to enjoy maths and enjoy the satisfaction of getting the answers correct and to understand the logic. It was no longer a series of ridiculous a's and b's but represented logic and a means of solving problems. It seemed to open up synapses in my brain that enabled me to deal with problems and for those who don't know it; this is the fundamental reason for maths. Mathematical equations have no real practical value to most people unless you are a scientist but it is enormously effective at developing your logic and therefore your problem solving techniques, logically breaking complicated problems down into manageable bite sized components. If you can learn this and understand this it is such a gift in life.

Robert was also doing well and we both got our heads down and worked diligently that term. I got distinctions for Math's, Trade Theory, Technical Drawing and Physics and I really loved it. Although this was a curriculum I should have found easy in that I was in Standard 9 and effectively went back to Standard 6, I needed the boost and needed to take three steps backwards so that I could make ten steps forward. The college itself was based in downtown Benoni in Cranbourne Avenue and I really felt quite grown up wearing whatever I wanted. Pauline's friend in church also used to go to the college and her name was Shona, a very pretty, petite girl and I couldn't take my eyes off her. I was still way too shy to strike up conversation with her though. Robert and I used to think it was just the coolest thing in the world to pop out for lunch and cruise around the town, have a steak pie and a game of pool before going back to studying something I was really interested in. It was wonderful and life was really, really good. One Friday afternoon Robert and I decided to buy a pack of Castle 'dumpies' from the local off-license and enjoy a few beers whilst having a few games of pool. Dumpies are basically a small 330ml glass bottle of lager which for someone who is used to the odd beer is a pleasant distraction and not too heavy but at 17 I wasn't too experienced in the drinking game.

We both had a pie to eat before embarking on our afternoon of drunken bliss and I must admit, I had never felt so wonderful in all my life, this feeling of being intoxicated was truly amazing and I thought I would explode with happiness. Could life *really* be this exceptionally good; I thought I was living the dream. I probably told Robert that he was the best friend in the world and that I loved him and that we would be Butch and Sundance for the rest of our lives. I was in ecstasy and that afternoon was truly fabulous as we potted balls and had such freedom, such fun. We were standing around throwing our heads back with laughter and having the time of our lives. After six bottles of lager and many games of pool I was ready to go home as my head started to feel as if it was a few feet above my body. When I turned my head it was as if my eyeballs followed a split second later which caused a bit of uneasiness. My head felt thick and there was this rushing of blood in my ears as I realized I had had more than I could handle. My mouth felt as dry as a desert sandal and I knew I had a long walk home in the hot sun ahead of me. I wasn't looking forward to it as I was really quite inebriated. I did think that perhaps the walk would sober me up a bit but the oxygen seemed to make me feel worse as I staggered home in an exhausted state of queasiness. I really didn't feel well at all when I got home but fortunately no-one was in when I spewed up in the toilet. My day had suddenly gone from utopia to becoming the worst day of my life as my stomach repeatedly squeezed every last drop of food and liquid out of it. I was a dribbling and unhappy wreck, arms clasped around the toilet with the jaunty toilet logo of 'Twyfords' making me feel worse. 'I am never doing this again' I thought to myself. The one small chink of light was that at least Mum and Dad weren't home. I got into bed in the late afternoon and felt rough. When Dad came home he was quite worried at first but then must have smelt the alchohol as he arched his eyebrow and said 'Been out for a few beers have you mate?' to which I weakly replied 'erm, no I think I had a dodgy pie Dad'. Needless to say, he didn't believe me.

What would Mal Bourne have thought, the preacher at the Church of Christ, I shudder to think. It was very much forbidden for the youth to go out drinking but there was no real hold over you as an individual apart from the psychological group peer pressure. I didn't really care too much to be honest; I was more concerned with not disappointing Mum. In fact I was getting to the point where I was old enough to make my own choices and still wanted to be part of the church group but not totally immersed in it. I enjoyed the social aspect even though it was fairly innocent stuff, I just could not stand the church service and the formality of the sermons. You could say that spiritually I was now treading water in a rock pool.

At this stage in my life Old Bens was becoming less and less of an influence as I stopped training and therefore couldn't get picked for games. It was a shame that it just petered out the way it did and I regret not really giving it more of a go. I wish I had given it everything I had and played to the highest level there but my mind wasn't on it any more. My attitude to it was all wrong and I expected to just play for the first team and unusually I didn't want to have to battle for my place. I think college and the seriousness of my academic future were much more important to me now than playing and I poured myself entirely into my studies.

From the age of thirteen I discovered my first pimple which was an alarming and unwelcome discovery; however my skin was to get worse and worse through my teenage years. This was another aspect that knocked my confidence as when I was attending college I used to suffer with horrible carbuncles on my neck and certain parts of my face. It was later to be diagnosed as deep scarring acne but for a few years I was always on some sort of treatment, whether it was antibiotics, tissue salts or homeopathic remedies. The antibiotics worked brilliantly to begin with as my boils would clear up but then my body got used to them and so the boils returned. The homeopathic remedies were totally useless I thought at first but knowing what I know now, we weren't patient enough and didn't allow them to work. I was expecting the instant miracle cure that homeopathy isn't and I soon got frustrated as my symptoms got worse. What I didn't know then was that the symptoms have to get worse before getting better as it is a process of reversing the imbalance from the body as opposed to patching over the issue as is the case with antibiotics. We were not to know as research then was not as easy as it is these days. Back then you just took what the doctor was saying as total gospel without questioning and basically your health was their responsibility not yours. I know this now to not be true.

Dad, by now was again starting to get restless, just when I was established in college and really settled in my life. Mum put her foot down though and told Dad in no uncertain terms that she wasn't going back to Cardiff again, she had had enough, loved South Africa and wanted to stay as we all did. We were all happy living in Benoni but Dad had a hankering to be closer to the sea, a need for his soul to be closer to the ocean. With Cardiff currently out of bounds I think Mum and Dad eventually compromised and decided that East London in the eastern Cape was to be our next destination. I was asked repeatedly by Mum and Dad if I minded or had any objections and whilst I did I didn't really feel it was my place to say 'No, I'm not going'. So I went along with it without really wanting it. We put our lovely house on the market and Dad applied for a transfer, which he was granted, but it was not easy. Some serious strings had to be pulled but it eventually got approved by the South African Post Office. I couldn't believe this was happening as me and Robert were really close, I was enjoying college and life was pretty good apart from the lack of girls and my teenage acne. Robert said to me 'Don't just go buggering off to East London without telling me alright?' And ironically that is precisely what happened as Dad announced that if we were to go to East London within the next couple of months, I needed to ensure I was enrolled in the East London Technical College for the following term. I had completed my pre N1 very successfully indeed and my next step was N1 proper which itself was equivalent to Standard 7. In between terms there was always a holiday break where Robert and I would do our own separate things. With each three month college term being the equivalent of a year's work it was really important I started the next term whether it be in Benoni or East London. Due to circumstances it had to be in East London and I had to make sure I was there ready to register for college.

I wasn't ready for this sudden change and it caught me off-guard, I wasn't able to get into contact with Robert, even having left messages with his Mum. Mum and Dad couldn't leave Benoni because they had to finalize the house sale, Pauline, being 21 said a flat 'no' to moving down to East London as she had by now left school and had a job at Standard Bank. Cei was only five so she was to stay with Mum and Dad. The net result was that I was going it alone to East London. This would be the start of one of the most unusual but productive chapters in my life. Dad made arrangements for me to stay at a South African railway hostel within walking distance from the college and before I knew it I was boarding an overnight train from Germiston to East London, a good twenty hour trip.

Chapter 16

Alone, Paradise and In The Living Years (East London – 1987 – 1990)

The train journey was quite an eye opener as I was in a sleeper cabin with three other strangers, one of whom looked like he'd just come in for shelter off the streets as he had a huge heavy coat, a matted beard and smelled of urine and alcohol. I admit I wasn't expecting the luxury of the Orient Express but this was a bit much of an induction as a teenage maiden voyage. I left in the early evening, waving goodbye to Mum and Dad with a lump in my throat but trying to be brave as there were other hardy souls in the cabin with me. The evening went by without too much incident apart from the occasional blanket-lifting farts from the 'Wildman of Borneo'. I did sleep, but not too deeply and it was a relief to get off the train at 2pm the next day. I was met by Graham Johnson, the preacher of the East London Church of Christ and although I had met him before I didn't know him well at all. He was a lovely man though, big and tall with a heavy drooping mustache and with a gentle giant kind of spirit. He reminded me of a big St Bernard dog, huge and affectionate and nothing seemed to worry him at all.

He dropped me off at the railway hostel with my case and I made my way up to my little room. The room itself was honestly the size of a prison cell with a single bed, a small cupboard to hang clothes, one chair and that was it. It was basic to say the least but it was a roof over my head and it was cheap. I used the 'tikky box' phone down in reception to call Mum and Dad and tell them I had arrived safely. As I didn't have a radio I used to call Mum on a Saturday night to get the Cardiff result and sometimes she would say 'Ooh, I'll go and ask Dad, I think they won'. I'd be on the other end of the line thinking 'Please can you find out for certain, this is really important to me'. It's true to say that football didn't run in Mums veins but she knew it ran in mine and that was good enough for me.

Naturally everything seemed strange to me at first and I felt like a fish out of water, I was seventeen and in a city 750Km's away from my roots having never really travelled alone before. On one hand it was exciting and adventurous but my overriding feeling was that of being lonely. I unpacked and went down to the 'TV room' which was in the basement and again the décor was very sparse. The room was dark and quite large and consisted of row upon row of soft office chairs that you would normally find in a Doctors surgery. The TV was bolted to the ceiling and I sat down in a middle row ready for the evening's entertainment. There was just me and another lonely soul in the room but then from nowhere Graham Johnson walked in and said 'What are you doing sitting here in the dark, come and have some dinner with us'. It was a kind gesture typical of Graham and I immediately warmed to him.

With my only mode of transport being my legs, it was difficult to properly explore East London but I gave it a good go. I wandered down Belgravia Road which joined onto the main East London thoroughfare called Oxford Street and continued to walk down into the heart of the city. Compared to Benoni it felt like more of a proper City with its own identity and feel, it was vibrant and busy. In Benoni we didn't often go into the town as it was more industrial but East London town centre was a central hub and a gathering place. In the months I was in the hostel I managed to explore quite a lot of the city but for now it was back to digs and focusing on the reason why I was there, College.

I was apprehensive and nervous on that first day at East London Technical College, the building was very grand and I was impressed by the look and feel of this well established institution. Roll call was taken for NTC 1 Electrical students and my name was called out. I was in, registered and ready to go. I wondered how I would cope with the new, harder level of work but my focus was absolutely clear, I was determined to succeed and show the world that I actually had a brain and wasn't just a football mad trouble maker. My minimum aim was to attain NTC 3 level which is equivalent to Matric or Standard 10. If I passed each of the courses consecutively from NTC 1 to NTC 3 I would catch up all my peers in Benoni High and finish Matric the same time as them. That was the drive and my ambition. There were to be no distractions at all since I had no friends apart from the Grahams. I felt resolute in my mission, I was there to study and boy was I going to give it a good go. I would finish college, walk to my hostel and shut myself in my room whilst I read and re-read through the Electrical Trade Theory text book we were issued. I divided the total amount of pages in the text book by the number of days that course would take and I memorized those particular pages on a daily basis. For me failure was not on the menu, only varying levels of success. My subjects that term were Maths, Engineering Science, Engineering Drawing and Electrical trade theory and apart from the latter, I got A grades in all of them, I was a boy on fire.

By this time Mum and Dad had sold the house in Benoni and they were on their way, the blue 1982 VW Passat groaning under the weight of suitcases and anything else Dad could strap to the roof rack like something from the Beverly Hill Billies. Mum, Dad and Cei arrived in early evening sometime in early November as Dad strode into the TV room and gave me a big hug along with Mum. 'Aah we missed you love, it's so good to see you', I had my family back and I was really pleased, I wasn't ready to go it alone just yet I thought. I was still a boy.

Fortunately for us we were offered the use of a 'flat' by one the pillars of the Church, Bill Ronson. He said to Mum and Dad that we could share the flat with him in Quigney in downtown East London and based on that description Mum felt a little apprehensive. A flat to share down town? None of us were enthused but our reservations were very much misplaced as Bill was a master builder and his flat was more like a luxury townhouse overlooking the ocean. Yes it was in a built up area but it was a beautiful place to live whilst we got on our feet. Bill said to us not to worry about Nessie when we got to the flat as he was apparently harmless. We were expecting to find a huge, sullen teenager with tattoos but were less relieved when we came face to face with a fearsome looking, stocky Staffordshire Bull Terrier. What a lovely animal he was though as he had such a gentle nature. He seemed to be the dog equivalent of Bill himself as he was strong, squat and full of enthusiasm. Bill reminded me of James Robertson Justice facially but his builder's forearms bore testament to a strong man. He taught me how to shake hands like a proper man and it became a challenge whenever we met, it was like putting your hand into a crusher and you had to match the force in order to keep your hand in one piece. I will never forget Bill as a wonderful man of the earth, a really genuine person with a huge and generous heart. Even though he was a bear of a man he was also soft and you would often see him welling up at certain times, especially when young children were singing.

We were only to stay with Bill a few weeks before Mum and Dad found us a lovely home in Reef Road, Vincent. It was the equivalent of Northmead in Benoni and we were all pretty happy with our new place as it was homely. It was a huge and airy house with front and rear gardens on a slope which hampered my outside football prowess but by this stage I was still more intent on doing well in college and gone were the hours and hours of football with a tennis ball out the back, even though I did still erect a miniature goal in the same manner as my goal in Benoni. The handy aspect of this home was that it was so close to a shopping mall where I used to walk to and read football magazines in the CNA (Central News Agency) for hours.

Now East London is a unique coastal city and quite isolated from the other main centres such as Johannesburg, Durban and Cape Town. You kind of felt like you were out on a limb living there, as beautiful as it was. Back when we were living there its immediate borders, North and South were the Transkei and Ciskei African states which were both very rural, traditional areas. The area is one of outstanding natural beauty and the beaches were just simply magnificent. You had all the wonderful bays such as Gonubie and Nahoon, the latter being a very well known surf spot and synonymous with huge crashing waves. Even Orient Beach closer to the city was a real gem of a place. It really was like being on permanent holiday living there. One aspect that took a lot of getting used to was the phenomenon of the 'Berg wind' which used to envelop us occasionally in summer. A berg wind is an unusually warm wind that blows from time to time and on a hot, sunny, summers day it is not the ally that you want. It feels like a practical joke at first because just when you are flagging due to the heat of the day and you find relief by going into the cooler kitchen, a berg wind will cunningly snake its way into your home and obliterate what little resistance you had left to the weather. It is honestly as warm as a hairdryer that wind, it really is quite unique.

I found the city to be very 'English' and traditional in its atmosphere, where all the boys' schools played rugby against eachother and there was massive rivalry between Selbourne College and Queens College, it was great and a real close knit community. There was deep rooted tradition which I admired and loved but I felt like the outsider that I was and so couldn't join in with the jolly banter. It was at times too close knit as I found it hard to break into the circles but by that time I had secretly resolved to become a loner anyway. I was tired of leaving places and friends, tired of uprooting and I had had enough. Emotionally I shut myself off in East London and didn't want to harvest any deep relationships. I really just wanted to plough myself into my college work but at 18 you need other social aspects, you need friends and hobbies to distract you. I needed an outlet and there were plenty available but I was thwarted by my own self-esteem and shyness.

Church was an option that was ever present in terms of socializing and in fairness this was my only way of meeting people. I had opportunities in college to go out but I was closed off from it and Church was where I had to be in a sense. I had formed the habit of church and it was a way of life for me whether I liked it or not. The East London Church of Christ was a lot more laid back than its more formal Benoni congregation but for me it felt like a waste of a Sunday morning to be in Church when a sunny beach beckoned. Under the leadership of Graham Johnson, however, the Church was liberal and free feeling and I did actually enjoy it at times. It was a smaller congregation but the families in it were really good, wholesome people. We would often go out on weekend expeditions with the youth of the church and it was really good fun but at 18 I really needed my own life, separate from the eyes of my parents and separate from Church. The only problem was that I had no idea how to build my bridge from being a loner to going out and experiencing life, going to parties, going to sports events, going to the movies, having a beer on a balcony overlooking the sea, having a braai on the beach. I wanted to do all these things with people and yet I didn't want to have a relationship with people who I thought would ultimately disappear from my life. It was an awkward time for me and I didn't have the emotional maturity to do anything about it at the time. Even though we were surrounded by so much beauty, I felt lost and alone in paradise.

Christmas of 1987 was a fairly arid time in the O'Conner household as Mum and Dad were still waiting for the proceeds of their house to come through. As it turned out we didn't have too much money over the festive period and I remember Dad selling a pair of his Post Office issued work boots in order for us to get food in. That sounds more dramatic than it was in truth because those funds soon came but it did leave us all feeling a bit sorry for ourselves in our isolation and let's face it, Christmas is about being with family. Around that time there were fantastic tunes in charts such as 'She Drives Me Crazy' by 'The Fine Young Cannibals' and Phil Collins's 'Another Day In Paradise'. For me though the song that reminds me mostly of our time there was 'Fast Car' by Tracey Chapman. It was a lovely song but it reminded me of loneliness and even now I find it depressing to hear it. On the other hand, however, there was a massive hit song that transformed my relationship with Dad. It was called 'In The Living Years' by Mike and the Mechanics and the words struck me so deeply. The song spoke of missing the opportunity to talk to his Dad when he had the chance, to tell him he loved him even though they had their differences. That song had me in tears and it still effects me to this day but when I heard it for the first time I had to tell my Dad that I loved him. I don't remember me saying that an awful lot to my Dad prior to that song but from that point on, I never lost an opportunity if that was what I was feeling. We just never know when loved ones will disappear from our lives forever as mostly they are gone unexpectedly and you never know which conversation will be your last. Always remember to tell and show those around you how much you love them, you just never know if it will be the last thing you say to them.

Chapter 17

I was to start NTC 2 in much the same way as I finished NTC 1, at a relentlessly hard working pace. In that term I met a young apprentice who worked for Eskom and was originally from Morecambe in Lancashire. He was a real character and had that typical footballers perm that was popularized by Glenn Hoddle and Chris Waddle in the late eighties. He invited me to come and try out at the local football club, Buffaloes FC. I couldn't resist and ended up there on Tuesday night being put through my paces in training. It was wonderful and liberating and just what I needed, banter with a few lads, of which there was a large British presence. Having spent months being a perpetual student, I wasn't at my fittest but that would soon change as our training would sometimes consist of running from the club to East London Golf Club and then onto Nahoon beach and running up and down sand dunes. It was totally exhausting and by the time we got back to the club we were usually out on our feet. It was a great distraction and I enjoyed it, it was my chance to do something by myself, for myself.

Unfortunately I still had my acne affliction so Mum decided to get to the bottom of it and booked me in to see a dermatologist. After taking blood samples and performing a thorough check it was established that I had deep scarring acne and the suggestion was to avoid sweets, chocolates and fizzy cold drinks. I diligently adhered and stayed off them all completely but there was to be no getting to the root cause of why I had it in the first place. Years later I learned that all of our physical afflictions are a manifestation of our emotional well being and that certain ailments can be traced back to certain thought patterns. In my case the pattern was not expressing my feelings and the skin is always the first to tell you if it is stressed and frustrated. I'm not sure if I was that stressed but perhaps constant studying took its toll and the fact that I didn't verbalize how I felt was a main factor.

Shortly after the dermatologist episode I became ill with Chicken Pox which resulted in me being covered from head to toe in red spots, including my face. It's not as if I needed the extra dermatological challenge, I had enough on my plate already. Anyway, an appointment with the Doctor was needed just to confirm what we already knew. I had never before met this Doctor and when I first went into his room to be diagnosed I thought 'The Fuhrer' had risen from the grave and was practicing as a Doctor in East London. His skin was quite pale but his hair was dark and swept in a rigid side path and, yes you guessed it, he had that little mustache as well. His piercing blue eyes surveyed me and he then asked 'So what seems to be the problem?' in a very Afrikaans accent. To which I cheekily pointed to my pulsating orb of a face and said 'I thought that would be pretty obvious don't you think'. His reply wasn't quite what I was expecting 'Oh I see, you have acne do you Mr O'Conner?' Well he was correct technically but that wasn't the reason I was there that day as at that point, for once, my acne had cleared up.

During my escapades up to the shopping mall I mentioned that I used to go to the CNA to look at the latest football magazines, the expensive monthly ones from Britain that were slightly out of my price range. Well during that time I noticed a very pretty young girl about my age working on the till. I doubt she even noticed me but I soon became quite smitten with her and used to go into that shop more than I really needed to. I would walk in and my heart would flutter as I walked passed her trying my utmost to look cool. I would glance through my periodicals then catch the odd glimpse of loveliness from the corner of my eye, stopping short of dressing in a large brown mackintosh and hat and cutting two peep holes into a newspaper. When it came time for me to pay for 'Shoot', my affordable football magazine from Britain, my heart would be pounding in my chest wondering if perhaps she could possibly feel the same about me. I longed for the exchange of change to be more than 'That'll be R2.50 thank you'. I wished I could be debonair and charming and make instant nonsense chit chat that would sweep her of her feet but I wasn't ready then. Week after week would pass by with the same pattern, the same magazine bought and the same predictable outcome. I looked myself in the mirror one day and said 'Liam, you are a man, you are 18 years of age now go and do something about this girl, one way or another'. I decided my best tact was to write her a letter and express how I felt but not to be too gushy and come straight out with the big question 'Do you want to go out on a date?' So without any external guidance or influence from my Mum and Dad, I wrote a letter in secret, folded it as perfectly as I could and sealed the envelope with a true loving kiss. My heart was fit to burst.

The big day eventually came where I had to go and deliver the letter. You can imagine how I felt as I walked into the CNA and flicked through my magazines for 15 minutes without actually seeing what was on the page, for all I cared I could have been thumbing through 'Huisgenoot' or 'Gardeners Weekly'. The moment came, my heart was really racing and I could feel myself going quite light headed as I walked up to pay for my single pencil. My mouth felt very dry as I walked up to the counter and engaged a glance at my far-away princess. I was next in line and I wondered should I still do this or not? As nervous as I was, I told myself I needed to for my own self worth if nothing else. The moment was excruciating as I lingered, trying to pay for a pencil whilst trying to grab her attention. She seemed so businesslike and unconcerned as I passed the note into her hand as I said I would be back the following day and to please just read what I had to say.

The following day I was on pins, it was worse than waiting for a football result for a game Cardiff HAD to win. I eventually made my way up to the CNA not knowing at all what to expect, half excited and half nervous. I think I bought a sharpener this time to go with my red and black Staedler pencil, I was prepared to flash the cash and impress this little lady, no expense spared. I looked over and she was on the till, my heart had almost jumped out of my mouth. I sheepishly went up to the till with my sharpener and my R1 coin and smiled at her with a look that said 'Please say yes'. She smiled beautifully and gracefully but didn't give too much away as she passed me a note of her own. I took it gratefully and decided I needed to read this in total privacy. I blazed a trail out of that shopping mall and speed walked home, those bum cheeks of mine wondering what on earth was going on, my legs a blur. I sneaked back in and went straight to the little room behind the garage that we called the 'servants quarters'. I went in here because I knew I could lock the door and be away from prying eyes. I opened the letter with trembling hands and my eyes couldn't process the words quick enough as I read and re-read the letter. She was such a lovely writer but eloquently said that although she really thought the letter was a lovely thing to do, that she already had a boyfriend and was quite happy. I was totally crestfallen and burst into tears in the confines of the room, surrounded by a lawnmower, strimmer and petrol cans. I was really and truly gutted, for the first time in my life I had plucked up the courage to do something about a girl and it had ended in failure. In the grand scheme of my life it was a small blip but at that moment it was hugely significant and made me feel I was not worthy. Now if you are thinking that this is a tale of woe, hold on, be patient because amazing things were to follow in my life, more than I could possibly have dreamt of. But for the time being I was down in a valley and needed to climb out.

I threw myself into my college work and the subjects I took didn't really stand much chance against my determination to master them. I was doing this with hard work and diligence and I got great satisfaction getting the results I craved. I didn't have a natural flair for the understanding of electronics or anything electrical but I was certainly dogged. The subject matter could at times be really dry and boring but sometimes it really took my interest. Irrespective of whether I enjoyed it or not though, I was succeeding. I flew through NTC 2 and in the process met some real characters in my class, such as Paul Wilkinson, Darren Boysie and Simon Poulton. Darren was possibly one of the funniest people I had ever met in my life. He was just so witty he was a joy to be around. His imitation of the lecturers used to have me in absolute stitches. Mr Webber, the electrical trade theory lecturer, used to be on the end of most of his imitations and it was made funnier due to the fact that Mr Webber was very strict and no-nonsense. He used to speak in a very droll, measured voice that crackled with irritation at the thought of disrespect for the subject. He loved electrical theory and just wanted us to do the best we could. Darren used to imitate him all the time and one day he got caught. Mr Webbers' wrinkled brow arched upwards as he said 'Oh we have a comedian in the classroom, hey? Well Mr Boysie, pack your bags and get out'. That would become a catchphrase for Darren in all the other lectures as we would be in hysterics listening to him mimic his exact voice. Darren was a lot older than myself being a senior apprentice for SAR (SA Railways) and all the blokes in the class loved him. His favourite thing was to pretend to be Dirty Harry and quote all his famous lines from that series of films. In one math's class the teacher was giving us a problem scenario of two cars travelling at the same speed with different levels of fuel in the tank etc… you get my drift. Near the end the two cars were in the petrol station having both filled up and as the math's lecturer was dictating the last line of the problem, Darren struck with perfect timing. The lecturer dictated to us '….and the owner of the Toyota Corolla was charged….' And Darren piped up 'with public indecency'. The timing in a silent classroom was just perfect and the whole class, even the lecturer, was laughing. To young fresh face lads, it was so funny.

On another occasion a Hardeedaa bird was outside making their unusual, indescribable prehistoric call that sounds a bit like laughing when Darren took the opportunity to rib one of the slower students, the unfortunately named Simon Poulton, Simpoulton for short. Simon couldn't quite grasp an electrical theory question and as he answered the question incorrectly, the Hardeedaa made its familiar call only for Darren to hold his head in his hands and say 'See Poulton, even the birds are laughing at you'. It was cruel upon reflection but really funny at the time.

Another more serious character was my friend from college Paul Wilkinson who was an apprentice at South African Breweries (SAB). He was a huge muscular rugby lad from Selbourne college with a very dry sense of humour and a pale complexion. Because he was quiet but prone to sudden outbursts of rage it lent him the nickname 'Psycho'. He managed to get me some work on the weekends at SAB helping out the apprentices and I was very grateful for it. I wasn't driving at that point so Paul would come and pick me up on the back of his motorbike at the crack of dawn on a Saturday. I was so pleased to be able to earn money, decent money, for the first time. I offered to pay for my tuition in college which Mum and Dad gratefully accepted, it was the least I could do since we weren't flush and college wasn't for free. It did of course mean working on a Saturday and Sunday which put paid to any football and church but I was more than happy with that compromise. For the first time in my life I didn't have to sit in church and listen to sermons, I was earning money instead. I must admit I did miss the social aspect of seeing the people in Church but the chance to earn money was too much to resist. It wasn't an easy introduction into working life at SAB as it was a huge factory with lots of machines and processes. On my first day I was asked to look after the main boiler in the boiler room of which I had zero experience. The experienced old veteran of the boiler room looked me up and down and said 'What sort of experience do you have in looking after this important equipment?' To which I honestly replied 'None at all'. He said he couldn't leave me to look after this by myself so he got me stripping down sections of the boiler, sanding them down and cleaning with white spirits. It was filthy dirty stuff but I loved it, I felt part of something trying to achieve a goal and it felt good even if I was the least experienced there, even of the apprentices.

I had other jobs that included mucking out giant trays ten metres up the side of a machine which were filled with thick grease, a filthy way to earn money. Due to limited access the only way to get the grease out was to scoop it out with your hands. Another job was unscrewing hundreds of brass nozzles that were all attached to a snaking brass pipe through which boiling hot water passed in order to clean empty beer bottles on a huge bed of rolling conveyers below. My job was to inspect each one by unscrewing it from the brass pipe and ensure any green algae sludge was removed.

They reminded me of mini brass shower heads. It was not a pleasant job but somebody had to do it, and that somebody was me and I couldn't have been happier. What a reward at the end of the week to have a pay packet with R300 in it, a real sense of achievement.

Meanwhile college was great and I was motoring along, picking up great grades and really feeling confident. I smashed through NTC 3 so was basically at Metric level now, along with all my peers in Benoni High. They had not left me trailing in their wake and I felt just as clever as them. That wasn't enough for me though, I wanted more. I was addicted to this academic success so I enrolled into NTC 4. This was the first part of a really valuable electrical engineering qualification at tertiary level. NTC 5 and 6 were treated with reverence in the world of engineering as it was and still is quite a feat to attain that level. With NTC 3 being a solid qualification for a career as an electrician, mechanic or plumber, NTC 6 was engineer level or above. There were grown men in my class in their late twenties and early thirties struggling with this type of work and desperate to get their NTC 4 in order that they could get a better pay rise. I knew I wanted better, I knew I could do more so I pushed myself even harder. Looking back though, I should have stopped at this point and focused on getting a job which would have given me practical experience alongside the chance to study N4, 5 and 6 on an 'en bloc' basis. The apprentices I used to study with usually studied solidly for three months then had practical tuition for another three months and that alternated all the way through their apprenticeship until they reached their academic plateau.

NTC 4 was to prove quite a leap in standard from NTC 3 but I still applied myself wholeheartedly and did really well, so well in fact that I won the trophy for the outstanding student of N4 and had my picture taken for the local paper, The Daily Dispatch. I was so incredibly proud of this achievement and it still ranks high on my list of never-to-be-forgotten moments, a real highlight. Mum and Dad were present when I went up on stage and accepted my trophy, the picture in the Dispatch showing me shaking the principal strongly by the hand whilst accepting my award. They were proud and so would Bill Ronson have been of that handshake.

I was becoming more and more independent with my studying and working weekends but I was to become more of a help as to Mum in this time as she underwent a very important operation. A hysterectomy is quite a major operation for a woman and it was to be no different for Mum. Mum asked that I looked after my little sister Cei as much as possible and this I did with pleasure. I loved my 'little plum' and would have done anything for her, even though I teased her so much. I used to make her sandwiches for school and make sure everything was ready for her just to go to lessons. I would do my own ironing, wash dishes and generally help out with as much as I could whilst Mum was recuperating. That brief spell taught me the importance of being domestically independent and to perform basic chores. I believe that all boys should be able to sew, cook and clean as in this modern world there is little need now for gender specific roles. The modern couple usually both works full time so as such it should always be a partnership when doing work around the house where possible. Whilst Mum was recovering in hospital after the operation Dad had tried his best to make her feel better by putting lipstick on her whilst she was still in bed. We were expecting visitors but Mum still felt quite ill and it was too soon really to be seeing people. When applying the lipstick Dad mistakenly used a flesh coloured anti-blemish stick which left Mum looking drained and deathly and as if she was in a more perilous state of health than she actually was. Already pale from the operation, she didn't really need the zombie bloodless lips makeover. Poor Adrian Le Roux had the shock of his life when he came in to the hospital ready to cheer the patient up with a bunch of grapes and some flowers. Instead of a recuperating, but healthy, woman lay what looked like a corpse. He was quite mortified until Mum greeted him and explained that she was actually alright. She was too drained to properly explain and Adrian left feeling grateful she was okay.

Another achievement for me was passing my driving test which is essential in South Africa since the public transport system is almost non-existent and the 'taxi service' is something to be avoided if you value your life. 'Taxis' in South Africa equates to minibuses which are mostly neglected death traps. Most are definitely not roadworthy and you genuinely take your life in your hands if you get in one. There is no stringent 'Hackney Carriage' license to adhere to here. In SA if you have at least one good working eye, with full vision from it desirable but not essential and you can drive, shoot a weapon, sound the horn and are totally ignorant of the rules of the road you have the makings of the perfect taxi driver. Another prerequisite is to have an unfeasibly long, rubbery right arm which you are required to dangle limply from the open side window as an act of bravado. Maintenance of your vehicle is considered a necessary evil and the less you pay with getting away with repairs the better. Some great examples of the taxi-driver looking after his pride and joy would be a spanner replacing a steering wheel or a pair of tights to keep the exhaust on, never mind the state of the body work or windows. A lot of taxis show the scars of multiple bullet holes so non-matching side panels is almost a luxury. A lot of taxis when viewed from the rear have a chassis so out of shape that you can see all four wheels at the same time, like a crab. Africa is not for sissies you know and this is why the youth choose to get that drivers license as soon as they are legally able to.

I was just about turning eighteen when I started having informal lessons with Dad in a quiet car park opposite the Joan Harrison pool in Vincent. Upon reflection Dad was a very patient teacher and really did well with me and if it were not for him I would not have passed my test. He did have his bouts of suppressed irritation after the fifth straight time of a bone juddering stall though. You could feel the silent waves of irritation as the car took off like a rocking horse on castors but generally Dad was brilliant. After eventually mastering the clutch and first and second gear in the car park I was released onto the open road where I could shift into the easier third and fourth gears. Dad was next to me with his foot on his invisible brake but I understood why. Mum then volunteered to take me for a spin a few weeks later when I'd picked up my confidence and she soon realized it was a mistake. After confidentially zipping around the streets in a rather erratic fashion Mum was a little ashen faced as I veered across a busy junction with a stream of cars approaching. She was biting her bottom lip saying 'Ooh, be careful love' with a stressed and blotchy face. Bless her; it was not a pleasant experience and proved to be the first and last time she gave me a lesson.

A few months later I was ready and wanted that license. I was in 'seek and destroy' mode and wanted that life changing piece of paper. I booked up, paying scant regard for the highway code, and got my test date. It was a Friday afternoon sometime in early April 1989 and I was almost turning ner, ner, ner, ner 19. Dad still had the blue metallic 1982 VW Passat estate, almost a family heirloom by now. I had been briefed by friends about the typical route the examiner would take me on so I felt I was ready. I was dropped off by Dad to the test station while he went for a quick beer. The crusty old Afrikaans examiner looked generally irritated by life itself without the intrusion of yet another teenage delinquent on the roads. He asked me six theory questions and I scraped through by getting three correct. Not great but just about competent enough for him to feel he could take me out onto the roads. He said prior to the practical test 'Ah khun see ahm waistink mar taahm' (I can see I'm wasting my time) which got my nerves jangling somewhat.

We got to the Passat and he surveyed the vehicle disdainfully before saying 'Please read the license plate' which I diligently did and managed to get correct. I thought to myself 'that's 4 out of 7 now mate!' He then ushered me impatiently into the car whilst he stood in the front and asked me to put the hazard lights on which I proudly did. Nerves still taught, he then asked me to show the indicators 'left' and 'right' but in my nervous state I selected the windscreen wipers instead, only for the dry wipers to rub lazily across the dusty windscreen. I thought he was going to jump into the car and strangle me as he shouted outside the vehicle 'INDICATORS MAN, INDICATORS!!' I got there eventually before he descended into the passenger seat, an heir of resignation about him. He was undoubtedly thinking 'what a waste of a Friday afternoon, I could be sinking a Lion lager now instead of driving around East London with this buffoon'. Well what followed was actually faultless driving as against all the odds I ignored the tension in the car and resolutely decided I was not failing today, not today pal. Today I'm not going to be a failure statistic. Reverse parking in Quigney, perfect. Three point turn in Nahoon, perfect. Emergency stop, faultless. My confidence was beginning to soar. We completed the circuit around town and made our way back to the test centre. By now his demeanor was a lot more relaxed as he sensed the pub was now within touching distance and he said 'Congratulations, you have passed'. I could have screamed with delight but instead cheekily said 'So am I still wasting your time then?' to which he replied with a grimace and a hint of a twinkle in his eye 'It's not too late for me to change my mind you know'. And that was that, I felt like I had earned my wings. I was so pleased and so proud of passing first time. Dad came back and we both celebrated by going for a quick beer together in a pub somewhere in Quigney, overlooking the Indian Ocean. Life was absolutely superb.

Meanwhile back in the land of college life was extremely demanding. It was becoming dauntingly difficult and every lecture was a series of complicated formulas on blackboards. This was serious stuff now, there was very little fooling around in class and the guys that were in attendance were serious and really wanted to get this qualification. It meant something significant, something few attained. If you passed NTC 5 your employer knew that you had what it took to become a top engineer in your chosen field. In NTC 5 the hardest subject of all was the fearsome Electrotechnics which is the study of heavy current principles and three phase power. Without going into too much technical detail, it was bloody hard, the hardest subject I have ever studied before or since. All of the formulas had to be remembered and virtually every component of a formula had another formula and often these formulas had their own formulas again. It was absolutely mind boggling and I'm still not sure how my brain coped with it all. If ever there was a subject I was going to struggle with, it was this. I would spend evenings pouring over formulas trying to get to the right answer to a proposed problem; it was real mental gymnastics of the highest level. The satisfaction I would get spending three quarters of an hour on one problem and then getting it correct was phenomenal. Most of the time I would be sitting there in determined anguish, unable to crack the code but eventually I would get it, no matter how long it took me. The other subjects of Digital Electronics, Industrial Electronics and Maths were all difficult as well and they all had their fair amount of formulas too, especially maths. Maths itself was becoming so complicated to the point of becoming illogical. I still enjoyed my mastery of it though and I wasn't about to let my nemesis control me ever again. As hard as it was, I had it licked mostly through hard work and a pinch of natural flair but not loads. The fact that we had a brilliant lecturer helped as he was to the point but extremely thorough. He would explain things in great depth but at great speed and if you didn't keep up it was as if you had tripped on an escalator, it was very hard to keep pace. The only way you could keep pace if you were not a genius was to put the extra hours in after college. That's what I had to do, I had little choice. Digital electronics was all about understanding maths in another language almost, but again I worked hard and mastered it. Industrial electronics was a slog of simply absorbing lots and lots of processes and how they worked, how they worked with other principles and generally just a load of circuits, definitions, diagrams and explanations to remember. My head felt full to capacity and I probably needed to ground myself but I didn't, my only real outlet was to internalize and make things, make models, make anything that gave me enjoyment. I didn't really have friends because I didn't want to commit to anyone and as such I didn't really have a lifeline to normality. The other lads no doubt would be letting off steam and going for a few games of pool and a beer or two I would imagine. I would be at home either going through more exam papers or making things but it was all alone. I had become a real loner.

Exam time is always stressful no matter what level you're at but NTC 5 was exceptional for me. I was well and truly stressed out but nonetheless ready for the challenge; the other lads were also in the same boat. They were walking around in a bit of a daze and trying their utmost to be relaxed but the strain took its toll. Eventually we knuckled down to the exams having practiced and practiced and practiced numerous old exam papers to the point of nausea. Our first exam was the huge shadow of Elecrotechnics and what an introduction it was. The papers were handed out; my heart was in my mouth, my stomach in a knot. This was it; this was the three hours of reckoning. Was I up to the challenge? I started eagerly looking through the questions and the first one was almost like a riddle. There were certain factors not given which we came to realize afterward that you had to assume. The first question was an immensely tricky one and I wasn't sure I got it right, it just didn't feel correct and I felt panicky. I calmed myself and went to question two, again another tricky riddle as if the examiner was trying to trip you up rather than test your knowledge.

I stumbled through this question but again I didn't feel confident. My belief was ebbing away, question after question as the intensity ramped up. I felt in a real panic as there was not a single question I felt that I answered fully and correctly. All this preparation and all those previous exam papers we had practiced were not a patch on this paper. This was the exam from hell and everyone in the class looked either bemused or ashen faced. We were looking at each other as if someone was playing a really sick joke. I completed the paper but truly felt that I had failed my first exam since the 14% in Biology in Standard 7. I was truly gutted and very despondent. All that hard work for months and to fail at the last hurdle. The other subjects were completed quite routinely and the exam papers were as we expected so I knew I had passed three out of the four at least.

It would be a long wait for the results before I could truly relax and for weeks I was on pins wondering what I should do if I had failed Electrotechnics. They wouldn't let me take NTC 6 without having passed NTC 5 and this was playing on my mind hugely. The pass mark for subjects then was 40% and I wondered what my grade would be along with everyone else. The day the grades came out I will never forget. There were handfuls of students making their way to an A2 print out on a cork board in the main foyer with all the results of East London technical college from Pre N1 right through to N6. All the N5 lads were craning to see their results and I noticed a good few of my class mates walking passed me back to their cars with disappointment etched into their faces. I finally got to the noticeboard and scanned down the list of names; Ranson A, Reinhard JW, Reece ST then O'Conner C. After all those months of toil it came down to just one line of results which read:

Mathematics 99%, Digital Electronics 66%, Industrial Electronics 74%, Electrotechnics 41%

I had passed! I had overcome, I had done it. I had passed that savage subject by 1% and was one of only two people to have done so in the entire year. I could not believe it! The relief flooded through me like a pain killer, it was epic and wonderful and I rejoiced. Oh how I rejoiced. I felt I had done something here of immense, life changing value. This was genuine, it was real graft and I had succeeded doing something insanely hard where other intelligent individuals had failed. No-one could take this away from me; I would have this embedded in my heart forever. I was on top of the world and ready to tackle N6, my last chapter at East London Technical College.

Chapter 18

During this time we used to spend some lovely weekends with people in the church, most noteably Bill Ronson at his country retreat in Chalumna on the Eastern Cape's wild coast. Bill, with his successful building business was a wealthy man but he didn't flaunt it and was very humble. He did, however, like his getaways to the country though to escape from the business of his life and we were fortunate enough to have been invited on a couple of occasions to his lodge on the banks of the Chalumna River. We would all set off in his fully laden Land Rover on a Friday afternoon for the hour and a half journey into the wilderness. The approach to his home was off the beaten track and you needed an off road vehicle to get there. Once there you were greeted by a well kept bungalow nestled into a wooded area right next to the river, it was idyllic and such a true getaway from normal life. We were blessed and lucky to know Bill and to have struck up such a relationship with him and his generosity was so unpretentious and appreciated by us. Also with us were the Lazarou family who were from the church and I struck up an immediate rapport with Jimmy, a very likeable student, the same age as me. He had a really unusual sense of humour which I thought was brilliant and we got on well.

The lodge itself was such a lovely rustic home with an open plan living room leading on to French windows which in turn looked out onto the river itself. The patio just in front of the French windows was where we used to braai and spend wonderful evenings chatting around the fire, Bill throwing back his head in laughter, Mum and Dad smiling and happy. Dad was especially happy because Bill liked a few beers and was really quite down to earth and not typically Church like and formal. It was wonderful and free and we would all go to bed when we were tired, not at any particular time. We would also eat when we were hungry and not at a certain time in the day. It was a good lesson not to be a slave to your routine and Bill just loved being wild and free. He used to tell us that he came to Chalumna with one set of shorts and T-shirt for the weekend and that was all he needed.

In the day we would go out in a small motor boat moored to the jetty just down from the front of the house and in front of the patio. We would be taken up to the mouth of the river to where it met the sea. Having moored the little boat on the edge of the river we would walk up the sand dunes and over onto the beach where we would walk and talk along the beautiful, wild and untouched bay with big foamy rollers crashing into the sand. In my eyes it could not have been any better and we all loved it. I look back at those times with absolute longing now for what was and I really hoped that I appreciated it as much as I should have. The only sour point of the trip was when Jimmy accidentally put diesel into the petrol engine of the speed boat which rendered it useless. This wasn't a high point for Jimmy but Bill was so calm and unperturbed about it and a short time later had the engine fixed. Nothing was a big deal for Bill and he took everything in his stride, he was such a good example of a man and I admired him immensely. The story of Chalumna is not significant in itself other than to regale what peace we all had there and how fondly I look upon that time. An interesting fact though is that Chalumna and the part of the sea that it flows into was the scene for an amazing discovery in 1938. This is where the Coelocanth, the prehistoric fish, thought to be previously extinct, was caught. It currently sits proudly in the East London museum but is now very much stuffed.

Again through the church, we met some people who invited us for an afternoon of sailing off the coast of East London and out into the choppy Indian Ocean. Now the part of the coast that East London occupies has a fierce reputation of being a churning cauldron due to the fact that it is where the warm Agulhas current meets the icy Benguela current. There have been numerous shipwrecks along this stretch of coast, most notably the Russian cargo ship 'The Orient' which sank off East London harbor in 1907. The beach to this day is called Orient Beach. And so with this in mind we set off from the harbor in a small motor launch which was quite exciting to say the least. I had just had a pie and fizzy drink so all was reasonably right in my word as I stepped onto the gently rolling deck. It was a clear and sunny South African day and I was really looking forward to this mini adventure. The little boat was coping easily with the six foot swells and I felt like I was on a Bucking bronco as the bow plunged headlong into the waves. I was thrilled as I stood, legs firmly planted to the deck and feeling like I was Sir Francis Drake, chin pointing upwards with pride, hands on hips. Then the novelty of the constant rolling up and down began to wear off as I started to feel slightly ill at ease. I thought to myself, 'When we get further out to sea it should surely calm down'. I was wrong. Those swells got higher and higher and I went to the stern to see if this made me feel better. It didn't. I was feeling decidedly green now as we plunged downwards yet again into the foamy, broiling water and up again a split second later as my stomach thought it was being ripped from its body. The inevitable hurling up of my pie and fizzy drink made me feel a little better for about twenty seconds as the seagulls swirled overhead, ready for an unexpected treat. It wasn't long before those feelings of nausea returned with a vengeance, the swells still constant and unrelenting. My head hurt, I was totally green in pallor, and I felt weak as I hung limply over the side of the boat, mouth dribbling. I didn't care; I just wanted this to end. No! I needed this to end.

I stole a glance at our captain and he looked at me with a hardy grin and said 'another hour and a half and we'll be able to turn back home sonny, we're almost half way'. We had only been out for half an hour and I felt like my insides were coming out of me as I was retching endlessly at the end of that Godforsaken vessel. Then another wave came and another dry heave with nothing to show for the disappointed seagulls. I was mumbling incoherently to myself as I willed this time to be over. A sideward's glance from the corner of my eye saw Mum and Dad sitting happily on the boat, totally fine. I was the only one on board who was affected in this way, I couldn't believe it. I wasn't sure I could do another three and a half hours of this torture. Mother Nature was absolutely relentless and unforgiving as I thought to myself 'surely this can't be good for me' 'what if my stomach actually falls out of me'. My career as a swashbuckling adventurer of the seas was a short lived one as we eventually made the return journey back to shore. Never in my life have I been so grateful to set my feet back on dry land as I kissed the ground when I got onto the harbor amid some good humoured banter from the experienced sea hands still on board.

In August 1989 after months of hard work and further exams I had achieved what I set out to do after having previously passed NTC 3. I had passed my N6 certificate and I was mightily pleased with myself as this was a qualification of some note, university level and allied with some practical experience I could go a long way. After two years of intense study I had come such a long way academically from the bumbling, directionless pupil of Benoni High. I was proud and confident now and felt I could get a good job in an electrical company somewhere; this was the next goal for me.

This proved to be more difficult than I thought it would be because all the big employers in East London already had their allocation of apprentices. Nestle, SAB, VW, Eskom, SA Rail and Mercedes Benz were all targets of mine but none of them were really interested in a lad who was nineteen with an N6. I was slightly too old to start an apprenticeship and my qualifications meant I would have to be paid above the normal rate for a trainee. I had become overqualified as an apprentice. Ironically my determination to succeed and to show the world I wasn't stupid had caused me to put myself in a difficult pigeon hole. I couldn't become an apprentice, what would I study? I wasn't attractive to employers because I had no experience. Companies wanted someone who had an N6 to have the practical grounding to back up the theory. I didn't have that. This made me feel quite isolated and insecure about my future as letter after letter of rejection came from potential employers. I tried absolutely everyone; I was constantly on the phone, trawling through the job pages in the Daily Dispatch and even asking my lecturers if they had any leads. One did and took me to a company to have a chat but it was very casual and with no real conclusion.

It was so disheartening but I naturally kept plugging away and, in fact, kept every rejection letter as a reminder to spur myself on. When I got that job, I told myself I would burn them. To further fuel my anxiety I had received my call up papers for National Service. I should have gone when I was eighteen at the end of NTC 3 but you were allowed to postpone for a year or two if you wanted to study further, which is what I did. My call up papers meant I was to be stationed in Heidelberg Signals Regiment. I was not too keen to spend two years of my life in the army but accepted that it had to be done sooner or later. It was with some dread when I opened my call up papers to confirm my start date of January 1990.

Of course by this time I had been in East London for two years, I had achieved some great things, Mum was doing some part time work at Graham Johnson's and Dad was still with the Post Office. We were happy enough but still quite unsettled with not much family around us. As beautiful as the place was we still felt on the outside looking in which was becoming a pattern for me. A pattern I didn't really want but reveled in my loner status. I tried to come across as dark and brooding with girls from the church, alone, an island. I'm not sure if they did think I was the tormented genius I wished to portray but suffice to say, I was effective in not making deep friendships. When Dad decided to take us to East London, Pauline stayed put in Benoni and eventually fell in love with Leonard, the second youngest brother of the Putney clan. We missed her and all her quirky ways, we missed the general atmosphere of Benoni, a really free and friendly place to live. I missed everything about Benoni, it became the place I wanted to go back to more than anything and my heart longed to go back. Now from a neutral perspective East London was a far more beautiful place to live in so many ways compared to Benoni, but Benoni was where my heart was.

Dad though was again having second thoughts and, yes, you guessed it, he was tinkering with the idea of going back to Cardiff. 'You must surely be kidding right!' you would be quite within your right to think. Dad had the chance to send us all on holiday back to the UK free of charge, paid for by the South African Post Office, if he were to sign another five year contract. We went through weeks and weeks of tortuous indecision as to whether we should stay in East London, go back to Benoni or return to Cardiff. I can't even remember which one I favoured, possibly going back to Benoni was mine but I didn't really know and didn't think it was my place to decide.

At one point we were on the verge of booking the tickets for a holiday to Britain and my head was swimming with excitement. YEAHH!! We were actually going to do this! I couldn't wait. Then the following day, Mum gravely said to me 'Dad wants to go back to Britain Liam......for good'. I was so irritated, annoyed and disappointed. I was in a silent rage for weeks, not being able to comprehend why Dad could be so unbelievably unsure. I felt really messed about and found difficulty processing the decision until I found two things to focus on; Cardiff City and that song 'In the Living Years'. I decided from then on that Dad was Dad and that I would love him no matter what, no matter how much he infuriated me. Dad could be indecisive to the point of absolute despair but he was warm and loving and would still have done anything to protect his family from harm, possibly not mental harm, but still. I say that with a smile to Dad. The other thing was the excitement of watching my mighty boys in blue, my beloved BLOOOBUURDS. I actually, literally dreamt of watching Cardiff City and it was top of my list of things to do. If we went back to Britain, this would give me some meaning in life. Even though they were riding the crest of a Barry Island style wavelet in the lower reaches of the third Division, I still loved and worshipped them. I drank in every result. I was ready to see my boys in the flesh.

After many months of anguish and indecision, we had finally come to a conclusion. We were on our way back to Cardiff but not before seeing the wonderful leader Nelson Mandela released from prison after 27 years on Robben Island. We were all huddled around the TV, mesmerized and mindful that this was a true milestone in South African history. We weren't to realize at the time that it would in fact have a worldwide impact as well. My respect for FW De Clerk for deciding this was phenomenal, my respect for Nelson Mandela even more so but I would only really come to appreciate the greatness of the man in much later years. 11th February 1990 will stay in my memory for quite some time.

In April 1990, after a short but wonderful spell in Benoni, where I got to see Robert Hair once more, we were at Jan Smuts airport once again for a trip to Cardiff, via Amsterdam. This was to be quite an eye opening weekend stay over for a naïve young 19 year old lad. Eventually, and after a fabulous weekend of Dutch sightseeing, staying at the Hotel Krasnapolski, we landed at Cardiff International Airport for the next exciting chapter of my life.

Chapter 19

TV's, Bluebirds and The Dog and Duck – The Rapids (Eiddew Street- 1990 – 1994)

We were met at the airport by Uncle Ben and Auntie Anne in a big minibus that took us through the South Glamorgan countryside. It felt strange and bitterly cold but welcoming none-the-less. I love the warmth and earthiness of Cardiffians with their sharp wit and this was Uncle Ben down to a tee. He was the epitome of a brash, opinionated but well meaning and truly funny man. It was a lovely landing to be chatting to him, talking about rugby and football. Aunt Anne was also chattering nineteen to the dozen to Mum and it's fair to say, the pair of them can natter.

We were dropped off at number 333 Cowbridge Road East with Uncle Vince and Auntie Heather once more, the same scene of eleven years prior. Myself and Jimmy were instantly re-united and he really made me feel at home. Although this was not a long stay, not like in 1979, it was certainly a welcome one. After a short stay of a few days here we took up the offer from Mum's best friend, Deborah Hopkins, and used her mother's old house in Lansdowne Road, Treganna, rent free. What a blessing that was, we had done it again; we had fallen on our feet once more. I lose count of the amount of money we probably saved during the course of our lives living rent free, Dad was quite shrewd in an oblivious way. 59 Lansdowne Road was to be our home for quite a few months whilst we got on our feet and although it was on a main road it was an instantly inhabitable house. When we'd settled after a few days and registered at the Job Centre we were able to start relaxing a bit. I had a knock at the door one evening and it was Jimmy. His first words were 'let's go for a pint Liam' which overawed me a bit. I wasn't used to this, I didn't have money and I wasn't sure I wanted to waste it on beers but I eventually succumbed and we both met Jimmy's best mate, Freddie Steele in 'The Insole' pub on an April night. I think I had two or three beers and felt decidedly light headed, Jimmy was an experienced drinker by comparison and he was quaffing them back with insatiable glee. Being a week night I wasn't going to overdo it so we left and I had a bag of chips from Sam's Fish Bar on the way home, doused with salt and vinegar. After a few beers is there anything better? I was hooked but still on a mission to start work and start my life. Living on a busy street in the middle of an urban sprawl in Treganna would previously have depressed me but now that I had direction and a goal, I was spurred on and focused on the things that I loved.

One of the first things I just had to do was to go and watch my beloved Cardiff City. It was April 16th 1990 and Easter time which meant a local derby at home against arch rivals and despised foes, Swansea City. To be quite frank both teams were poor as they were both flailing in the lower reaches of Division 3 but I didn't care, I just wanted to see my boys for the first time. I paid my money on the turn style and managed to drag my cousin Jimmy along as well. The eight and a half thousand fans that were in the ground didn't witness a classic but I was enthralled none-the-less. The smell of cherry tobacco, alchohol, greasy beef burgers and chips added to the cocktail of my senses. I was seduced by the songs, the banter, the wit and the enthusiasm of the Bluebirds fans. Even the sound of the ball as it was being effortlessly launched around from one pristine boot to another was fascinating to me. The professional footballers who were being paid to play this beautiful sport were real athletes who had mastered the art of football (many cynics would be laughing out loud at this point with 'Cardiff City' and 'mastered the art of football' in the same sentence) and I admired them so much for having reached their pinnacle, they were not at the top of the football ladder but they were being paid to do something they loved and that was wonderful in my eyes. The power of the chanting from a chorus of hard core supporters made me feel as if I was part of an army, a small Blue army. It gave me shivers down my spine. The sight of the lush green pitch, like a green, smooth carpet sent my pulse racing. The sight of the beautiful goals with fine blue and white mesh net was also another aspect that, believe it or not, I thought was a thing of beauty. The stadium was old and bitty and not a futuristic bowl but d 'you know what? I felt like it was my home, my Ninian Park. I loved it, I loved the Bob Bank that I used to mostly stand in, I loved the little Canton Stand and uncovered Grange end. The main stand was grander by comparison and where you would watch a game if you wanted to be away from the rabble and had enough cash to do so. I can still taste the peppered Bovril drink and warm meaty pies that I used to devour. I was absolutely smitten by the whole match day experience and the evening games I found to be even more thrilling with the floodlights beaming onto the green carpet and making the arena look supernatural, it was my holy of holies. So my first experience in this derby match was such a deflating and somber let down as I witnessed my first, but certainly not last, crushing disappointment at Ninian Park. The final scoreline said it all: Cardiff City 0 Swansea City 2. I felt as if my home had been robbed by an unwelcome intruder, I felt sick to the stomach and like my castle had been breached by a cheeky and unworthy invader. I have never handled defeat at home very well; it's a slap in the face for me. Jimmy and I trudged home and he vowed he wouldn't be back and I believed him. I vowed I would be there for the next game against Walsall on a Tuesday night and I believed me too. This was the start of a beautiful relationship.

On the job seeking front, my 'Income Support' money from the job centre was to be £75 every two weeks whilst I feverishly looked for work. Now whilst most people would have complained that it wasn't enough to live on, I was actually really grateful and really excited at the prospect of being able to save money as I was living at home. The job centre suggested I register for a refresher college course at the Coleg Glan Hafren which I accepted gratefully. I was given a £3.75 per week 'travel allowance' which basically paid for the bus to and from college. I decided I was going to save this money so instead decided to ride a bike to college, I was determined to save some money. Jimmy's Nana in Ely asked for help to clear her garden for £10, everyone turned their nose up except me. I jumped at the chance to earn extra cash even though it was back breaking and thankless work. I just loved the power of that Pound coin in my hand. Coming from South Africa with a fairly weak currency to Britain with the most powerful currency in the world made me feel more powerful and I became hungry for success.

Meanwhile my spiritual journey was reaching a spluttering plateau and had been ever since the latter days of East London and SAB. The Cardiff Church of Christ had shrunk in numbers quite drastically since Jack and Val Davies left there to go back to the US. There was, however, a hardy bunch of never-say-die Christians that were the remnants of the original cast of 1980 still worshipping in a rented leisure centre room in Fairwater. It was more desperate and dire than even Moira Terrace and the total congregation numbered about 12 people and the sermons were a grueling hour long drone of uninspiring biblical drivel. The same person who preached also led the singing with the amusing accolade of being tone deaf. As a man he was a solid and wonderful person with a heart of gold. He was certainly dogged and determined but also very definitely dogmatic in his Christian belief. I used to sit in my grey, plastic leisure centre chair with face resting on my fists fighting the urge not to drop off as the hypnotic tone wore me down to the point that I actually bashed my forehead on the chair in front as I startled myself awake. With such low numbers and such dry content even Mum eventually gave up. I mean let's face it; a leisure centre was not the ideal spot to go to church. I used to squirm with embarrassment as I sat in the little room with my 'Sunday best' on as people in swimming trunks and squash kit would walk past the window with quizzical looks at these people dressed 'up to the nines' sipping miniature glasses of wine and eating dry crackers in the table tennis room at 10am in the morning. It was all a bit bizarre and it couldn't really last.

As a result, Mum decided on opting for the more vibrant but not quite scripturally correct Baptist Church in Treganna, next door to the old Woolworths. I went along but at twenty, I was doing this to please Mum and had absolutely no inclination whatsoever to be there. I had absolutely had enough of Church and vowed one day that I would not return. I was a young man with a lot of catching up to do; I was discovering girls, drink and football and my life was beginning to really blossom socially. The last thing I wanted at that point was to be going to church. At this point in my life I knew I believed and loved God, this has never changed, but what I wasn't sure of was religion in any way shape or form. I felt suffocated and oppressed when in a church room and the feeling got stronger and stronger until the point came where I had to say to Mum that I wouldn't be going to church any more. Mum was a little upset I think but deep down she knew. In a Christian sense I had 'fallen away' as they say. I felt a large amount of guilt but this emotion was not greater than my desire to start living and having fun. I was tired of having to be a sensible Christian boy who would 'hopefully' grow up and marry a sensible Christian girl. I craved freedom and expression and the need to feel like I was breaking out of my normality. I wanted to drink and swear and stay out late, I wanted to earn my own money and spend it on me enjoying myself. I was twenty after all and most British youths were where I was at twenty when they were sixteen. I had some catching up to do and it wasn't going to be through a Church youth group. This was the beginning of the end of any regular church going and spiritually I entered a kind of Sahara desert which would last over ten years, but it did mean I would start to find my true self.

The first job I applied for was at the 'Top of the Shop' restaurant in David Morgans in the Hayes where I would be a part time kitchen porter whilst I studied my refresher course at College. I was happy to ride my bike into town on a Saturday morning and start washing huge pots and pans to earn some much needed money. I was going to put the cash towards a Cardiff City season ticket; I had already made my mind up. The work was new to me and although not exactly mentally challenging, it most certainly was physically. I had to wash huge empty, burnt encrusted curry pots, piles upon piles of dishes and endless heaps of cutlery. One of my duties was going into a deep freeze the size of a room and getting whatever the chef asked me to get such as boxes of fish, beef, and chicken. It was one of those rooms you see in films, the one where the idiotic guy gets locked in somehow and almost freezes to death. I know what you're thinking and no it didn't happen but I could not stop thinking that 'what if' just what if that door was slammed and locked and I was trapped without anyone even knowing. Top of the Shop was a lovely, vibrant place to work and for what it was, it paid well and I was overjoyed at receiving a pay cheque for £320 for washing dishes for a month of weekends. I was asked to work two weeks solid as an attempt to make me permanent which I happily did for the money, but knew this was not really my chosen career path.

During that time I was still applying for many jobs but the job market seemed more alive and vibrant in Britain as opposed to South Africa. There were many opportunities and I was encouraged by college Glan Hafren to go to the University in Cardiff and look at what was advertized there. There was a lot of investment in South Wales at the time, especially by leading Japanese firms so there was plenty of scope. I filled out an application form for a company called 'MELUK' whom I had never even heard of. MELUK is in fact the unique local factory name for the Cardiff facility but representative of a more global corporate electronics giant that goes by a much less clunky name. I also applied to the Japanese electrical giants 'Sony' based in Bridgend as well as Philips in Cardiff. Meanwhile I went to the RAF recruitment offices in town and applied to join up there as well. I first underwent a medical which went rather well and was told I was in perfect health and had 20/20 vision which massaged my ego a bit. Subsequent to that I was to have an aptitude test to see if I knew my electronics in order to become an apprentice aircraft test technician. Happily, it went very well indeed.

I then had three letters within the space of a few weeks all requesting me to attend an interview which I thought was quite amazing and I could not believe my luck. The three were Philips, Sony and this little known company called MELUK who in fact were another Japanese electronics giant and whose brand name is very familiar to the world. The Sony interview went okay but they offered shift work and I didn't have a car so it was less than appealing. The Philips interview in Penarth Road was really very interesting indeed and the job was to be looking after the maintenance of transmitter masts in South Wales and the West, but only after a further two years of study in University and on the job practical training. It was really tempting but I really did not want to study any further, I wanted to start my life now, start earning money, start living. Finally I had my interview at MELUK with Paul Stroller, Gerriant Jones and Mr Nagasakiya. It was a tough interview and Gerriant Jones spread a huge schematic diagram out in front of me and said, 'Do you know how that works?' I gulped inwardly and said honestly that I recognized all the symbols and circuit configurations but didn't really know how it worked, instantly and at a glance. He didn't seem to mind and appreciated my honesty. Paul was the 'good cop' who asked all the questions I was comfortable with. Unfortunately Mr Nagasakiya was the 'tired cop' as he proceeded to use this half hour interview as a chance to catch up on some lost sleep. I was half way between bemused and amused until he woke from his slumber and asked 'Liam, prease exprain the piezo erectric effect?' which happened to be a subject I had studied in depth in East London and therefore reeled off the answer quite impressively. At the end of the interview I wasn't completely confident but thought I had done okay. I was asked back for a second interview and this time it was Paul, Gerriant and another manager called Barry Davies who took the interview. Barry was MELUK's answer to Clint Eastwood as he looked at me with narrowed eyes and with cigarette smoke curling around his face. I could barely make out his face behind the whispy vale of blue smoke but did catch a glimpse of an Eastwood styled snarl as he asked in a broad Cardiff twang 'Liam, do you feel lucky huh punk?' Not really of course but this is what I imagined. Again that interview went well and so I waited at home, wondering what the outcome would be with all of these irons in fires.

I eventually had post from all three and they all offered me work but my heart was set on MELUK for many reasons. They offered me £700 per month to start with, which was quite a nice salary then for a 20 year old with no financial commitments. Also they were based in Cardiff so no need to get up at a stupid time, I could at least catch a decent timed bus or two to work. And they also wanted me as I was, with no need for further study. The hours were also attractive, 7:45 to 4:30 Monday to Thursday and 7:45 to 13:30 on a Friday which meant no shift work. An early finish on a Friday was a very attractive feature and I happily accepted.

Meanwhile I had an offer also from the RAF which included nine weeks training up in Lincolnshire with a view to being permanently based in Weston-Super-Mare when I'd finished. I was tempted but not really enough for me to go for it. I do wonder how that would have panned out though because my temperament and personality would have fitted in well in that sort of establishment. It wasn't to be though, I wanted to live and work in Cardiff and that was that.

Chapter 20

Prior to all those interviews I had saved up enough money to buy myself that £240 season ticket for the newly, gloriously relegated 'Bluebirds'. They were in the fourth tier of English football for the first time in their history so the women in the ticket office must have thought I'd lost the plot a little with my boundless enthusiasm for my boys in blue. I happily handed over my cash which meant I was officially in the club. I was now a fully fledged Bluebird. My first away game was at Lincoln City's Sincil Bank in early 1991 and I was fully kitted out with cap, scarf, badges and replica club shirt. What a thrill it was to join an early morning throng of passionate supporters at the club waiting to go on the long journey, all like minded individuals who just wanted to see our boys win. I looked around me and there were tired faces of men and boys seeing their breath in the crisp, cold January air and ready to board the Cardiff City Supporters Club coach. There was no cheering or over-exuberance at 7am in the morning, just quiet anticipation of an exciting day. Now trust me when I say this, there is nothing at all romantic or glamorous being pent up on a coach for hours on a freezing cold morning but for me there was something magical, adventurous and exciting about the whole experience. Eventually everyone in the coach came to life at about 10am when everyone had eaten. I had not had breakfast at the early hour I awoke so tucked into my cold, hard pasty from the corner shop. Usually pasties are tasty when warmed up but at this temperature all I could taste was dry, hard pastry with a splendid mix of meat, potato and fat. The fat left an unwelcome film around my mouth for a good while but I was exuberant and happy and I didn't really care. The other lads on the bus were all singing the anti- Swansea songs by now with full gusto and it was livening up.

We eventually arrived at Sincil Bank which was basically a building site of a stadium with three very small terraced sides overshadowed by a huge single grandstand directly opposite us visiting fans. It was standing room only for us back then in a little isolated corner of the ground where there must have been about 500 Cardiff fans. I felt proud and as if I was in a little army, I had people around me who loved the Bluebirds as much as I did which was a rarity. For ninety minutes we never stopped singing and chanting, having a laugh at ourselves, our team and our surroundings and trying to get the opposition fans to join in. In a very drab encounter we drew 1-1 but I was thrilled to have witnessed it and sampled the atmosphere. I was hooked and wanted to do it again.

This is difficult to describe to someone who has never loved a football club or sports team, even harder still to describe the love of a team who are not very good and didn't, at that point at least, look like getting any better. Why did we do it? We were the epitome of the term 'die hard fan', not just a supporter of a successful team in the premier league, which takes little commitment or effort, we were the real deal. We were there week in week out, watching woeful games of football in a big stadium sometimes containing just 3,000 people. Why? Because all we wanted was for our boys to put the ball in the net more times than our opposition and if we managed it, it was pure joy. The reason we turned up every week could for me be summed up in one word, 'HOPE'. Every week there was hope in our hearts that we could win again and start climbing the league. Dare we mention the word 'promotion' to the next level; it was the holy grail of football fans. I saw it as a lot like life itself, a never ending yearning for betterment and whilst we enjoyed the moment, enjoyed the game itself (sometimes) we were still looking at what our status would be come the end of that season.

I decided I would join the Cardiff City supporters club team which played on Astroturf and also in the colours of the team, wearing the actual strip. What a thrill that was. I hadn't played for about two years so was a bit rusty but I soon got back in to it. I was invited down for a game at Sophia gardens for a friendly where I said I was most comfortable at right back. I was never a speed merchant but what I lacked in pace, I made up for in tenacity, determination and a ruthless streak to stop the opposition at all costs that earned me the nickname 'Psycho'. I honestly took it as a personal insult if a player beat me or got past me and I was aghast if ever they went on to score. I took pride in what I was doing with passion and commitment and to me I was representing Cardiff City, I could not have been more proud. I was fortunate enough to have done well enough to make it straight into the first team because the coach loved what he saw in me. After one full blooded aerial challenge for the ball which meant me having to take a knock to the head as well as my opponent, the coach grinned from the sideline and said 'you're a nasty piece of work you are mate'. I was in and I was to always keep my place from that moment on. I never took a step back and gave everything I had to that shirt I had temporarily inherited. We were to play a lot of other supporters teams, which meant when the real Cardiff City went to play away, we would play the supporters of their team which was again a real thrill. On one occasion Cardiff were playing Walsall away up in the West Midlands which we were all going to attend but instead of playing the Walsall fans, we were pitted against the more illustrious Wolverhampton Wanderers supporters team. We were all very excited and nervous but my mind was focused and ready. We were to play in the morning, a few hours before the real game so we arrived at Molineux, the real home of Wolves in our little white mini bus with our kit bags. When we got to the stadium we saw the team bus of our opposition, a huge black and gold coach in the colours of their club. Everyone looked at each other and took a collective gulp but I was having none of it as I cajoled and got everyone 'up' for the game. From their coach out stepped a huge striker they nicknamed 'Tango' and behind him was the trainer. He came up to us and gave us all programs for 'Wolverhampton

Wanderers Supporters Club versus Cardiff City Supporters Club' which contained a light hearted bit of banter along with a team sheet with all our names on. I was absolutely gob smacked and impressed, so were all my team mates, so much so that they started to feel that we were about to be taken to the cleaners. All this gear, the kit, the coach, it was all very impressive. However, we were a good team, a solid unit captained by Kit Purse at the heart of the defence. I have to say it, he was more passionate and determined than me, and that took some doing. We looked around the dressing room and there was a quiet, steely resolve with all of us. We kicked the game off and I was marking the giant 'Tango' who everyone said looked liked the legendary Wolves striker, Steve Bull. We went a goal down very early on and Tango scored, I was quite gutted but more determined than ever to stop him.

I decided that any niceties had to go out of the window as Tango picked up the ball on the by-line with me in hot pursuit. With everything in me I lunged to win the ball in a fair and square, full blooded tackle. I was in a red rage inside and I wanted to stop this man at all costs, I wanted him to know that I meant business, even if it *was* a friendly. The timing of my tackle was absolutely perfect as I scythed down man and ball and sent Tango into orbit for a fraction of a second. This was an element of my game I would come to perfect, that well timed tackle at a crucial moment. I heard a collective 'Oooh!!' from all the players and spectators and waited for the reaction from player, team mates and most of all, referee. The referee immediately awarded them a throw in and Tango eventually got up, brushed himself off and said to me 'bloody good tackle mate' in a broad Brummie accent. I smiled inwardly but didn't want to give too much away; I didn't want him to think I would give him an inch. He didn't get another sniff of the ball that day as we ran out 6-1 winners, with all the boys looking to me and that tackle as a pivotal moment of inspiration. Often in a game, when the chips are down it takes a spark from a certain individual to set a fire going throughout the whole team. That spark can be in the form of a flick, a moment of genius, a rasping shot at goal or pretty much anything really but that day it was from me and took the form of a tackle. That fire, that determination and passion transmitted itself throughout the team and I was delighted to my very core to have been congratulated for such a good defensive performance. We came off the pitch exhausted and happy and went for a good few beers with our Wolves supporters who were absolutely brilliant hosts and taught us all a lesson in how to welcome an opposing team. Tango and I chatted and we both knew there was a wonderful, sporting, mutual respect. 'This was the life' I thought as I sat in the bar area in a beer filled blissful mood.

During a fun packed, wonderful footballing summer of 1990 I learned that my start date at MELUK was to be the 6th August and I was to begin as an Assistant Technician in the technical department. My job was to help the technicians and engineers test prototype TV's before they were released to mainstream production and my immediate boss was the fearsome, rugby playing Gerriant Jones who had quite a short fuse and took absolutely no nonsense. Under his watchful eye I would be prodding and poking around the chassis of a TV set trying to know what I was doing. It was a really steep learning curve and I felt ill equipped to deal with the practical side of electronics since all my experience up till then had been theoretical. Basic things such as using meters and oscilloscopes were new and alien to me but at least I had good help from peers in the same boat and also the technicians. Although I was being shown the ropes on how to perform tasks I never really got enough confidence up to play and experiment with the product which is an essential part of learning and growth. I was too scared of making a mistake and didn't really fully grasp the practical elements of what I was doing and why I was doing it. I didn't realize it then but I was more of a 'see, touch, feel' sort of person and needed to hold an item in my hands in order to understand it. Electronics is very much an application of mathematical assumptions and I found it really difficult to translate theory into practice. I tried and tried but it never fully 'clicked' so after a good few months of training I was moved to the chassis group, still within technical, but more concentrating on the mechanical build of electronic circuits rather than how they worked. To be quite frank, I discovered very early that I had very little interest or enthusiasm for electronics and it didn't fill me with wonder, I had no inclination to ponder complicated problems. I wondered why on earth I had spent so much time studying this when I had so little passion for it. I did not think this at the time but later on I vowed that I would always tell my children to follow their passion, follow their heart and listen to what makes their wings soar. I had played safe and studied hard at something I thought would be a good source of income. I was focused on the misguided notion that 'electronics is where the money is' and 'you won't go far wrong in the world of electronics'. As some of you may or may not know, the real truth is that if you follow your passion eventually the money will flow to you providing your mindset around money is healthy. It absolutely doesn't matter what it is you love, you just need to love it, live it, breathe it and enjoy it. Abundance will attract itself to you if you are living a passion and abundance doesn't mean just money, it means health and happiness and living in a state of serenity.

However, my MELUK days were just about to enfold and although it wasn't particularly electronics that would keep me there for over a decade, it was the fascination of putting things together that did. I was genuinely more interested in mechanical assemblies rather than sitting behind a TV. I was now a chassis member in the technical department and I was starting to enjoy myself as at times it meant technical drawing which was a keen interest of mine I should have pursued further. I was to meet some absolutely brilliantly funny individuals in my time at MELUK and with a total workforce of about 2000 people, there were plenty of characters, it was like a small town. Because of my mainly South African upbringing I was never really exposed to the typically intelligent wit of the Welsh. I have never before or since laughed so much generally in my life as much as I did in those years since the humour was so varied and clever. I learned a lot from my peers in that respect. One particular occasion springs to mind when I first started and it involved me having a conversation with Mal Davies, a chassis group Engineer from Taffs Well. When someone in Wales is unwell or sick they say 'I'm bad' (I'm baahhd). Well I was telling Mal about my passion for Cardiff City when he looked at me with a naughty twinkle in his eye and said 'I wouldn't go and watch them, they don't come and see me when I'm bad'.

There were so many other people and so many other stories that I could devote an entire book on this part of my life, such was the richness of my experience there and it was during my time here that I dipped in to my repertoire of mischievous pranks. All through childhood I would be winding Mum, Pauline, Cei or even Dad up in any slight way that I could but now it was time to take my skills to the professional stage. It was as if I had a mind full of ideas and creation that could best be expressed through joking around. I was always doing things as a boy like putting salt in the sugar bowl, swapping the bicarbonate of soda in a 'Leo dried peas' packet with an extra strong mint (they looked identical), putting mustard underneath the butter on toast for Mum. Even putting tea leaves in the granulated coffee. The list went on and on. So by now, working full time, I had graduated to become a very good prankster indeed and I used my skills as often as I could. I could almost describe it as a hobby.

I equipped myself with a mouse-trap styled, cap gun incendiary device which basically meant that you put a cap gun cap into a small metal, spring loaded clip in the 'open' position. Because of the spring it naturally wanted to close back on itself so if hidden underneath something, when that something was lifted the spring would snap back, forcing the clip onto the cap, resulting in a loud bang. This was just up my street and so working with TV's and the precarious and volatile nature of electronics, the scene was set. Martin, a very skilled, very passionate and very serious technician had his head in a TV with the chassis out as he probed and measured. With his face deep in pouting concentration, he was on a mission to fix this TV no matter what and he was in the zone. He left the workshop for some reason so I pounced like a true opportunist that I was. Against the clock I quickly lifted the chassis he was working on and inserted the 'cap trap' in its open position underneath the plastic support frame. I returned quickly to my workbench before he entered the room, a picture of innocence and concentration. As he started work again on his repair he lifted the chassis very gingerly which resulted in a loud 'CRACK' which made him drop it instantly with a look of ashen disbelief on his face. He must have thought a big capacitor had blown. I was in hysterics, my head bursting with the pressure. He looked at me with a fair amount of disdain and just said 'Nice one Curley' which almost made it even funnier.

I came close to being seriously disciplined once when I put a sulphur bomb in my boss's cigarette 'for a laugh'. Barry 'Dirty Harry' Davies was my boss and he used to smoke like a trooper. There would always be blue wisps of smoke curling up in front of him at his desk as he flipped through parts lists, throwing back luke warm coffee from a plastic cup. For a good while he vacated his desk so I pounced. I took a cigarette from his packet, containing only a few, and I inserted the little grey shaft that looked exactly like a pencil lead into the end you light up. It was thin enough to disappear into the leaves, like camouflage and without compromising the cigarette itself. I put the cigarette carefully back in to the pack and forgot about it, hoping he would light up in the office in front of all the lads. Unfortunately for him, and nearly for me, he went to a management meeting with a lot of other Japanese bosses but I didn't think he would actually pick the doctored 'fag' and smoke it in the meeting. Well obviously he did as he strode back into the office, white with rage and although he didn't know for sure he correctly blamed me for making him look ridiculous. 'Liam, you could have got me sacked there!' 'That bloody cigarette stank the f@#*ing meeting room out, it was stinking of eggs in there and everyone was looking at me like it was me'. I feigned mock concern as I failed at stifling a laugh. It was such a funny episode that all the lads were in stitches. Barry eventually saw the funny side as well.

There were so many other crackers I pulled as well, like painting polo mints with Typex and seeing the resulting white flakes on the lips of my victim, with not a hint of concern for their health and safety. Another good one was pressing the silence button on the shared telephone when one of my colleagues was on the phone to production. The silence button was so that the person on the other end couldn't hear certain bits of conversation when the button was pressed. Mark would have the receiver in his hand, facing away from me, with the body of the phone near me so that he couldn't see it which meant all the buttons were within easy reach of me, including the silence button. As soon as Mark got to a crucial part of the conversation, where he was delivering an important part number that the production manager needed to implement, I would press the silence button so that the person on the other end was unable to hear the crucial piece of information. This must have been hugely exasperating for the poor production manager as Mark would be repeatedly spelling out 'It's fi…..…………… ohms Mike'. 'IT'S Fi…..……OHMS MIKE!!' The production manager would be irritated as he thought Mark was messing around and Mark would be irritated with the production manager because he thought he was being slow on the uptake or hard of hearing. For me it was the perfect wind up, it was sadistic of me but at the same time really, really funny.

There were always prank calls to the auto insertion department where I would ask the girl in the office to put a call out for a 'Hugh Jardon' or a Spanish contractor called 'Manuel Hung'. It was all good fun, especially when I got my friend Richard, who was a bit of a ladies' man. He used to dress to impress and wore some beautiful silk ties with matching shirts because the look was everything. On a hot summers day as he had just come back from production I noticed he had an open can of Coke on his desk. As he left his desk once more I took my Stanley knife and cut a slit vertically down the wavy line of the can, between the grey and white so he wouldn't notice. Crucially it was just below the lip of the can and when Rich came back, sweating profusely and panting for his drink, he grabbed the can and took a gulp, spilling all the way down his tie at which point he thought he was just being clumsy. He dusted himself off and took another gulp with the same result. This time a few expletives were thrown in to berate how idiotically clumsy he was. Then finally on the third failed attempt, now with shirt and tie stained with brown liquid, our office model looked at me witheringly and said 'Curlo, you're a prick'. Again, my head hurt with laughter and by then everyone knew it was me, I had become infamous.

A very memorable wind up was when I overheard a conversation between my good friend Craig and a supplier of wire braided harnesses. Craig already had a short fuse with this particular supplier since they had bungled a few previous approval samples already. This particular day he was at pains to point out exactly what he wanted and this was to 'please solder the fly leads on, do *not* under any circumstances crimp these parts on'. He left it at that with the supplier and asked them to please fax down a drawing of confirmation for him to approve so that they manufactured the sample right. Time passed and I didn't plan this but took my opportunity when it arose later that day. I was at the photo copier and noticed a fax coming through from Craig's suppliers. It was the fax drawing of confirmation of the braided cable assembly being soldered, not crimped so they had understood and got it right. I just could not resist though, I took the fax, made a photo copy of it and proceeded to expertly doctor it so that it read 'crimp' instead of 'solder'. These were the days when fax's came through on that shiny, thin, heat sensitive fax paper so I had some work to do in order for it to look authentic. I had to manually cut out bits of words from other sections of the fax and glue it onto the copy and then send it back through the fax machine in order to copy it for it to look original. The end result was a perfect counterfeit fax reading the opposite of what Craig wanted. I kept the original in my top drawer until I had had my fun.

Next was to place the fax on Craig's desk without him knowing it was me who put it there and wait for the reaction. I was sitting a few seats down from him when he came back to his desk and looked at the fax on his desk. He picked it up and started reading it in disbelief as his face started to turn red with anger. He was in a rage as he started saying 'I cannot *believe* these morons have got it wrong again, I couldn't have been more clear, for f@$&s sake'. Well within an instant he had the phone in his hand, contacting the beleaguered supplier and when he got through he couldn't help himself as he said 'Bill, what don't you understand about my drawing?' 'I explained *exactly* what I wanted and yet you send me this crap'. There was a period of silence as the supplier tried to explain that he did in fact understand the drawing and couldn't understand what was going on which made Craig feel even more frustrated. It was at this point that I cracked up and couldn't stop my laughter any more. Craig knew me well enough by now to realize I had pranked him as he stopped dead in his tracks and said 'Bill, I think someone has been playing silly buggers here, I'm really sorry mate, forget what I've just said'. Needless to say, Craig was not too impressed with me and vowed to get me back and boy did he do that, and didn't I deserve it.

After a good couple of years of practical jokes and wind ups I had my comeuppance and little did I know it at the time but it was orchestrated by my good friend Craig and Barry 'Eastwood' Davies. The MELUK site had bought an adjacent building which was empty, dank and run down and little bit creepy. We were to turn one small section of the huge building into an archive room which I was asked to do. The approach to the little former office where the archives were to be housed was surrounded by a cold, dark series of empty corridors and rooms. The little room I was to work in was filled with boxes of files and my task was to get it in some order. After chatting to myself for a while and getting on with the task eventually I managed to make some headway. I had my hands on my hips for a moment whilst I pursed my lips in concentration. I felt a cold eerie presence around me in the sea of cardboard boxes and I felt a little uneasy. As I turned to go and get a screwdriver, from out of a box roughly thigh height, out popped a satanic sounding Jack-in-the-Box. In the split second instant I saw a tall thin man with dark hair propelling himself out of the box like a possessed demon. His face was contorted like the evil face in the painting 'The Scream'. I screamed like a little girl then collapsed with laughter as I realized milliseconds later that it was Craig. He and Barry had colluded in order to get me back and they were both flat out, clutching their bellies, faces red with laughter, eyes brimming with tears. It was such a sweet victory for them and I loved them all the more for having 'played the game' with me. I was on the wrong end of a hammering but I loved the camaraderie it created. Other people would also get their revenge on me as one lunch time I was man-handled to a workshop chair and cable tied to it for the entire half hour. These were fantastic times and although I did work hard and the stress of keeping your products going was immense, it was all within a backdrop of a good social set up. The size of the workforce lent itself to the feeling of going to work in a small village where everyone knew one another. People would fight and bicker and backstab but likewise they would also bend over backwards to help one another when the chips were down. It was like a huge family and all that families went through and it was a unique community and one that has never really been replaced in my heart since. The quick witted boys from the Welsh valleys with their self depreciating humour were an absolute joy to be around. I loved my life in work and I was also progressing quite nicely as an assistant Technician.

Chapter 21

Mum and Dad eventually bought a house in Eiddew Street, Treganna, number 25 which was the end house in the terrace with front door opening straight out onto the street and all the houses all joined up. It was a lovely little home and one which I would become very attached to later on. Again, Dad did a fair bit of work to get the house nice and solid and I can only admire him for teaching me how to be practical and resourceful. Dad was and is a good teacher and I will always respect and love him for these qualities.

By this time I was going out with Jimmy more and more to pubs and clubs and I was absolutely having the time of my life. On a Friday night we would all go down to the Clive Arms for a good few bevies before having a bag of chips and a pie after 11pm. It would be the usual crowd of Treganna lads, mostly all of Jimmy's buddies that I inherited. It was an instant, ready-made, package deal and it's what I really needed back then to bring me out of my shell. Remember that I still had all my inferiority complex issues buried very deep within me by now but I brushed that aside as the feelings of having fun and gaining acceptance with my peers became a stronger force. I loved the feeling of having drank a few beers and the feeling that the world was all wonderful and rosy, that feeling of oneness with your mates when you were asked what you wanted at the bar. I'm not glorifying drink and its perils but at that time of my life, I needed to be a part of that scene. I needed to visit this pleasure park and it's what I did with both feet first. I also felt safe in a crowd of lads and I mixed in well, I became one of the team, I was normal, I fitted in. My hair was short and cropped to the extent that you couldn't tell if I was ginger, strawberry blond or just blond. It didn't matter as I started getting interest from females whatever colour it was. I didn't quite know what to do about this interest but I was none-the-less ecstatic to be getting attention from them. For the first time in a long time I felt as though I belonged and since I was now an adult under my own steam and earning my own money, I was not going to let that go. I was a normal 20 year old doing what normal 20 year olds do. Having fun!

Saturday nights were a bit more of a serious affair as we would dress in smarter trousers and shirts and start off in the Clive Arms on Cowbridge Road or at Llandaff rugby club and end up in town, Cardiff town with all its thrills, spills and delights. Oh what a night we would have there! I found it *so* exciting and enthralling, Cardiff these days being one of the party capitals of Britain. Initially Jimmy and I would meet up with Howard Gore and Tony Ferreira in Tony's Dads house in Grangetown where we would go to an off-license, buy a few beers and spend a couple of hours gulping back tins of cheap lager whilst listening to Billy Idol, Madness or whatever else we fancied at the time. Tony was a more introverted person than Jimmy and Howard, Howard being obsessed with Billy Idol to the point of looking like him and acting just like the superstar. He was a brilliant character, larger than life and full of over-the-top expression. We all loved him for the way he would loudly exaggerate any story for maximum effect in his broad Cardiff accent, he was brilliant fun to be with. With Jimmy's natural funniness the four of us would be in absolute hysterics going out on a Saturday night. It really was such a great time we had and we imagined we were part of the group Madness, miming to songs and basically acting idiotically. When I look back now, if it wasn't for Jimmy I'm not sure I would have come out of my shell as quickly as I did because he was the sort of person who was really popular with people and seemed to know everyone, very handy when you were as socially naïve as I was then.

Obviously with a group of lads there would be friends of friends and girlfriends until quite a social network was created. For me this meant meeting girls without having to chat them up in a noisy nightclub or bar, it meant I could be me in the group, having fun, whilst inadvertently getting to know that so far elusive and beautiful creature called 'a girl'. Because we were all just having fun there was no pressure to be seen to be 'dating' anyone and there were no awkward dynamics in play. We all just got on with it and had a good old laugh, whether the opposite sex were watching or not. It was the perfect introduction for me and I gradually gained more confidence around girls.

Considering my previously near paralysis around girls up until now, I had really come out of my shell and whilst I wasn't 'Don Juan' I was enjoying myself in an innocent way but with wicked intent. There were to be many drunken face-latching episodes onto the lips of other drunken Cardiff girls which left me quite thrilled. I had never before kissed any girls in any way so to steal the odd kiss in a darkened night club or outside pubs was as if I was in Rock 'n Roll heaven. At the time they were of course all beautiful, in fact the more I drank the more exquisite they became. There was one occasion at the Cardiff City Supporters club dinner where one of the female supporters thought I was one of the youth players. It was amazing to mingle with my heroes but even more fantastic for the girls to think I was a player. I got on like a house on fire with a certain beauty from Bridgend only to realize the following week that she reminded me of the eighties iconic footballer, Glenn Hoddle, when I next met her. She had looked completely different the previous week in a drunken haze at a dodgy Grangetown dive as drink is very much an anesthetic to our senses. My first real encounter with a girl was brief and very unromantic but considering my slow start in the world of romance, I was more than happy.

It was approaching Christmas time 1990 with all the atmospheric festivities in full swing where I would be going to the MELUK works 'do' at the Royal Hotel which in itself was like going to an extended family reunion.

151

By comparison to more conservative and sensible places of work that I have recently become more accustomed to, MELUK was like a family occasion. Often with these office parties most of the fun was on the night itself with the remainder being discussed as to 'who did what' on the Monday afterwards.

Christmas came and went as I was able to lavish expensive gifts on Mum, Dad and Cei for the first time in my life. I was working in a well paid job and had little outgoings, so I was determined that Mum and Dad would have nice things such as proper leather gloves, lovely perfumes, Turkish Delights, Chocolates, Black and Decker adjustable work benches. I loved giving and I think Mum and Dad were pretty appreciative of it as well. I'm not sure if Mum ever got the hang of the work bench though.

On New Years Eve all the lads and ladies piled into our favourite haunt, The Dog and Duck in Womanby Street. This place suited us all perfectly because it wasn't pretentious and definitely wasn't a posers paradise such as Jacksons on Westgate Street. It was more of a relaxed, down to earth student-like sweat pit with drunken throngs of girls and raucous rugby boys looking to snare their little fillies for the evening. It was a night club on three floors with different genres and eras for each of them so if you got bored you could always go somewhere else within the club. It was so crowded that pints of beer were not a practical option if you wanted to dance as well. Bottles were more popular but didn't last too long in a hot and sweaty club. I started dancing with this pretty, dark haired Scottish 'gerel' (girl) and quickly found her to be warm and funny, almost laddish but innocently charming. It was a brief episode in a blur of an evening and I may possibly have kissed her.

I was to find out that she was a friend of a friend of Jimmy's and was excited at the prospect that we would all pile back to Tony Ferreira's house in Grangetown after the club had closed. After a heavy evening of drinking at the Dog we usually dined out in luxury at 2am in the morning in the exquisite Caroline Street, otherwise known as 'Salmonella Street'. The huge red sign of 'Tony's Fish Bar' was our version of the Star of Bethlehem where we would end up and join a queue waiting for

'Chicken Curry off-the-bone' served in a bulging polystyrene tray packed with chips, chicken and curry sauce. Trust me; food has never tasted so good at 2:30am in a litter strewn back street packed with drunken revelers. Stabbing greedily with a plastic fork at the last little remnants of chips meant it was time to make our way back to Tony's where all I wanted was a cup of tea. The Scottish girl was with us and I immediately warmed to her when she asked everyone 'Who wants a cuppa?' I thought to myself 'That's my kind of girl'. She was in her late teens and pretty in a cute sort of way with dark brown eyes and hair. I immediately took to her and we struck up a conversation easily, making each other laugh. After a night sleeping at Tony's house with bodies littering the bedrooms and living room it was time to get a taxi home to Treganna in the wee hours of a January Sunday morning. The girls name was Leanne and this was the beginning of my first love affair.

After the dust had settled in the new year and we were all back into the swing of things I started asking about this new girl on the scene who they predictably called 'Jock'. Jimmy knew her but not very well, she was more of a good friend of Tracey, Jimmy's Tom-Boy buddy from around the corner. At first I wasn't too bothered if I saw this girl or not but always had a good laugh when we were in each other's company. It was all very casual at first but becoming more serious, for me at least. I was getting to a point in my life where I wanted a relationship, something I had never had before. Leanne and I were not an item, nowhere near it but I did secretly want it. We would often end up kissing at the end of the night in a night club and I was falling in love without realizing that Leanne wasn't. She had other issues to work on which I was happy to help her out with but for now I had to be content that it was what it was, a weekly 'cop on'.

They say youth is wasted on the young and I have to admit that it's about right. When I look back now I wished I'd been a bit more patient with relationships and not rushed in so quickly. I was so keen for a relationship just so that I could feel wanted by a girl which to be fair was what I never had when in school. I don't have any regrets about the girls in my relationships but I do feel I should have remained single for a lot longer instead of committing to a long term relationship from the age of 21. It's easy to say that now but at the time I was following my heart, which is what I still do today and what I will always do.

I was smitten by Leanne and I knew she liked me a lot too, but it was still all very casual and open ended. I wouldn't go as far as to say I pined for her in the week but I did look forward to the weekend and getting together at the Dog 'n Duck. I remember one Sunday morning after another good session in town the previous night, I decided to go and knock on Leanne's door as she told me she lived in 'Ivy Road' in Penarth. I thought to myself 'what an amazing coincidence, I live in Eiddew Street, Treganna and she lives in Ivy Road, Penarth. Surely this is meant to be?' So I got on the bus to Penarth and looked for Ivy Road. Bear in mind that this was 1991 and before the invention of street maps so I used the age old custom of asking strangers where somewhere was. And yes, I was being facetious with my previous remark, of course street maps were around back then, I in fact had an A-Z of Cardiff but for some curious reason, didn't bother checking it.

The first few strangers I asked wrinkled their noses up at me with a glazed look of confusion when I asked 'Do you know where Ivy Road is?'. After the fourth time of asking somebody which was an old man with a hearing aid, I started to feel a bit deflated and forlorn when they said such a place didn't exist. The last throw of the dice was a rough looking thug who wore a shell suit accompanied by the matching cigarette and can of Stella. 'Hiya mate, do you know if there is such a street called EYE VEE ROAD?' I said. 'Nah mait! Oooh you aahftah' was his unusually helpful response in a very broad Cardiff accent. 'Erm, Leanne, she's a Scottish girl who said she lives in Ivy Road' I replied. 'Aaggh! Yoo mean Jocks daughter dohwn yoo' he said. 'Err Yeah?' I replied. 'Aye, she lives in IGH VIEW mait, not EYE VEE, follow me, I'll show yoo'. As I was following the flammable tracksuit bottoms I realized I had been caught out by that Scottish accent, not for the first time and definitely not for the last either. You see 'High View' in English translated into 'Igh Vee' in an Aberdeenshire accent.

As I followed this helpful athlete up numerous flights of concrete stairs I was caught off guard by how desperately depressing and poor this grey council estate looked. There was no grass to be found, just row upon row of grey, three story blocks of flats. There were the odd burnt out wrecks of cars where they had previously been stolen and then set alight, children of eight years old looking at you with hardness in their eyes as if they had lived a life of crime already. The children had a wild feral look about them and it made my spirits sink. Welcome to the notorious 'Billy Banks' I thought.

I managed to be escorted to the right flat and I knocked on the door, it was late morning by then. Someone came to the door after I found myself being scrutinized behind a tiny security glass, those useless tiny magnifying glasses the size of a five pence piece. The door opened and this tiny gypsy-like woman stood before me, one hand on her hip, the other with a long cigarette as she surveyed me with cold disdain. Her hair was long and black and she had quite a hard face with pale coloured eyes. Her skin looked tough and well smoked. I nervously said 'Erm, Hello, is Leanne here?' She immediately bellowed up the stairs 'LEANNE! THERE'S A GINGER BOY DOWN HERE WANTING TO SEE YOU'. She didn't take her eyes off me and it was if she was actually shouting at me. I'm not entirely sure what I was supposed to do here apart from silently acknowledging that she was indeed correct on all counts but could have been a little less abrasive with her summary. As the awkward silence descended on us I heard Leanne slowly making her way downstairs which broke the silence. 'Ooh Christ' I heard as Leanne realized who it was whilst she mumbled something about not being ready. I was invited into the house, past the gypsy bouncer and up into Leanne's room where we lay on the bed and chatted for hours. I think she must have thought it was all a bit strange but sweet, this lad coming all the way from Treganna on the bus to see her for a chat. It was nice though and felt like a beginning. We got on well and it was different to chat without the noise and dark humidity of a night club.

Me being a rank amateur in the love stakes, I was not aware of the game I was letting myself into by pursuing a young girl who was free and essentially single. For some unknown reason young girls seem to go for the 'bad boy' who hurts them and they get hung up on this, thinking it's going to happen every time. I wasn't interested in games and the thrill of the chase that some people love; I just wanted a warm and loving relationship and thought I had a lot to offer. Leanne had already loved and been hurt before so she was cautious and I couldn't entirely read her properly. I know she laughed a lot and put on a brave face but underneath I sensed there was some sort of hurt. Being a man I wanted to fix it straight away but I wasn't sure what was broken. I couldn't if she didn't let me in. I was like an eager young Labrador puppy whilst Leanne was more like a frightened kitten. During this time the phrase I became accustomed to and ended up with a deep loathing for was 'I'm confused'. As we all know, men and woman work differently but I wasn't aware that we had a different language as well. So when it came to asking Leanne out for a meal or a date she was saying she felt 'confused' which frustrated the living daylights out of me. Confused about what! It's either yes or no, we can either do this or not. Obviously as we men grow up a bit we try our hardest to understand and sometimes we get it right. Eventually I figured it out that being 'confused' meant that she was not entirely committed to the relationship because she had feelings for someone else or at least thought she did. It was all making sense, kind of.

I was to eventually realize that I was just being too enthusiastic, I was too nice, too much of a gentleman and generally too eager to please. Woman, especially young girls, don't often appreciate these traits in guys, especially if their first love had been a womanizer. I had always grown up to believe that woman should be treated with gentleness and care which I still feel is true but the Yin to that Yang is also needed in that a woman also needs to feel danger and excitement and to think that their man has another side to him. That there is real substance beneath the gentle exterior, steel hand, velvet glove.

For months during that summer of '91 we still flirted and kissed and laughed and cried and became really close. We really were an item but not quite officially. We would have the most amazing heart to heart discussions at all times of the day, morning or night and we really grew into eachothers being. It's a cliché but Leanne grew to be my best friend first before anything else, not that this was what I wanted but it was just how it happened. I was reasonably happy and really wanted to take the next step and become an item but I don't think Leanne was too sure.

Chapter 22

I was really becoming my own man by now but still at that awkward stage of living at home. I was under Mum and Dad's roof and paying rent to help them out with the mortgage. I had my little room and generally loved being at home but knew the time would soon come when I would need to leave. I was independent, had my own decently paid job, could drive but didn't yet have my British license. Since I had already passed my test in South Africa my international license was valid for one year, within which I needed to pass my test.

So the main aim for me was to pass this test as quickly as possible and get it out the way, tick the box so to speak. I had been driving for over two years by now so was confident and brash. I saw this test as a nuisance but necessary and I needed to do it in order to become a legal driver. I was eager but unprepared and not aware of what I was up against. The British driving exam is generally a rigorous and thorough test of your ability to drive safely on the roads with the emphasis on the word 'safely'. I booked my test without having had any lessons, bought a theory book to brush up on and waited for the day, nervous but confident.

I took Dad's 1982 VW Passat estate to the test centre in Fairwater and gave the examiner my details and South African drivers license. He looked a little bemused by the little paper document in my ID book but carried on regardless. As we walked out of the test centre he stopped and said to me 'Please could you read the registration plate of that car in front of us please?' The car was about twenty metres away and I could easily read it but in order to break the tension I jokingly said 'Which car' which went down like a lead balloon. He gave me a withering look and told me to get into the car. We pulled off and as far as I was concerned I was doing just great, cruising around the streets of Cardiff like I owned the place. My reverse parking was spot on, the three point turn in Ethel Street a synch. Reversing around a corner was a bit tricky but I thought this was pointless and not like I would ever really do it much so didn't worry too much about it. I was a bit arrogant, it has to be said. Half way round the examiner said to me he was going to hit his book on the windscreen which was my signal for an emergency stop. I completed this with aplomb and I felt confident, especially after my hill start went well. There was an occasion where I eagerly entered a round-about and caused another driver to hoot his horn at me in exasperation but I thought nothing of it. 'This is what happens on the roads' I thought 'get over it'.

Near the end the examiner told me to stop at a convenient place which I thought meant 'emergency stop' for some reason. Yes, I know, I have no idea why because I'd already performed it, but I was actually still quite nervous. So half way up a quiet suburban street in Fairwater on a sunny summer afternoon I suddenly jammed on the anchors as if an invisible child had ran out into the road without warning. The poor examiner wasn't expecting this as his upper torso was almost catapulted through the windscreen, clipboard flying out of his hands, head jolting forwards. So we were stopped in the middle of the road as I looked to my left to expect a 'thumbs up' for an excellently executed emergency stop when he said 'No! I meant park in a convenient space'. I parked up and he looked at me gravely and uttered those dreaded words. 'Unfortunately you have failed to meet the requirements of the British driving standards, you have failed on four major points'. I was incensed and really irritated at this and just wanted this idiot out of my car so I could let off some steam. I could not believe it! However, I had to gather myself and drive back home and tell everyone the bad news.

That very evening I vowed to get straight back on the horse and get this damned test passed so I applied for another as soon as possible which turned out to be a few weeks away. In that time I brushed up on my failure points and felt confident for my test. The same thing happened; I failed, but this time for other points. I was taking this personally now so again went and applied straight away. I channeled my disappointment into working hard to get another date. This time I dragged Dad along with me so we could brush up on all my points of failure and yet again I sat the test. Yet again I failed and for entirely different things so this was becoming a big problem for me.

I had to get off my high horse and get help, help in the form of driving lessons by a professional instructor. Since I could drive, had a license and had been driving trouble free for two years, it was a blow to my ego. I booked an instructor who came highly recommended from my cousin Amelia and he took me on a test drive. Mike was his name and he was a brilliant instructor and explained to me that he would get me to a level way above what the national level was so that in the event of a mistake or slip up due to nerves, I would still have done enough to pass. I felt confident in him and he was very honest with his assessment of my driving at the end of the test drive. 'Liam' he said 'I can see you've been driving for a couple of years and you are an experienced driver. The problem is that you've slipped into bad habits that you're unaware of and it's up to me to help you iron them out. I don't need to teach you how to drive; I need to teach you how to pass the test'. And that's exactly what he did. After eight intense lessons he said I was ready for the test.

Now how about this for a bit of irony? The same driving examiner that failed me on my first attempt was testing me again this time. On this occasion I was much less brash and very well polished in the art of passing a driving test. After fourty five minutes driving around the west of Cardiff I did everything perfectly and he congratulated me on passing the test. I could have kissed him but just about held my emotions in check as I had something up my sleeve. Mike was waiting back at the test centre like an expectant father, hoping to ensure he kept his 100% pass rate intact. When I got out of the car I pretended to look crestfallen and dejected. As I crossed the road I could see him looking concerned as he asked 'How did you get on?'. 'I PASSED' I said with a huge grin on my face to which he replied 'Ooh, you bugger, I thought you'd failed by the look on your face; well done Liam'. It was a satisfying conclusion to an unexpectedly hard journey, one which I took too lightly at first but quickly realized that complacency had got the better of me. I went out with Jimmy and Michael that Friday night and celebrated at the Clive Arms.

Life was going well, I was 21, had passed my driving test, had a good social life and had a good job which I was enjoying. The only things I thought I needed for life to be perfect back then was for me to be in a relationship and then have a car of my own and to get a place of my own. The situation at MELUK was that I had had successive promotions to take me up to becoming a grade 4:2 assistant technician. One more increment meant I would become a fully fledged technician which was my minimum target. Apart from all the jokes and wind ups in work and general social club atmosphere it was an important role which I had. If I didn't do my job correctly it meant that thousands of TV's would be made incorrectly so I had to be thorough. The way it worked was that the technicians would be responsible for the main model for the UK market and any European derivatives of that product would be the responsibility of the assistant technicians. If the TV's were made wrong for any reason it would be picked up whilst being tested on the production line but by that point it meant a lot of rework and a lot of time lost so it was not a desirable scenario. I was in charge of producing drawings and ensuring that all the drawings for the assembly of the product were clear and understandable. I was responsible for the list of parts that went into making the TV, called a 'parts list' (funnily enough!). There were literally hundreds of components that went into making a TV set, some very big and obvious, others tiny and seemingly insignificant. If you were to get one part wrong it would have an impact either serious or superficially but nonetheless a change to what was specified.

If the design department decided they needed to change something that affected the picture or sound quality or anything else for that matter, it would be down to me and a test technician to ensure that this information got to the line. This change could take the form of a tiny value change on a single printed circuit board or a huge mechanical change and the information to the production line would be in the form of an 'alteration report' or 'concession'.

There was one occasion where my TV range for Italy had a 'buzz elimination' countermeasure to stop certain channels on Italian broadcasts from sounding as if there was a giant hornet in the TV set. A succession of errors between design and us in technical eventually culminated in the modification not being applied when it should have so it meant hundreds of TV's in Italy would be affected as they had already been built and shipped. I was not entirely responsible but had to shoulder some of the blame. It ultimately ended up in hundreds of TV's having to be reworked in a MELUK warehouse in Milan so a task team had to be assembled in order to go out and get the job done. My manager Gerriant Jones asked me 'Liam, is your passport up to date?'.

Although the reason we were going out was not exactly of a productive nature I couldn't have been more excited at the thought of visiting a foreign land. I had never been to Italy for any reason so I was going to enjoy the fortnight that we were to be there. The team consisted of Graham from production, Steve from engineering, Sue from production and me. We landed in Milan on a bitterly cold Sunday evening in February, were picked up by our Italian contact and checked into our hotel which was better than I could have expected. It wasn't the Hilton but it was certainly no railway hostel either. I felt quite the jetsetter, quite man-of-the-world-ish. We were taken by taxi in the morning to the main Milan warehouse and introduced to a few key people before being shown the enormity of what we had to actually do. There were literally hundreds of TV's in boxes waiting to be unpacked, dissembled, offending PCB removed and capacitor modification applied. We had a crew of Italian casual labourers who were there to provide the muscle and become a human conveyor belt. They would unpack the TV's from the carton and place it on a long bench where another would screw open the back cover. Someone else would be removing the B-PCB whilst Sue then removed the can on the board itself under which the modification was applied. My job was to apply the modification to the B-PCB by soldering a few capacitors to the board, after which Sue put the can back and the whole sequence was reversed thereafter. We looked at the sky scraper of TV's in the dark foreboding warehouse, blew our cheeks out and got cracking with the work. We had an exhausting two weeks ahead of us. We would usually finish late, at 6pm or thereafter and go straight for a good few beers in reception back at the hotel whilst eating bar snacks for a few hours. For one reason or another we would not usually have an evening meal due to expense, saving money or simply feeling too tired. Having a few well earned beers became our treat, our habit at the end of a long days work. In the morning I would be ravenous and help myself to as much of the buffet as I could physically muster. A full English breakfast followed by croissants, cheese, hams, coffee, orange juice and more toast. It was quite a feast and set us up for the day in some style to the point where we didn't have to have lunch, or if we did, very little.

We were taken to lunch one day in a little café in the city that had a wonderful view of the alps in the background. I had a meal called 'Veal Saltimbocca' which consisted of veal and prosciutto in a white wine sauce. My word I had never tasted anything so delicious and it brought it home to me how passionate the Italians were for food. It opened my mind up and I fell in love with Italy, how seriously they took eating and therefore living. It was their attention to detail, their acknowledgement of how sacred meal times were. It was never about grabbing a quick snack, shoveling it down your throat and getting back to work. I noticed that the people were deliberate and relaxed when they ate, they would not be rushed. I loved it and admired it and wished to live like it too. I was also surprised at how simple their pizza's were compared to the very Americanized ones we got back home. Initially I was disappointed at how bland they appeared but soon changed my mind after tasting one. Everything seemed fresh and delicious.

It was a wonderful time, very hard work indeed but a real eye opener. On the middle weekend I wanted to go and watch a game of football. I had to; I was in Milan, a hotbed of football fanaticism. I was lucky that it was Inter Milan playing at home that weekend because if it had been neighbours AC Milan, I'm not sure I would have been able to get a ticket as it was a golden era for the Rossoneri with the likes of Marco Van Basten and Ruud Gullit playing for them. Instead I was able to get a ticket to watch their fierce city rivals, Inter, the Nerazzurri. All week the Italian labourers had been calling me 'Bergkamp' the famously gifted Dutchman who played for Inter at that time. It was only because I had a vaguely similar look in that I was fair haired and ridiculously handsome that they called me that. Well that's what I kept telling myself anyway. It meant I was going to watch him live against Torino at the famous San Siro stadium. Myself, Graham and Steve wanted to go to the game so we all managed to get tickets at the stadium after a long taxi ride into the city. It was a bitterly cold day and we got the cheapest tickets possible, somewhere up in the stratosphere of the stadium, looking down at the little Subbuteo figures, or so it seemed. I was loving it, loving every kick of the ball, fascinated by the surroundings and at how different it was to watching football back home. Graham and Steve weren't avid football fans and were there for the experience. I knew I wouldn't be back in a hurry so just wanted to lap up the atmosphere and take in every minute. Torino were 0-1 up in the game with Inter chasing shadows and pressing hard. The other two lads were becoming restless as the game drew to a close but I wanted to see every last minute. I wanted Inter to win but the game was reaching its conclusion. On either side of me I was hearing 'Bloody hell it's cold, can't wait to be back in the warm hotel' or 'D'you think you've seen enough Liam?'. I stuck to my guns initially and told them to man up but eventually relented when there were three minutes to go on the clock, the score still the same as it was. We left our seats where I took a final mental snapshot and started to exit the beautiful stadium. I was resigned to an Inter defeat and as we were half way down one of the 'turrets' we all heard a magnificent roar as Inter equalized. I could not believe it as I looked at the two half wits next to me, smiling sheepishly. I was so disappointed to have missed a goal by Inter. Then as if Murphy himself couldn't add insult to injury more, as we got into a taxi I heard another volcanic eruption of emotion as Inter scored the winner, a penalty it turned out, from Dennis Bergkamp. Inter Milan 2 Torino 1 the final score. Well, the taxi ride back to the hotel was a joyous occasion as I shot Stephanie and Lady Earl Grey daggers. All was forgiven though as we went back to the hotel for a couple of beers. The following week we worked extremely hard and got everything done that we had planned. It was a successful mission and one we could all be proud of but I was ready to come home. It was only two weeks but Italy changed my perspective on life.

Chapter 23

Meanwhile, the situation with Leanne was reaching a crescendo and things came to a head. I had asked her out for a meal at the 'Model Inn' in the centre of Cardiff in order to spend some quality time with her, like really get to know her without the distraction of alcohol and friends. It was a Saturday night and the evening was lovely, me cracking jokes and Leanne throwing her head back with laughter. It felt warm and intimate and just what was needed but we decided after the meal to go out to the Dog 'n Duck to catch up with our buddies. This was a mistake. I was feeling warm and intimate and could easily have gone home and cuddled up on the sofa but I was also easily swayed to stay out and have a bit of fun.

We both went into the club and chatted for a bit before going our separate ways which left me a bit flummoxed but I thought nothing of it as I caught up with all the lads and started swigging back the beers. After a few hours of oblivion I went looking for Leanne, only to find her chatting to a group of her work friends. Male accomplices! I felt like I had been smacked in the face as I saw her laughing and enjoying herself with these guys. I felt a jealous anger well up inside of me as I shouted something at her and left. She came after me but I was in a blind rage and totally lost it on her. I don't know what I said but it wasn't pleasant and she went back inside rather muted. I walked home in a temper and stupidly punched a small tree covered in rain water which soaked me and Howard Gore walking in the other direction at 2am in the morning. It was a chance meeting and I remember seeing him but not acknowledging him. When I lost my temper it was explosive and destructive and not at all pleasant.

I heard through a few friends that Leanne thought I was 'too nice' which was giving her cold feet. Perhaps she was right and I was just being way too eager to please. It was probably too soon to be getting so settled and familiar but I was so naive, I was a rank novice at this game and didn't really know what to do or how to act. I thought I had to play the game, not realizing at the time that I just should have been me. But as it was I felt quite devastated that I wasn't wanted and my fragile confidence had taken a knock. The sebaceous cyst of insecurity buried deep within me had momentarily resurfaced like poison. I still felt in love with this girl but my heart was breaking inside because she didn't feel the same way back and I wanted her, I didn't want to wait. I was too impatient and I felt hurt and withdrawn. The worst feeling for me was that I felt rejected.

The following Saturday I was out with all the boys and determined to enjoy myself with or without Leanne, which, to be fair to me, I was succeeding at quite a break neck pace. By the time we got to the Dog I was in great spirits but still guarded against Leanne and anything she wanted to talk about or do. I was not in the mood for games any more, I had tried and had not succeeded, and I was hurt and down but by no means out. When I saw her I greeted her politely but coldly and she immediately got the message. I went off in the other direction and started enjoying myself, chatting to other girls, dancing and really letting my hair down again. I could feel someone's eyes boring into me but I didn't pay too much attention and carried on having fun. Leanne had seen something in my eyes when she first saw me that night that let her know I was not to be messed around with; she quickly discovered that although I was a decent, nice person and fun to be with, I had another darker side that wouldn't tolerate any mind games. I was still fuming inside but it wasn't going to ruin my night and if truth be told I was using it to get answers as to how she really felt. Hypocritically I probably was playing my own game but I just needed to confirm if the relationship had a tiny flicker of life or if it had been extinguished altogether. Tonight I would get my answer, tonight I would know if Leanne cared enough to be devastated or would she just drift off into oblivious laughter with her other male friends.

It turned out to be an emotional end to the evening as all the friends piled out of the club in the early hours. We would normally hang around outside the Dog in small groups waiting to go for something to eat in Caroline Street but today was different; there was something to be resolved. Leanne was looking at me with her hurt puppy eyes and I could tell she was emotional and raw. She seemed to be reaching out; she seemed to want me and I needed to be wanted in return. I was still acting stubborn though and would have just walked home and left it at that but a few friends, including Jimmy, encouraged me to just speak to her. I relented and we talked, with Leanne assuring me that she could be with no other. She was honest enough to tell me that she thought we were going too fast and that initially she did think I was too nice but that she had seen another side to me, a side she needed to see. I had no pre-conditions; I had no real expectancy other than to have a close companion to call my 'girlfriend'. It was the 21st September 1991, a date we were both to acknowledge as the first time we were a couple. As a little boy I didn't ever feel worthy of a relationship, I felt inferior and withdrawn. Now though, I felt acceptance. I felt warmth and love and I didn't want to let that feeling go. I was still a little boy with lots of insecurities in reality, but I think that by having a relationship I was able to mature and face new emotional challenges which would shape me. It didn't feel like it at the time but I was at the foot of a mountain, an emotional Everest that I am still climbing. It was a start for me.

I have always felt that relationships are our greatest teacher, whether we accept those lessons or not, whether we feel bitter or enlightened is our own choice. There will always be chasms of turmoil between the wonderful plateaus of contented happiness. It is during these hard times that we learn most about ourselves, we learn the parameters of our being. I had so much to learn about life back then, so much to experience with the opposite sex and how they think and I am still learning, believe me. The moment we think we know everything and stop learning is the moment we stagnate. As human beings we are meant to learn of the infinite knowledge that exists in the universe. Our minds have infinite capacity if we are open to it. In later life I realized that any problems we have stem from our own issues and even though we feel the other person is at fault for the relationship breaking down, we still need to look within and learn our own lessons.

Relationship issues are never one-sided. If you take this advice you become a better and more confident person. If you always blame everyone else for break ups there is to be no growth, no moving forward in a spiritual sense. Therefore with this pattern the issues will inevitably end up being repeated in further relationships as we sit with head in hands wondering why we always choose a person who ends up hurting us. If there was no such thing as love and relationships we would not have the desire to learn about ourselves. I think that love is the blood that courses through the heart of learning. Learning is why we are alive.

This was my start and Leanne was my first real relationship. We were about to have a wonderfully fun few years of freedom, laughter, tears and soul mate closeness. We both had a lot to learn and I was happy to be with her to do it. In a spiritual sense I was by now in a complete wilderness where I had very few thoughts for church or anything Christianity related. I felt a lot of guilt for not going to church but my feelings for freedom, expression, fun and liberation were greater still. I didn't at all feel bitter about church; I was just too distracted by life to care. Leanne worked for the Hotel Elang as an Accounts assistant and I used to pick her up from work and go for the odd beer in the Elang Tavern. This tavern soon became a favourite meeting place for all our friends before going clubbing in the evening.

The time soon came where I needed to move out of Eiddew Streetand away from Mum, Dad and my little sister Cei. Life was never to be the same again, mostly for the good but it was tinged with sadness for me. It was desperately sad leaving home as I knew it was forever or at least intended to be. Mum and Dad took it well but understood, they were upset but they knew it had to happen. I had always been really close to Mum and it was such a wrench to leave, even though I was only moving about a mile away, emotionally it was the other side of the world. Mum made me a photograph album showing progress from new born baby to current young man. She put a poem in the album talking about a relationship between a mother and son and it made me cry so much. It was such a beautiful send off and I was grateful for Mum being the wonderful person that she was. It was touching and I shall never forget it, I still in fact have the album with the poem in. Dad was practical with his advice and the ultimate protector as usual; Mum was her usual soft, gentle presence with her brilliant sense of wit.

Leanne and I moved to a flat in Llanfair road, Pontcanna. I can't remember the number but it was right on the bend. We moved in with another couple, two friends of ours, Dhana and Gwen. They were both close friends and Gwen was also going out with Howard Gore, our Billy Idol lookalike mate. It was exciting and new and I felt liberated. I had a good job, had bought my first car from a work colleague (the one whom I put a cap under the chassis he was working on), had a girlfriend, was living in a lovely flat and had a good social life which included going out for drinks on a Friday or Saturday, sometimes both if we were flush. Plus I was able to watch my beloved Bluebirds. Unfortunately, and I do slightly regret this, I didn't play football for a few years because of my new found relationship. I drifted away from it, away from the grit and physical demands of the game and into a warm, cozy relationship. By this stage I wasn't a season ticket holder at Cardiff City but I went to enough home games to have warranted one. I travelled to the odd away game but not half as much as I used to.

One statistic I'm not very proud of is that I have travelled away to watch the Bluebirds on over twenty occasions and never seen them win. I had watched them at places such as Lincoln, Swansea, Wrexham, Burnley and Brentford to name but a few and never seen the team pick up maximum points. I had seen them draw a few and lose plenty more, but never that elusive win. I did, however, come agonizingly close in Wrexham on Saturday 17th April 1993, just past my 23rd birthday. The Bluebirds were flying high in Division 3 and looking like gaining promotion under Eddie

May, it had been a wonderful season. Some of the Bluebirds mad faithful at MELUK had organized a trip on a coach up to North Wales, leaving the factory at 10am, fully stocked with lager and cider. Only those with tickets could attend, and I had mine along with the rest of the coach. It was going to be a special day in the spring sunshine, Cardiff clinching promotion on the ground of their North Wales rivals if they won. I couldn't wait for it; I was champing at the bit to get the day underway. These magical days with workmates having a common interest and all being together have proven to be few and far between in my working career.

The banter and drinking started as soon as our bums hit the coach seats with Vincent the coach's ringleader and unofficial bar tender. 'Evrywun awrrayy fur booozz?' he asked in broad Cardiff accent. Out came the cans of Carling and Strongbow and we were now aboard a Bluebirds party on wheels, there was no turning back. To be fair, I did pace myself quite sensibly compared to others who were intent on not actually being able to see the game. A good four hour journey later with many pit stops for bladder bursting relief and we were in the heart of Wrexham. Even though I had taken it easy I was still quite inebriated as I got off the coach wondering why the steps seemed narrower and steeper than when I first got on. We all spilled into this welcome little pub for a bite to eat and more beers along with a few games of pool. Some idiotic guys from the coach decided they wanted to fight the first Wrexham fans they came into contact with. I was not at all going to be involved with this and distanced myself from them, this was not the reason I was here and I looked down at people who did this and who brought the name of my club to shame. Me and a couple of others agreed that we should just head off to the game and soak up the atmosphere in the stadium rather than be involved with any trouble.

As we left the little pub my head was swimming as the oxygen hit me. We had about a fifteen minute walk to the ground and I was full of banter, bravado and beer as I sang 'BLOO ARMEY' over and over again, passionately. I had been drinking quite a bit so I was probably louder than I realized as my weary legs propelled me along the pavement to the game. My mouth had that parched feeling to it and I felt that glow of alcoholic warmth envelop me. It felt strange to feel like this in the middle of the day, the bright sunshine felt a bit surreal as we walked to the game. Anyway I was by now walking on the curb with hoards of Cardiff fans on one side of the street and hoards of Wrexham fans on the other. We were divided by a thin blue line of Police constables keeping order. They were situated in the middle of the road where some had police dogs, others were on horseback with most of the officers on foot. You could see the police just wanted to shepherd us to the ground with a minimum of fuss in a quiet and peaceful way which is what most of us wanted as well. This was when my perfect day started to go horribly wrong.

I was still in fervent banter mode, singing my Bluebirds songs and randomly shouting 'AAARGH' at the top of my voice. A female officer gave me an icy stare and said in a stern voice 'No more of that, okay son'. I acknowledged what she said for a brief couple of minutes and then started to sing again, full of the joys of drunken life. It wasn't that I was thick or looking for trouble, it was just that my brain had forgotten what the officer had said barely two minutes ago. Another burly officer warned me 'Oi, any more of that and that'll be the end of your day'. 'Whoopsey' I thought, I was just having a bit of light hearted fun. The two warnings weren't quite enough for me as I kept on singing and bantering again. The police obviously thought my behavior was threatening and for me it was 'Strike 3'. Before I knew it a female police dog handler had released an Alsatian onto me. The dog launched itself at me and took a bite out of the back of my right hamstring and just held its grip there as the police officer said to me very calmly 'You're coming with me'. She instructed the dog to let go and I was embarrassingly escorted to what is known as a 'meat waggon'. This is an armored police, riot van containing eight tiny cells with barely enough room for a single person to sit. I couldn't believe what was happening and in my dulled state I asked the officer if I was still allowed to watch the game to which she wryly replied 'You might get to hear the score later sunshine, if we decide to let you out after the match'. I could not comprehend what was happening, yes I had been a bit stupid by repeatedly not listening but I wasn't *really* a threat to the peace I thought. In the eight celled police wagon there were three Bluebirds and five Wrexham fans. I felt ashamed, stupid, gutted and a bit scared to be honest. I had never before been anywhere near being arrested and now here I was, a football hooligan. The very idiots I despised for bringing the game to its knees, I had become.

The more it sank in that I wouldn't see the game the more I felt like I wanted to cry. I didn't because I had rival Wrexham fans goading me in the opposite cells and they were really annoying me, really merciless in the safety of their little cell. We arrived at the police station where an officer took my belongings and a brief statement and I was locked up in a dingy little cell. I was thinking of being cheeky by voicing my thoughts that I was hardly going to hang myself for being arrested for shouting in the street, them having confiscated my belt. I thought better of it as I lay on the concrete slab of a bed. I looked at my surroundings in disbelief as I registered that I was in a prison cell, all alone in a strange place. I wasn't so much afraid, just really disappointed and ashamed of myself. I knew I wasn't going to prison but it did make me think that I had been really stupid. Alcohol had got the better of me and unfortunately not for the last time.

I lay there minute after minute, hour after hour, staring at the grayish green walls, absently seeing patterns and maps on the grubby tiled ceiling. My mouth was dry and my lips parched as my mid afternoon hangover began to take hold. My head began to ache and my mouth felt like I had just eaten a kilogram of mature cheddar cheese. Next door I heard somebody shouting and swearing in frustration whilst I just wanted to be quiet and disappear into myself. Every fifteen minutes an officer would pull the tiny door hatch to see if I was still alive. I asked him 'any news of the score officer?' which received a stony disapproving look, as if that mattered at all. My headache was getting worse and I was starting to sober up which is never a pleasant process when you are still awake. I was wondering when I would get out of this prison cell. I knew they would let me out but I had no idea when. Then it struck me. Would I even make it onto the coach back home? I started to worry as the realization set in that I may not be able to get home that night, at least by the same means that got me here in the first place. It was still during the game but I figured there wasn't much time to go. I didn't have a watch on me or a phone so I had no clue what the time was.

The match would normally have finished at just before 5pm and as I lay there it felt way past that time as an officer opened the cell door. 'You'll be happy to know that your lads won the game two – nil' he said. 'YEEEEEAAAASS' I shouted and then remembered why I was in there in the first place. I sheepishly collected my belongings at the front desk, had my dog bite wounds checked by the doctor and I was free to go. It was just after 6pm and I had no idea where I was going or even how to get there. I asked an officer which direction I should walk in order to get back to the ground and he sent me on my way. A good 20 minutes or so later I was at the ground, the scene of one of Cardiff City's greatest triumphs and needless to say I had missed it. I looked around the deserted streets desperate for signs of blue life but my boys had long gone.

Just as I was wondering how on earth I was going to get home with little more than £20 in my pocket I spotted a coach around the corner. It was a wonderful site although it wasn't my coach. It turned out to be an Adar Glas Caerdydd coach, another branch of the supporters club from the South Wales valleys and it had broken down. I didn't care, it was a godsend. There were throngs of Cardiff fans waiting outside for the vehicle to be repaired so I just coolly walked up the steps and into the safety of the marooned coach and took up a seat somewhere near the back. I wanted to be inconspicuous, unnoticed but most of all home. Eventually the coach roared back into life, everyone piled back in and we were on our way. A lot of singing and banter and four hours later we were back in Cardiff where I walked home from Ninian Park. It had been a very long day and I *still* had not witnessed Cardiff City win away. A tender, worried ear bashing from Leanne was all that lay between myself and my bed.

Chapter 24

After a few months in the shared flat we decided that it was time we moved into a place of our own because by now, the novelty of flat-mates was wearing thin. Gwen and Howard were on and off in their relationship and that took its toll on the dynamics of the small space we lived in. Howard, although a brilliantly funny character, was quite a womanizer and I would listen to tales from Gwen about Howard. We got quite close, too close in fact. Eventually it was time to move on and myself and Leanne found a lovely little flat in Treganna, 5a Poolside Road near the Corporation Pub.

Now this is not a cowardly excuse for me to use but as much as I was in love with Leanne, by this stage I knew that the full overwhelming sexual attraction was not quite there and never really had been from the beginning. Being inexperienced I just kind of accepted that it was how it was and that I was lucky to be in a relationship. How limiting and desperate that sounds but it was what I thought on a subconscious level. The issues we both had regarding that most intimate of human traits didn't enable us to really explore the fullness of our relationship. I was certainly attracted to other woman without taking action on it, I just didn't see it as an option back then. With perspective now, I was a 23 year old man with a girlfriend who was more of a friend than a lover and I knew this and should have had the courage to end the relationship before I hurt anyone. Unfortunately, though, I was too comfortable in this hard fought relationship to let it go and the seeds of doubt were there even though we did settle well into our life together in the second floor flat. Leanne and Gwen were good friends but not completely and utterly bosom buddies. Gwen was a pretty, dark haired, petite girl from Llantrisant, just north of Cardiff. She had a lovely soft nature with a wicked sense of humour and we made each other laugh a lot. We got on very well and I found her vulnerability irresistible. Howard had long ago lost interest which hurt her but she was on her way back and she would spend many a long time at our flat just passing the time, chatting, smoking and drinking, having a laugh through glinting eyes.

It was something that distracted me from my own relationship and although the flat belonged to me and Leanne, all three of us would more often than not be in the flat together. It felt as though we were all three friends together. Gwen did have her own flat with her sister Joe, but she spent so much time at our place. She would curl herself up on the couch like a little cat and chat with myself and Leanne for hours. When I write this it sounds really weird and I feel apologetic about it but this is the ugly truth and this was how it was back then. It was normal to me then and it was my life. It was getting to the point that I would be really disappointed if Gwen didn't come over for whatever reason, it was getting bad. I had real feelings now and it worried me. We were close and exchanged some very knowing looks to each other on so many occasions. I felt guilty but a real excitement at the same time. Nothing happened initially in the first few months but the inevitable was only a few pints of cider away on any given weekend.

The inevitable became reality in the summer of 1993 as a group of us would drink in The Kings Castle and The Forresters Arms with many of Gwen's student friends there. We had our regular clan and from the surface myself and Gwen were 'friends' having a heart to heart. After regular 11'o

Clock chucking out time we would get something to eat and go back to our little flat where we would all talk some more and have a good laugh. It was after one of these innocent chats that it was decided that I should walk Gwen home, at Leanne's insistence. I could hardly believe my luck as we walked back together, the 20 minute walk to her house taking longer than it should. It was then that it happened and as ashamed as I am to have cheated on my girlfriend, it was the most amazing and exciting thing I had done up until that point in my life. I was exhilarated by her response as we kissed passionately in her street, both laughing drunkenly. We were like two naughty children and it felt dangerous.

This pattern was to repeat itself often after that to the point where I felt I needed to end things with Leanne. I was falling in love with Gwen and she consumed my every thought. I wondered in work when I would see her again but this was all very unfair on Leanne even though our relationship was great, as friends. She was the innocent and oblivious victim of my carnal desire or so I thought. I was looking through an old drawer one day and found a very recent photo of her and her friend from work out with two Italian lads, having ice-creams. I could not believe it and felt totally betrayed. They were obviously hidden from me and it was fairly obvious that it was some kind of date that went on. When I confronted Leanne about them she started giggling nervously until she came up with a whopper that 'they were all just good friends on an afternoon out'. She denied it completely that there were any wrongdoings on her part and I eventually, stupidly accepted it. Looking back on things, our relationship should have come to an end, regardless of the Gwen situation. Leanne and I still loved each other though and the link was strong.

Things with Gwen were getting fraught as well and I was fully prepared to make a go of it with her if she wanted it. I was ready to give everything up with Leanne. Unfortunately her better moral standing didn't allow her to fully take me away from Leanne, she just couldn't bring herself to do it. She knew on some level it was wrong. I was absolutely crushed and spent a long time getting over her, whilst still in a loving relationship with Leanne. How screwed up is that? I couldn't grieve publicly either as it was not a relationship in the eyes of the world or even our friends. Unbelievable but true. It wasn't to be and Gwen left the scene and moved away from our immediate circle of friends. In a way it was just as well I guess, she was a vegan and although I totally respect that form of diet, I don't think I could ever have put up with it. There was an occasion once when she had curry sauce and chips from a chip shop and was tucking into it in her girly sort of way. Out of the blue she started sobbing uncontrollably and I wondered if she had just heard that she had three weeks to live. It wasn't that dramatic, she had merely found a faint slither of chicken in her sauce.

Leanne and I stayed in that little flat for a while longer and had the opportunity to buy it but chose not to as it didn't have a lot of selling potential being on the top floor. It was a good decision retrospectively as my angels had something else in mind, something better. Apart from a less than perfect relationship things were pretty good. I was progressing well in work and had become a fully fledged technician. I was really pleased, it felt like I was worth something, it felt like I had a career now, rather than a job. I was no yuppy but I was a young and upwardly progressive person. I knew I had more to give but that would be later.

Now if you're wondering why you haven't heard much from Mum and Dad in this chapter, fear not. They were to break the inevitable news to me that shook my foundations but shouldn't have been a real surprise to me. Yes, you guessed it; Dad was unsettled and wanted to go back to South Africa. He was still the restless soul, still chasing his tail of happiness. By this time I was an onlooker and had no interest in going back to my adopted country. Mum and Dad asked if I wanted to come out with them but they probably knew the answer was always going to be a firm 'no'. I was settled and happy, established in my job and in a routine, I had no intension of going anywhere. My relationship was not perfect, which bothered me, but obviously not enough to do anything about it. Not at this stage in any case.

Leanne and I had only been in Poolside Road a short time and I was thinking of buying a house or flat but we hadn't exactly been saving money in order to get a deposit. Dad then gave me the opportunity and idea which would give me such a head start in my life. Dad wanted me to have the house they were living in; he wanted me to have 25 Eiddew Street. His decision to go back to South Africa was vindicated if he knew a part of himself was still going to own a tiny part of Britain. That part of him was me and I was only too pleased to accept.

The only problem was that we didn't have a deposit since Leanne and I weren't really saving for anything in earnest and this departure by Mum and Dad was all decided rather suddenly. This was a problem as a minimum five percent deposit was required from the bank in order for us to qualify for a mortgage. Leanne or I didn't have that sort of money to hand but Dad was determined that I would have the house, if it was truly what I wanted. And it was truly what I wanted. So Dad devised a cunning plan and put the house up for sale for £44 000, £2000 more than the estimated market value. He also didn't have £2000 to lend me in order to give me a deposit so took an overdraft out with the bank on the proviso that it was clear again within a couple of weeks. He drew the money out and gave it to me, I then put the money into my account and paid my solicitor the five percent deposit in order to secure the house. When the eventual transaction completed Dad had got what he wanted from the sale and he had ensured his son would have his first house. Never has this epitomized Mum and Dad's care and generosity more, it was typical of them and I would be forever grateful to them both. I had been given a precious foothold on the ladder of life and it was down to my Mum and Dad.

Eventually the time came for my parents and little sister to leave Britain behind once more and I wasn't sure how I would handle it. On a Friday evening in early summer 1994 I took Mum and Dad to Cardiff International Airport for their trip to Johannesburg. It was a somber but exciting time for all of us and Dad was doing his usual thing of explaining last minute instructions in intimate detail which were completely irrelevant, things like 'Oh, and don't forget that in about October, just before winter, make sure you bleed the radiators, but don't take the bleed screw fully out or it'll be murder to get back in, Alright mate?' This was as we were all teary and trying to say goodbye in the busy and bustling airport. It was Dad's way of avoiding an emotional situation. As they waved a final goodbye I didn't feel a great deal of emotion, I felt as though I had become King and needed to take responsibility for my people and show strength and purpose. Half an hour later at home I was crying my eyes out after a delayed reaction and a realization of how much I was going to miss my family. I felt all alone, not for the first time in my life but this time it felt as though I needed to grow up.

Chapter 25

Restless young man (Eiddew Street– 1994 – 2000)

It would be seven years before Mum and Dad came back to live in Britain, and they would turn out to be seven very turbulent years for them and my sister Pauline. That in itself is another long chapter of despair and tragedy in someone else's book but thankfully my immediate family made it through but it was almost impossibly difficult for all of them.

Myself and Leanne settled in well at Eiddew Street and we were so happy to call this our home as it was ideally situated in the heart of Cardiff near Forrest Park, near all the local shops and pubs and on all major bus routes. It was absolutely perfect and I was delighted with our little home. It was my first house and was a three bedroom, end of terrace with front door straight onto the street. The back garden was average to small in size but big enough for us to be able to entertain in summer if we wanted.

In terms of myself and Leanne's relationship, this was a massive distraction and took my mind off anything or anyone else. Leanne and I, although never apart for any reason, felt like a real item once more. The relationship never hit the heights of passion but what we did have was a lot of love and friendship between eachother which was what made it last so long in the first place but at the same time also created my own self-inflicted prison cell. That sounds harsh and indeed is but only given my perspective now. At the time it felt wonderful and warm but I was prone to a wandering eye and on nights out with the boys I sometimes couldn't resist if an opportunity arose. It was hardly the basis of a good relationship.

Now the nineties for me was such a magical time of freedom, discovering myself, brilliant music, excitement and naughtiness. The era reminded me of when my parents would talk about the swinging sixties with nostalgia in their heart. The nineties were my 'sixties' if you want. We had the likes of Blur, Oasis, Supergrass, The Stone Roses, The Verve, The LA's, Cast, Happy Mondays, The Farm and all those magical indie bands of that era. I was lost in a wonderful forest of beautiful music, sweaty, dark nightclubs, the smell of hops and tobacco. It was all so atmospheric, so rich and my head swam with delight. One song epitomized that era for me and it was James's 'Sit Down'. I would sit down on the grubby floor of the Dog and Duck and hold hands with the person next to me, whether male or female. At first everyone thought I was off my head until they all eventually joined in as well. I was in my mid-twenties and I felt like I was in my prime, I felt I had the world at my feet but in fact it was probably someone's cigarette butt on the floor. I felt as if I wasn't such an ugly duckling anymore, my character had burst forth. I was being me and I was expressive, I had become confident, at least the outer shell was in any case.

I'm convinced that one of the things that picked my confidence up was how I talked to myself. Now back then I had absolutely no clue of positive affirmations towards oneself but I did very often jokingly say to the girls in work things like 'If I was chocolate I'd lick myself' or if someone showed me any interest I'd say to the person telling me 'well she's only human'. I wasn't really that arrogant or conceited as it was just good fun but it did lend me an aura of confidence and when someone is confident it becomes attractive. I would often sing the chorus of a well known song 'Wind beneath my wings' by Bette Midler and instead of singing 'Did you ever know that you're my hero, and everything I would like to be' I would sing 'Did I ever tell you I'm your hero, I'm everything you wish you could be' and I would laugh my head off thinking I was hilarious. Another funny one was a song or book by David Hasselhoff called 'I love being me' and I needn't say anymore on that regarding a massive ego. All these funny little things helped my psyche even though I wasn't being serious.

Now Eiddew Street was at the end of a terrace adjacent to a relatively busy pedestrian route into Treganna, especially for new found friends of mine. During the course of drinking in the Clive Arms we got friendly with a great bunch of younger guys via Jimmy, of course. I was in my mid-twenties but the 'new wave' of the clan consisted of Keith Green, Andy 'Hughie' Lonsdale, Frankie Harley, Walter Johnson, Ray Bonner and Keith's lovely sister Carly who were all in their late teens or early twenties.

They were a brilliant bunch with each one of them a real character. Keith was like 'Face' from the A-Team, a handsome young man and with a brilliantly funny wit about him. I really loved him and got on well with him; he was and still is a good friend. Enter 'Hughie' who preferred being called that instead of his real name and I still have no idea why. Hughie was a lanky, moon faced oddity who everyone loved. He was soft and charming and had a heart of gold but he could also be street-wize and very cheeky when he needed to be. Hughie was completely off the wall and was an outrageous character who was perpetually 'skint' and lending money from people. I'm pretty certain he still owes me a fiver which I will at some point get off him. A typical Hughie move was to go to the local chippy (chip shop) after a few beers on a Friday night and ask for chips but tell the bloke serving that he only had 50p. George the chippy would begrudgingly give Hughie the chips, thinking him hard up, and the next thing you know Hughie was saying 'Mmm, these chips are a bit glassy in the middle mate'. He would also have the cheek to go up to a burger van on a Saturday night, somehow manage to barter the vendor down to a half price burger because he was skint and then say 'Oooh, you couldn't put an extra bit of cheese in that could you'.

If our group of friends could be epitomized as 'The Beatles' Frankie was the George Harrison of the group in that he was the quiet one. He was quiet but he really had a dry sense of humour as well. He could also be a sort of Inspector Clouseau character in that he would do some really daft things such as when he went on a first date in his VW Beetle. That in itself wasn't the issue, it was more the fact that his side window didn't work. He pulled up at the NCP car park in the middle of town to woo this special lady of his and as he went to extract his parking ticket from the roadside dispenser he realized he couldn't open his window. Further still he couldn't open his door because he was too close to the same dispenser but to complete the scene he couldn't reverse either because there was a queue of cars behind him waiting impatiently. A slight bit of maneuvering back and forth, with exasperated drivers behind him having to inch back, and he was able to eventually open his door. I can only imagine what was going through his mind, the minds of the people behind him wondering 'just open your bloody window' and most importantly his date. When he told us he was in stitches of laughter as we all were. Fortunately his date was just the same as him, they were two peas in a pod and the evening was a success. They were to be inseparable and as far as I know are still happily together. Sometimes life has a way of making us laugh at ourselves.

Walter Johnson was Mr Smoothe and absolutely super mellow. He was Keith's best buddy; they grew up together in the Treganna area and were always an inseparable twosome in the early years. He reminded me of a cuddly little bear who just wanted to have fun for the rest of his life and he more or less succeeded.

By this time Jimmy was still on the scene but was fading out of it due to him meeting his wife-to-be Anne. Jimmy naturally knew them all and they all loved him but he was obviously becoming more and more serious in his relationship which was totally understandable. Anne, though, although a pretty blond girl, just did not seem like a girl Jimmy would go for. She was very serious and extremely difficult to get to know. She would come across as being incredibly aloof and cold and once, whilst passing her in the street, she looked right past me, I was incredulous. Anyway, it wasn't my place to judge, I just wanted Jimmy to be happy, and on the surface he was.

The new gang and I would often go out to the Clive and Dog 'n Duck and things were really great, life was coasting along quite nicely. My relationship with Leanne was comfortable and routine and with both of us in decent jobs we were reasonably okay for money without ever being well off. When you smoke and drink it's amazing how you always have money for that pastime, equally you rarely have money for much else. Unfortunately I did adopt that filthy habit of smoking which I am never proud to admit but it's who I was back then.

Everything in my life was good, even my relationship, but it was bothering me. I wasn't entirely happy, I knew there was more for me out there. I knew I wanted to sample more of life, to see other girls and to sow my wild oats. I would look at other woman in work and socially and they would occasionally look back. There were mutual looks of desire at times but I never acted on them, well mostly I didn't and I cannot confess to being an angel in these years. I knew that what I wanted was freedom to go out and have fun but at the same time I loved the safety of the nest I was in with Leanne. I never went actively looking for women but if I just happened to be out with the boys on a Saturday and something exciting happened, I wasn't about to refuse. It wasn't healthy and I didn't feel too great about myself.

The summer of 1995 was the beginning of the end for me; I had had enough and needed to tell Leanne that we needed to part ways. It was the single biggest human issue I had had to deal with so far but Leanne deserved my honesty. I needed to break free; I desperately needed to be on my own and to not feel guilty if I wanted to be with another woman. As I prepared to tell my little puppy dog eyed Leanne I felt a lump in my throat, a real heaviness in my heart and hollowness in the pit of my stomach. I asked her to come for a walk with me and we talked for hours in Llandaff fields. It was heart wrenching in the bright spring sunshine of those beautiful fields. We were both torn in two. I was in tears and so was she but deep down I knew this needed to happen. I wanted my freedom and I didn't want to stamp all over Leanne to get it. Summer was fast approaching and I couldn't wait to get out there and be single, it was as if I had been unhappily married for years and now I was having my mid-life crisis. We both agreed it was the right thing to do even though I knew Leanne would willingly have stayed together if it was just her decision. By the end of our chat in Llandaff fields we were both exhausted and spent, drained of emotion. We went back to our house and had a bottle or two of wine, as good mates do, and agreed on our break up. I was free and I was happy.

Chapter 26

That summer was one of the most brilliant summers for me as I was always out and about doing my own thing without a care in the world, walking through the sunny parks of Cardiff and loving my life, my new found freedom. I felt truly liberated and 'at large', it was as if I had a huge noose lifted from my neck.

Later that summer I eventually took Hughie in as my lodger and it was a mutually beneficial relationship as Hughie needed to move out of his place, 50 meters or so down the road, and I needed the money. Unfortunately for poor Hughie, I still hadn't fully grown out of the habit of playing pranks on people and often he was the hapless victim. One memorable one was when he drew a bath to relax in and when he wasn't looking I poured a load of bath oil in just to see if he would notice. I personally couldn't stand the stuff as it left me feeling dirtier than when I got in; I wasn't keen on scraping a film of grease from my hairy body to be truthful. With Hughie being of a similar mindset I was excited to gauge the reaction of my tenant in this domestic experiment. Now Hughie is a really laid back person mostly but sometimes some things could really stoke the fires of his temper. Slipping in an oily bath and almost breaking his neck fell into the category of 'How stupid could you be you bloody ginger idiot'. It tested the relationship and indeed the landlord – tenant partnership for about, ooooh, ten minutes? He calmed down and started to see the funny side after I had apologized through stifled and barely suppressed laughter. I did acknowledge that his observation of me being a less than typical landlord was correct and that perhaps I should start to behave myself a bit better. One condition was that he kept himself and his clothes clean because this was a particular pet hate of mine. I couldn't stand being dirty, there was no excuse in my mind, we weren't living in medieval Britain and to keep clean was a bare minimum. Hughie struggled to raise himself to the challenge and often I would tease him about his stinky feet and used to tell him his big toe looked like a London Bus, which tickled his sense of humour. Sometimes the smell of his gorgonzola feet would enter the house before he did they were that bad. He did eventually comply though and with the motivation of attracting the opposite sex, he had subscribed to a better way of thinking, oil free baths and cleaner clothes.

Leanne, in the meantime, had met another guy in work already and they were advancing quite rapidly in their relationship or so it seemed. I was genuinely pleased for her but thought it was ironic that, even though I was the initiator of the break up, it was me who had barely kissed a girl in this time let alone actually settling into a new found romance. Gareth Barland was the young man's name and he also worked in the Hotel Elang on reception. They were head over heels in lust and I was pleased that she was getting on with her life but at the same time a little concerned that she was diving into a murky pool of unknowns and not giving herself time to take stock and be independent within herself, be her own woman, not having to be with somebody to justify her worth. She was happy though and eventually wanted to move in with Gareth in Barry but I wasn't too sure it was wize. At the same time I would be out clubbing with the lads and just having casual, very brief flings with girls but nothing that even remotely suggested a relationship. I was still happy and content with my new found status; I was meandering down a tranquil river and felt no need to change anything.

I hadn't found anyone to love, I hadn't even found anyone to start anything at all but I didn't care, I was happy to be free and for relationships to happen if and when they did, I was in no hurry. So the next turn of events was perhaps one of the strangest and stupidest things I have ever done but at best case it reflected a soft nature and a terribly indecisive and unworthy nature at worst. Leanne's relationship with Gareth had hit the rocks and she no longer wanted him as much as she thought for reasons that were explained to me at the time but which I don't recall now. As a 'friend 'I was disappointed for her but knew it wasn't terminal and that she would find another relationship pretty soon if that was the object of her desire. What happened next though took me by surprise. Leanne, in an alchohol fuelled evening of outpouring, started to plead with me to take her back. I said I didn't want to and that it wouldn't work but she made a commitment to change certain aspects of herself in order that we make it work. I told her that she should just be herself and that I wasn't looking for a new Leanne, I loved and respected her as she was but not in a way that would work. Now don't get me wrong, it wasn't all her, I too missed her as a closer than close friend and I would often have lonely evenings but I was expecting that and ready for it. She was insistent though and I agreed to take her back but as I think back now I cringe at how soft I was.

But that wasn't all of it, better was to come. Leanne told me that she was pregnant and it didn't take a lot of working out to know that the little person was created between Gareth and herself. I was a little dumbfounded to say the least but agreed to take her and the little bump on. At 25 and single, in a good job and with the rest of my life stretching ahead of me I took the very unusual decision of accepting back a girl I had finished with but included the extra bonus of her being pregnant by another man. Yes, most of you will think 'Liam, what on earth were you thinking?' and to be honest I have asked myself the same question. The one answer that always comes back though is this. Because of the birth of this little person, it changed my life for the better and I honestly would not have changed a thing. For the brief period that this little mite was in my life I am grateful for and will never forget it.

Was I ready for the commitment of a new born child in my life? No, not really. Was I unhappy with this new situation? Not particularly, I wouldn't have done anything to have deliberately made me unhappy. I did tell Leanne though that I wanted the eyes of the world to think that I was the father, I was the real Dad. That was certainly my male pride coming to the fore. I didn't really want all my friends and family knowing that I had taken back a woman that had fallen pregnant by another man because it just painted a totally crazy picture of me being soft and weak in my mind. However, the reaction of many women I told the tale to in future years was quite the opposite. They thought it was strong and noble and such a show of love and commitment. Male friends didn't say it directly but they thought I was off my rocker. The truth is somewhere in between I suppose.

Chapter 27

The date was the 3rd March 1996 when little Calum O'Conner was born into the world at 8:05am in Llandough Hospital on a beautiful, cold but crystal clear spring morning. Leanne had been induced early, following a routine check, due to a preeclampsia scare which caught us unawares so I hurriedly went back home and packed everything I thought she needed. It was a Thursday afternoon when she went in but it would only be the Sunday morning when she gave birth to a beautiful little boy. I was instantly awestruck and tears overflowed as I held this tiny life in my arms. Babies are the most compelling of life forms, from the tiny little dry lips, mottled cheeks and little finger nails that resemble tiny pieces of tape to the miniature legs and arms that stretch and start to be used outside the womb for the first time ever. I was asked if I wanted to cut the umbilical cord and I was only too happy to do so but was surprised at how hard it was to cut through it. I imagined it to be like cutting through a hot dog sausage but it was more like cutting through a hose pipe with a blunt pair of scissors. Having cut through my face was sprayed with a little blood but I loved it, it made me feel as if this was some sort of Celtic warrior ritual between father and son. I was astonished at how instantly I could love a little being. Leanne had had an epidural and gas so she was totally out of it. Her Mum was also there to give a really motherly helping hand and her help was genuinely and absolutely invaluable. It was typical of her to be dishing out the ciggies in celebration and even though I was a casual smoker at the time it wasn't really the welcoming ceremony I had in mind for the little man. It didn't really sit well with me that we should celebrate the birth with a 'Red band'.

Prior to the birth I had completed the obligatory decorating of the nursery with the help of Walter Johnson and a few beers. The neutral green wallpaper looked very soothing and new and it was lovely to create this little oasis for mother and baby. We were all set. As Calum was born a month early, his lungs weren't fully developed and so he would often have croup, that dry, painful, barking cough that frightens the life out of new parents. I certainly think cigarette smoke didn't help the cause either but we managed to pull the little mite through with numerous late evenings spent with him in my arms, stood on the edges of the bath with steam from the shower rising up and soothing him.

Calum was a lovely little baby, as I am sure all parents think, and he really felt like mine even though biologically he wasn't. I bonded instantly with the little man and there was never any issue of me not accepting him fully. Leanne and I were also close and things were wonderful for a good few years between us. After a very unusual and unconventional start, we were a family. Leanne eventually needed to get back to work as did I and a new routine was set. Fortunately Leanne's Mum was happy to be our child minder as she didn't work full time but this meant me taking the little blighter from his cot whilst he was still sleeping in the morning and drop him to the other side of Cardiff before heading off to work. Leanne would then finish her shift early in work and then head back to Penarth to pick Calum up where she would catch the bus back home. I was grateful for the help that Kirsten, Leanne's Mum, gave but the chain smoking worried me with them both being cooped up in a third floor flat. At this stage of my life, I didn't have a vision of my perfect baby-sitting scenario but I knew this wasn't it.

Calum's biological father, Gareth, left the Hotel Elang after being deeply hurt by Leanne and was never to see her again, as far as I am aware. Life continued, we were both still young and still needed to be out and about at pubs and clubs but much less so and certainly not as intensely when we did manage to get babysitters. In fact a lot of the time we would go out with Leanne's side of the family which was Kirsten and Angus (Mum and Dad), her brothers Nicholas, Josh and Lewis along with their partners. Nicholas was always in and out of relationships and the less confident of the boys, the runt of the litter so to speak. Josh, the oldest son, was solidly in a relationship with the love of his life, Hayley, the Grangetown girl. Josh was a decent guy but always seemed on edge to me, as if his temper could blow at any minute and as if he had a point to prove, but we got on well and played many games of pool together and at one stage were gym partners. Lewis, the rebellious, youngest and best looking of all the boys was a real character, larger than life and sometimes overwhelmingly hyper active. He had a brilliant personality, was a clever young man but had a self destruct button which would trip him up time and again. I noticed he had brilliant potential but he preferred to red line it with the law and this distracted him from achieving anything of note. He needed to have the right influences around him but he unfortunately attracted the last thing he needed, a light fingered friend who would eventually lead him all the way into a young offenders prison. Not the end of Lewis's story by any means but a real shame for a bright young man and very inhibiting in terms of future employment.

Leanne and I would, as I mentioned, go out with Angus and Kirsten quite regularly having secured the services of a neighbourly babysitter who would always jump at the chance of spending time with Calum. I thought a lot of Leanne s' Dad, Angus, who was a large, tough Scot with a no nonsense attitude. He had spent a career in the Scots guards so knew how to handle himself and his quiet menacing presence would enter a room way before he did. He would keep himself to himself for large periods but if you crossed him or his family, you had made your first mistake. It took a while for me to gain his trust as he initially warned me that I needed to look after his one and only little girl. I promised I would but the only currency when trying to gain trust is action, not words. Angus absolutely loved Kirsten as well and would never let any harm come to her even though they didn't get along all the time. Kirsten was a simple gypsy like soul with an appearance of jet black hair and wild pale eyes set into very high cheek bones. She had a type of inherent tan, even though she didn't particularly worship the sun and she was a hard woman as you would have gathered by my previous descriptions of her. She would swear like a sailor and drink like one too and for a woman with a tiny frame she would drink way too much Southern Comfort and at the end of an evening she would be embarrassingly paralytic. When you are talking about a mid-week couple of casual, social beers it was not something I used to look forward to, having to listen to Kirsten's slurred uttering's. Angus used to tolerate it disdainfully but didn't really make the effort to discourage the flow of the destructive amber spirit. Amazingly I accepted that this was life and it in turn went on.

Now there are certain parts of this book that I am not proud of but regardless of this, I promised myself I would put all the detail in if I thought it was relevant to my story, 'warts and all' so to speak. Throughout this book I want to paint a picture of how I was and how I matured, and indeed how I still am maturing since I know I am flawed and am constantly learning lessons. A theme I hope you notice is the destructive nature of drinking and smoking in every aspect. It is destructive to your health, your finances, and your general aura of spirit not to mention the cleanliness of your home. I was not immune to these destructive habits but being a young man, I thought I had it all under control. I remember Dad telling me once 'It's fine to have a few beers but don't let it start to control you and beware of drinking spirits'. That was excellent advice which I acknowledged but ultimately ignored to my peril.

Now don't misunderstand or jump the gun here, I am not saying I became an alcoholic but the sheer volume and strength of liquor I was consuming on a weekly basis eventually became a worry to even me. The reason I know I was not an alchoholic was that I could simply stop whenever I wanted to and didn't really crave it in a physical sense. During the week I think I still wanted to be on the same high as I was on a weekend which would become a very expensive pastime and certainly not sustainable for anyone who had ambition, which I did, but it was buried under a pile of comfortable living and middle of the road security.

I needed a wakeup call and one such moment was amply supplied to me on a night out with the boys and girls from MELUK. It was a Friday afternoon early drinking start at the Village Inn in Pentwyn and intending to go right through to pub closing time (11pm back then). This time we had all booked to go ten-pin bowling at the Superbowl on Newport Road and we were all in good spirits. I'm not sure what sort of rocket fuel I was drinking but I think it was a brand called Red Stripe or Hurlimans and I was throwing the beers back with relaxed abandon as the strikes piled up as well as the missed duds that rolled harmlessly down the sides. By the early evening we had bowled our last balls, for that evening at least, and headed on into town for further unbridled joy at the Owain Glyn Dwyr pub in the middle of town. By now I was at the stage where I had had too much but was still functioning on three of my four engines. My grip on reality was getting less and less with every drink as the early evening descended into a hazy, slow motion of slurred speech and frequent trips to the toilet to relieve an over active bladder. At this point, I should really have got an early taxi home but I decided to follow the lads to a very popular night club on Queen Street, this being my first error of judgment.

Having got to the night club, all the lads were being ushered in by the bouncers and piling in like sheep into a dip. Unfortunately I was the unlucky black sheep who was halted in his tracks as the bouncers noticed that I was much too worse for wear to be frequenting their already throbbing club. I was incensed and embarrassed at the same time and took real issue at being snubbed in such a way, my reaction naturally magnified by the booze. I felt they had singled me out at the time but on reflection they were doing their jobs and were correct not to let me in. I left the door in a real temper as I staggered back up Queen Street with my tail between my legs. Now the next action is a blur to me and I'll never really know what the intent was, if indeed there was any. From the shadows of a darkened doorway to my right as I walked back towards the castle end of Queen Street I saw two figures side by side walking towards me at an angle and about to intersect my path. It seemed to me at that point as if I was going to be mugged but if this was the case they had chosen the wrong person. I can't be too specific as I was in no real state to be dissecting what happened but basically I swung with my right fist towards one of them so that the victim received an almighty uppercut. Now whether they were up to no good or not I will never know but the guy fell like a log to the ground and split the back of his head open on the pavement, I was to learn later. It was an alchohol powered rage and I almost instantly regretted it. For a split second my world stood still and then I heard footsteps running toward me as the bouncers from the same club came to intervene. I attempted to run away in what must have looked a comical site, given my drunken stupor, but eventually succumbed to an overgrown tree root from a tree I didn't even know existed. The burly bouncers picked me off the floor and marched me back to the club into a holding cell. Ever the optimist I joked that I had indeed made it into the club after all but they didn't look impressed and at one point I thought I was in for a hiding in this cell. What seemed like an age, a police officer came into the dingy little room, hand-cuffed me and shoved me into the back of a police car which was waiting on Queen Street. For the second time in my life I was banged up in a police cell but this time, in the early hours of the morning. It was horrible and I was ashamed of myself. I was asked if I needed legal representation which I accepted gratefully. By this time I was humble and apologetic and just wanted to erase everything I had just done. What a bloody idiot I had been! Having been charged I was released pending a court hearing, I was free to go, for the time at least.

My court hearing was set and my solicitor advised me to plead guilty and show real remorse. I had no problem with either as it was both genuinely what I was going to do and indeed what I felt. In fact I asked the solicitor if I could make contact with the victim and apologize but he warned me against that saying that it could do no good as far as the case was concerned and could even be perceived as threatening to the victim. My solicitor looked quite soberly at me and informed in no uncertain terms that this young man could have lost his life. He had fallen to the ground and split his head open and received 40 stitches to the back of his head, he was lucky it wasn't worse. My stomach churned and a deep sense of shame engulfed me. Shame, guilt and pure worry as to what my fate was to be. It was a horrible, long wait for my court hearing and I wasn't sure what the outcome would be. I was in anxious turmoil for weeks before my hearing and I didn't sleep too well. My work also suffered as a result but I was too ashamed to mention it to my boss, even though he probably already knew, such was the efficiency of the MELUK rumour mill.

Eventually the day came and I went into court as humble and ashamed as I could genuinely be. There were a hand full of people in the courtroom with one or two interested spectators. There was no grilling, just a confirmation of events on that evening and some witness statements with eventually my plea of 'guilty'. After a five minute wait outside the courtroom I was called back in for them to deliver their verdict. I was charged with 'Actual Bodily Harm' and fined £375, of which £300 went to the victim, the rest being court costs. The sentence was suspended for two years in which time I needed to clean up my act. I was relieved and pleased to pay the fine and put it all behind me.

I was a Dad now so I had to grow up and start acting like one, getting arrested for acting like a thug was not part of the image I had for myself. I needed to make some changes but amazingly enough I still wasn't prepared to give up alchohol, even considering the damage it had so far caused me and others. I wasn't happy with myself and I knew I was a lot better than this but I took the stance that I had simply overdid it on that night and had drunk the wrong sort of alchohol, it was an isolated incident and I vowed I would not do this again. It was an episode I wasn't proud of but I felt I had learned a valuable lesson, that lesson was that I couldn't just drink whatever I wanted without consequence, I had limits and I reached them that night. I understood that the alchohol I drank changed me into a character that was alien to me, or more precisely put, it brought to the fore a part of me that existed and is real, a type of dormant anger that I didn't want to possess. It was a closed episode.

Chapter 28

I committed to throwing myself into my work and had by now started working on a brand new product concept for MELUK. It was the new age of the digital TV set top box and I was involved with the introduction of this product into MELUK but before doing so meant I needed to be trained up and there was no better place than Japan for doing this. I had been selected to go as a technician with Bruce, my equivalent in the test section and I could not have been happier or more proud. Going to Japan for two weeks was a chance of a lifetime, a real gift. It's not the sort of destination I would have chosen to go on holiday to be honest but in retrospect this was the most fascinating and interesting trip that I could have experienced in order to give me a broader perspective of the world.

Before going I was given a list of do's and don'ts and certain protocols to perform alongside some traditional routines but by and large the emphasis was about observing the Japanese way of working and then also advising on build design issues based on my experience in the UK factory. It was exciting and daunting all at the same time but I was ready for it and I couldn't wait. The destination was Ibaraki, home of the sprawling town-like MELUK plant. The hotel was already paid for and I had an allowance of £40 a day for living which was generous considering that breakfast cost me £1, lunch £2 and evening dinner £10 or so depending on how extravagant I was feeling. The trip from Heathrow to the futuristic Kansai Airport, with runways built into the sea, was a grueling one. Initially the thought of flying over the Russian Steppes was exciting and intriguing, especially since I could actually see the snowy tundra below in all its white, powdery majesty. But after four hours of seeing the same landscape mile after mile it was as if the same bit of film was being repeated over and over again. It brought it home to me how incredibly vast this land was and how unforgiving it must be. My companion on the visit was Bruce, a somewhat eccentric but loveable character from fairly well to do Cowbridge stock. He exuded an air of aristocratic confidence which really made me smile, nothing seemed to faze him at all. He had the brazenness to ask the air hostess on the flight if we could go and take a look in the cockpit since his own father had been a pilot as well before he died. The last comment contained no element of truth at all but it managed to get us into the cockpit to talk to the captain and his vice. It was interesting to see how small and cramped the room was, rather different to the rooms you see in airplane crash films where there seems to be enough room for three or four people. It was less a room and more a couple of luxury chairs with immense instrumentation in front of them.

We eventually landed in Kansei Airport which was a feat of civil engineering in itself. The runway was basically a giant, man-made jetty going into the sea and rather bizarrely looking like a cul-de-sac floating on the surface of the ocean. The airport itself was like a giant, floating letter 'H'. Just over an hour later having navigated safely through passport control we had arrived by train at Ibaraki train station and then a short taxi ride to our hotel. When I say short taxi ride, what I really mean is a 'ridiculous waste of money' since the hotel was a mere 200m from the station. Neither of us realized though but at least we were safely in our hotel, our little home for two weeks.

Everything about Japan was completely different from what I was used to, it was a total and utter culture shock. Apart from the obvious differences in building structures and streets, everything seemed fast paced and bright. There were neon signs promoting various casinos day and night, there were plenty of bars to go and relax in and sing the odd karaoke song. The Japanese had perfected the art of karaoke, not for their beautiful singing but for the way in which it was organized. One could hire a room with a capacity of fifteen or so people for a set party and browse through reams and reams of possible songs and artists to sing along to. On an evening out with members of the work force I became the star attraction by belting out 'Let It Be' by the Beatles, 'Still Haven't Found What I'm Looking For' by U2 and other various favourites of mine. I really went for it and my audience wanted more. It appeared my voice wasn't too bad and I felt really pleased with myself. Truth be told, I felt kind of liberated and invisible because nobody really knew me. I had no-one to be embarrassed in front of, it was brilliant and I enjoyed myself thoroughly. I finished off my session with 'Green, green grass of home' by Sir Tom Jones, the unofficial King of Wales.

On the second night, still suffering from jet lag, I decided I was going to have a massage and an early night. After a round of charades with the hotel manager, who didn't speak a lot of English, I gathered that I should stay in my room and wait for my masseur to come to me. Fifteen minutes passed when I heard a soft knock at my door. I sprang up and opened it to find the oldest, tiniest little woman I had ever seen, with these huge glasses. I awkwardly motioned to her if I should take my top off but she firmly waved her hand to dismiss that question so I kept my clothes on. I wondered how this little woman could actually do anything with me fully clothed in my tracksuit but I soon wondered no more. I lay on the bed face down as she set to work pummeling me with these little stabbing motions with what seemed her thumbs. I was expecting my muscles to be rubbed in a rhythmic motion with oils but this was just as effective. She went over my whole body in this kind of mechanical motion as if I were a pin cushion but, oh my word, was it lovely. My whole body afterwards was completely and utterly relaxed to the point of my mouth dribbling onto the pillow. I paid the old lady and had the deepest sleep I could have wished for. It was an amazing experience.

One thing I found strange was that there would be vending machines on the pavement selling cold cans of drink. I found the trust in that the machines would inevitably steer clear of any vandalism quaint and reassuring, totally refreshing in fact. What wasn't so refreshing was my first experience buying a tin of what I thought was ice cold fresh orange from said vending machine. After walking the streets of Ibaraki on that hot afternoon I was craving something cold and thirst-quenching but as I took a grateful gulp from the tin it turned out to be carrot juice. I really enjoy the stuff now but back then I wiped my mouth in disgust at the thought of drinking a vegetable. Needless to say the Japanese writing for what it actually was got lost in translation.

It was time to go to work and myself and Bruce caught the MELUK bus to the main factory. You were able to get on the bus if you showed your company badge which I found hugely impressive in the same way that little boys find flashing an FBI badge cool. The headquarters of this manufacturing plant was massive and the fact that they had their own dedicated bus system reflected the firm's status within the country, let alone the city. When we got to the factory I was expecting a single, huge building but of course I was wrong. It was more like a town with numerous buildings, each its own factory and with several floors. I never did ask exactly how many buildings there were on the site but I remember being in building 'H' and on the second floor. There were five floors in that building alone. The magnitude of the place was staggering as there were streets that connected each building and vans that transported various goods from one building to the next. There was even a full sized football pitch alongside a baseball diamond for lunchtime activities. Believe it or not there was even a Do-Jo on the site but I didn't use it. One strange tradition was for an early morning stretching session to get the blood flowing to your muscles which I didn't partake in but probably should have. Even more weird for me was for a siren to sound at 8am and for everyone to stand to attention, put hand to heart and sing the company anthem with vigour. Naturally I didn't know the words but I did stand with a look of vacant commitment to the cause. The first few notes reminded me of a Walt Disney tune which didn't help when trying to portray a look of serious loyalty.

Eventually we got down to the serious business of work and I enjoyed the fastidious and meticulous manner in which the Japanese folk went about their business. I really felt that this was just up my street and I enjoyed learning the different technologies and processes that they employed. There was no trick to what they did, just a measured and methodical application of common sense. It wasn't only just learning that I was there for, I also had to impart some experience of my own in order for this marriage of information to work. This I did to some good effect with some quite different ideas, some being readily accepted as a good improvement without question, others having to be sold on the idea. Indeed there were a few ideas that were simply too unconventional to be considered and which were dropped straight away. It was said by some emerging Engineers that the Japanese way could sometimes be too conservative when it came to radical thinking. This may well be true but the proof of their success stands for all to see, conservative or not. Ultimately I was happy to have given a few ideas which were implemented and effected positive changes in the manufacture of products back home.

I really came to love the people and the way they were so open and giving but seemingly without the need for repayment. I was so incredibly impressed with the reliability of their word in that when a person said they would do something that it actually happened exactly when they said they would do it. I wanted to be like that, I really admired that sort of integrity. I was invited out for a meal at Mr Mukai's house who was one of the guys in work. Myself and Bruce were invited along where we took our shoes off at the front door and sat down at the dinner table which unfortunately was shin height for the two tall Westerners. I am a pretty big guy and found the going hard sitting cross legged all evening, but Bruce was a lot bigger and he struggled with the whole concept of not sitting on a chair to eat one's dinner. After a few hefty grunts of discomfort he managed to slurp up his noodle soup but not without splashing himself in the eye trying to use the chop sticks. Bruce was great fun and larger than life and he wasn't afraid to be the clown in company, a sort of posh clown that everyone loved. It was a lovely evening and Bruce made us all laugh with his antics; we had made some good friends.

One weekend Bruce and I were taken out by Mr Sakakibara to Nara which I didn't realize was previously Japans ancient capital. It was a beautiful oasis of countryside with deer roaming around and plenty of Buddhist temples to see. We all went into the temple and I was taken aback by the ominous presence of the biggest statue of Buddha I had ever seen. Dark and atmospheric, the figure was so huge I almost didn't notice it within the dark confines of the temple. One of the wooden supporting pillars measuring roughly a metre in diameter deliberately had a huge hole through the cross section at the base. A plaque above it read something along the lines of 'if a person is able to pass through this hole they are pure of heart'. Indeed only children were able to fit through or somebody not possessing a skeleton. I loved the simplicity and wisdom of the Japanese and I really learned a lot on that trip.

Gratefully, on another weekend, we were invited out to watch a game of baseball at Koshien Stadium. Now I have never been a great lover of cricket or baseball but I was grateful to be invited to what is an important sporting tradition for the Japanese. They really do love their baseball almost on a par with the Americans. I'm no expert but someone who was more knowledgeable than me on the game said that the American game was all about power whereas the Japanese game was more about finesse. We spent half the day watching this game which eventually concluded with a home win, which about sums up my attentiveness for the game itself. More interestingly for me was to watch everybody else watching the game. The Japanese were amusingly disciplined and ordered in their support for their beloved team. It made me smile when I compared it to a game at Cardiff City where people bought a ticket which gave them a license to purge all the frustration of their working week on the hapless referee, linesman, a lazy midfielder, our clueless manager or even the police. It didn't matter really; as long as the team wasn't winning they spewed a torrent of vitriol at somebody even though it was mostly harmless and very funny. When we were winning of course it was entirely different where we would sing in unison 'We're the greatest team in football the world has ever seen' to the tune of 'And it's no nay never, no nay never not I' by the Pogues.

In Japan it was a lot more conservative and very well organized as you can imagine. Within each block of seats there was a cheerleader in official uniform with white gloves to hold the team flag and he would start a chorus of support to the tune of 'Old MacDonald had a farm'. Everyone dutifully joined in at what seemed like perfectly timed ten minute intervals. Some were enthusiastic to the point of a rabid and frothing frenzy whilst others seemed to be going through the motions, much like a Roman Catholic Sunday mass service singing 'I'm happy today, oh yes I'm happy today'. I was wondering if some poor person might be escorted from the premises by a couple of men in dark suits and sunglasses if they stopped singing. Needless to say I joined in but wasn't too sure of what to sing so nudged Bruce in the ribs and sang 'And on that farm he had some pigs, eeh aye, eeh aye, Oh'. I managed to survive ejection. My first experience of a professional sporting event in Japan was interesting and fascinating but it didn't get me hooked on baseball as such.

A massive highlight for me was food and how they prepared it or for that matter didn't prepare it, in the case of sushi. Naturally we were taken out by work colleagues quite often during our stay which enabled us to sample things we would not normally have initiated by ourselves. One of these experiences was the wonderfully delicious Shabu shabu which consists of very finely sliced beef (thinner than bacon) boiled in water with stock and dipped in various delicious sauces such as soy sauce or the like. It was absolutely melt in the mouth delicious and the format was that you paid for a slot of time, such as an hour, rather than your actual meal. During that time you were able to have endless trays of beef appearing in front of you whilst you washed it down with an ice cold Sapporo beer. Needless to say, with Bruce and myself in the team line up we polished off a fair few plates.

Another enjoyable concept for alternative eating was Yakiniku meaning 'grilled meat' or in a South African sense 'braai'. However instead of the braai being out in the summer sunshine, it was an indoor affair and also included a stunning array of grilled vegetables. The way this worked was that you again paid for an allocated slot of time and helped yourself to the fresh produce which was presented on a counter in a market style. On the counter were all the marinated meats, fish and vegetables that your heart could desire which were then taken to your table, in the centre of which was your round, dustbin lid sized grill. You and your friends would then grill your food together whilst sitting down and chatting happily and then move it to your plate to consume. It was a great concept and a fantastic way to socialize. One drawback was that you looked quite conspicuous if you had gone back up to the food counter for the fourth time which is what Bruce and I did as opposed to our more nimble Japanese colleagues who stuck with one round, possibly two at a push.

Now no Japanese cuisine round up is complete without mentioning Sushi and Bruce and I were lucky enough to have been invited out to a very up-market Sushi bar after work one evening. We had both made friends with regulars of the Kakehashi bar which we frequented most nights. These 'friends' of ours consisted of Mitch and two other ladies by the name of Yuki and Chendo. I'm not entirely sure what the relationship was between Mitch and Chendo but I have a feeling that she was his official mistress.

So we all met up at the Kakehashi bar and were driven to the restaurant which was quaint to say the least. The fact that it was packed and we made up seventy five percent of the clientele that night suggests at how compact the establishment was. I wasn't entirely sure what to expect from this experience and neither was Bruce by the look of his ashen face. We sat on bar stools, all in a row, facing a counter with a giant fish tank on it. It was all very surreal as we witnessed live fish being whisked out of the fish tank and beheaded within our line of sight, if not right in front of us. The slain Salmon was then filleted, sliced up expertly and then inserted into Maki roles within a matter of minutes. This I found delicious and couldn't get enough of it but Bruce was struggling, he had reached his Japanese cuisine adventuring threshold. He did however give the vegetarian Maki versions a go as a token of politeness. Our hosts were impressed by my willingness to eat anything that came my way but were amused at Bruce and his typically Western response to things like eating a raw baby squid, seconds ago roaming freely in his watery, glass jail. His response at being encouraged to at least try a little bit was to feign deep disappointment and clutch his side saying he had no spleen so it was dangerous for him to eat raw food. He really was not enjoying this at all to the point of almost retching and he wasn't afraid of showing his hosts either.

I must confess that this was not my most favourite food experience on this trip as I treated it more of a challenge that I could overcome rather than enjoyable dining. Having passed all the tests so far, including that baby squid and various other weird combinations it was time for the piece-de-resistance. I was beginning to reach my threshold as well with Bruce sat beside me in a state of weak surrender and viewing my heroics with disbelief and disdain. A real delicacy in Japan is to eat a raw king prawn, freshly slain from the tank and this was to be my final challenge. I was asked to select my victim from the tank and I did so with something approaching deep dread but with a determination that I would rize to any challenge thrown before me. With groans of disbelief from Bruce, the 'chef' grasped innocent little 'pinchy' from his synchronized swimming practice and dumped him in my dish. With a rapid twist of the head I suddenly had two bowls, one with a twitching body in it, no it wasn't Bruce, and one with a king prawn head in I assumed would be for the bin. Chief chef then broke the spine of pinchy in several places to stop the twitching and gleefully presented me with my last few mouthfuls of despair. With a deep breath in and a shudder I picked up my little friend by the tail and decided to just get this over and done within the quickest time possible. From the corner of my eye I could see the look of horror on Bruce's face as the little carcass disappeared down my throat. I crunched and swallowed as rapidly as I could and wondered how on earth any Japanese person could think this even remotely enjoyable. I almost heaved as the tail fluttered down my throat, apparently the spinal cord not being severed properly I was to discover shortly afterwards. Having labored my way through this crunchy fish fest I felt triumphant that I had beaten the challenge. But wait! This was not the end. The real delicacy, I was told, was to now eat the head, including brains and eyes, the thing I thought could only now be fit for the rubbish bin. I politely declined; I had reached my limit as I said 'Ooh, I couldn't eat another morsel'. I had to pick Bruce off the floor as we departed shortly afterwards. That was quite an experience indeed.

Amidst the work, eating exotic foods and the weekend frolicking I also had the weekday evening distraction of the Kakahashi bar as I mentioned previously. This again was a tiny little bar with a capacity of no more than eight people hidden down a secluded lane. 'Mama' was the owner and bar tender who smoked heavily and looked a bit like a drag queen. She had a lovely personality though and was naturally welcoming. Regulars were Mitch and Chendo along with their friend Yuki. The way the drinking culture worked in Japan was that normally you bought yourself a bottle of your favourite Bourbon or Whiskey from the establishment which stayed behind the bar on a shelf with your name on it. Normal beers were bought from the bar but the tab settled at the end of the evening along with your karaoke song purchases. Having explained I was from MELUK in the UK I was afforded special treatment and shown bottles of Whiskey on the shelf belonging to colleagues back in Cardiff. After several cold Sapporo beers I was in full voice on the karaoke and belting out my old Beatles numbers which are hugely popular in Japan. I was learning as much local dialect as my brain would take in and the locals absolutely loved it.

Now, although I felt no shame at the time, what I did on those business trips to Japan was morally wrong and these days, now that I am much older and a little bit wizer I do feel shame in what I did. I could argue that I was trapped in a relationship without any sexual chemistry and that I deserved to sow my wild oats but I know now that that was a flimsy excuse. They say cowards hurt people the most and at that point in my life I should not have been in a relationship with Leanne, this was clear. I was in a relationship though and I cheated on her. I justified to myself that I was thousands of miles away and that this meaningless affair would be brief and last as long as I was there, which it did. I knew what I was doing was wrong but I didn't care, I felt like I was a star in a foreign land and I was taking advantage of my moment of popularity. This is me and this is what I have done and it represents one of the dark shadows in the painting that is my life.

The girl in question was Yuki from the bar and although her English was poor we got along very well and managed to converse easily enough. There would be many a drunken evening in the bar where 'Mama' would be encouraging me to kiss one of the local girls, much to my initial shock but eventually getting used to the fact with very little encouragement. I spent many a long evening with her, with her sometimes leaving in the early hours of the morning from the hotel whilst I dragged myself into work which didn't seem very professional. I tried hiding it from Bruce as much as I could because he mostly didn't come out in the week nights but he knew what was going on and I knew he abhorred what I was doing. He was a good man and he must have thought I was less than worthy to be in a relationship with someone who loved me dearly back home. He was right as well.

Knowing myself as I do, this was out of character for me and something I never did repeat in my life in any subsequent relationships so this was an act in isolation and reflective of my being in a relationship I should never have been in. Near the very end, after Leanne and I had broken up for the final time and were actually friends I had to tell her and even though it was years on, I still think it hurt her.

So came to an end an amazing and life changing Japanese adventure. I had achieved everything I wanted to on the work front and come back with lots of homework to implement back in Cardiff. On a personal front I had had one of the best holidays of my life and it hadn't cost me a penny, in fact I had managed to save some money since Mama usually wavered my bar tab for some reason. In fact Mama was to buy me a mock Samurai sword which was quite a job getting through customs. I said goodbye to the clan at Kakehashi bar and to Yuki, I said goodbye to all my wonderful colleagues in Japan. Bruce and I were heading home and I was physically and mentally exhausted. For me the flight back home was a blur of one glass of white wine after another and by the time I got to Heathrow I was slightly inebriated. My body said it was Kakehashi bar time but on the clock in Paddington station it said 9:30am. I boarded the train in a warm, hazy pre-hangover state where I wasn't paying too much attention to the carriage I was getting into; I just picked the first carriage which seemed rather sumptuous. I looked around me and noticed that the carriage was very silent, with only the sounds of the pink financial times rustling in the hands of gentlemen in pin striped suits and bowler hats whilst the train awaited departure. I could not believe my luck as I noted the rather swanky, luxury chairs and was mildly amused as I thought you only ever saw bowler hats in films trying to portray London businessmen but here they were *actually* in my carriage.

As I settled down for the journey I envisioned a luxurious couple of hours back to Cardiff but was soon jolted back to reality by a looming ticket inspector. He checked my ticket as I handed it to him, drunken and oblivious. He arched an eyebrow before glancing at me a second time and saying 'You're in the wrong carriage mate, this is first class, you're in economy'. I sheepishly gathered all my baggage together, including Samurai sword and staggered to the back of the train. By now the train was at full speed so you can imagine the picture of me swaying down the narrow aisles, in a by now, packed train. Additionally my hangover headache was just starting and I was gasping and sweaty as I man-handled the heavy suitcase, kit bag and Samurai sword through the train. Each and every chair was filled, much to my dismay, as I went through carriage after carriage. My arms were by now aching and I needed to sit down somewhere, anywhere. Eventually, with dry mouthed and burning arms, I spied an empty chair where someone had cheekily left a bag on it. I moved their bag with a big radiant smile and managed to find some space to put my baggage. Trying to put a heavy suit case up onto a baggage compartment above head height whilst the train rocked back and forth was what I thought surfing might feel like. As I did so I managed to bump a seated man on the arm as I dragged my bags up above his head, much to his silent annoyance. With everyone settled in their seats and trying desperately to ignore my puffing and panting I managed to stuff my belongings away at last as I settled into my seat. Then as if in slow motion my heavy Samurai sword managed to work itself free from above my case and crash onto the head of Mr Irritable, making a loud cracking noise. I was filled with silent laughter as I picked up the sword and apologized profusely to which there came no response as I think he was too angry. Moments later, as I sat behind him and across the aisle, I saw him rub the top of his head again which made me cry with silent laughter. The spirit of the Kakehashi bar was still with me, Mama would be proud. 'Welcome home Liam San'.

Chapter 29

It was an emotional homecoming and I was glad to be home with Leanne and Calum despite my wayward ways. Naturally such a monumental trip changed my perspective on life but somehow not enough for me to consider going it alone in my life. Despite my philandering ways in Japan I was still comfortable in my relationship with Leanne, but comfortable is not always healthy. When I look back with perspective this all seems so wrong and unhealthy but at the time, amidst my normal life I didn't question anything, I didn't want to upset the equilibrium. I was happy in my job, in my relationship, had a lovely little home and a little family. My social life was great and I was starting to play football again after a few years of being distracted by my relationship and having a family. On the surface all seemed perfect, which is what all my friends used to think. They used to see Leanne and me as the ideal couple, solid and homely. And we were, but underlying for me was a longing for a physical relationship. I knew I *could* have it but I knew I *didn't* have it with Leanne, as much as we both tried.

It was shortly after my Japan trip that I was awarded the position of Manufacturing Engineer within the chassis group which I had to apply for. I had come a long way since starting as a naïve, fresh faced scholar in 1990 and I was really proud of my progress. My goal was always to become an engineer and I never really harboured any ambitions of becoming a supervisor or anything remotely managerial which naturally would be the next rung on my ladder. I didn't ever really want to be parted from the practical, hands on role which I was accustomed to and didn't think I had the qualities to lead people but having said that I was still doing a lot more paperwork than I would have liked. Little did I know it but I had reached my peak at MELUK by becoming a senior Engineer, or rather more accurately a plateau since I held that position for a few years. A tiny crack of discontent was forming in my career and it was this invisible milestone that signaled the beginning of the final chapter of my long and exciting MELUK career, not that I knew it at the time.

With my home life and work life very much settled and going in the right direction it must be noted at this point that I was still deep in a spiritual desert and was blissfully unperturbed that I wasn't attending church or practicing anything remotely religious. My main aim in life was my family and their security, my work and my football and in that order. I was, as I mentioned, getting back into football having started playing casual Sunday league games for my local pub side, The Clive Arms.

One of the lads from that team said I would be good enough to play for their Saturday afternoon team called 'The Villa'. I wasn't too confident as I knew the standard was fairly decent but I said I would come and have a crack at it. Owen Thomas, who was to become a very good friend of mine, encouraged me back into playing and although I never told him, I had the utmost respect for him and his committed and passionate approach to the game. He was the heart and soul of the team and the type of player who would run through brick walls for his team mates. He was a midfield general with no real silky skills but a fantastic ball-winner and distributer who made the team tick. I loved him and his style of play and if it weren't for him I wouldn't have signed for the Villa. 'Dai' as we called him, was the most senior member of the team and although he took a lot of stick and good natured teasing he was the man that led us and galvanized us all. He was the sort of person you thought of when you thought of the term 'grass roots football' because he would be the man to arrive with all the freshly laundered kit and the man with the corner flags and nets. He would be the first out onto the pitch warming up and he was tough and gritty. He never backed out of a tackle and he made me want to be my best. I wanted to play for him and not let him down; I wanted to run through brick walls for my team mates as well. He was such a good example and I'm glad he asked me to play for the team.

When I started playing for The Villa in 1997 I was 27 and in football terms in my prime, so to speak. As a footballer I had decent enough skill levels but I was built for power and strength. I was never blessed with pace but my reading of the game was getting better and my timing in the tackle was really good and quite intimidating for the opposition. When I started with The Villa they were playing at the top of the fourth tier of the Cardiff & District football league and meandering along in more of a relaxed, social manner. The Villa was a team based in the affluent area of Whitchurch with their headquarters being the Three Horshoes pub on Merthyr Road. Dai, a Treganna lad like myself, had different ideas though and was determined to bring more success to the club and started to bring in players from around the city who he knew were of the right ilk to achieve this. I was one of them and I was happy to pull on the claret and blue team strip and represent what was effectively Whitchurch's finest.

During our first season together we had mixed fortunes but were a decent team, hard to beat but lacking goals up front. I had cemented my place in the side playing either at right back or centre half and built up quite a reputation as a no-nonsense defender who didn't like conceding goals and never came second best in a tackle. In a 50/50 tackle I was always confident of winning the ball and for those of you who don't know what a 50/50 is; it means two opposing players coming from equal and opposite directions and competing to win the ball. They say most injuries occur when you are indecisive or 'bottle' a tackle. I never did. On the pitch I was very vociferous and encouraging and constantly organizing everyone in my vicinity. As soon as we lost possession of the ball I was calling team mates back to get behind the man they were supposed to be marking like a sergeant major. I would talk constantly through games and always let my teammates know I was there or if they were out of position, letting them know in no uncertain terms. I was dedicated to being my best, to winning and to not concede a goal. For me, it was such a bonus to walk off the pitch having won without our goal having been breached; it was the ultimate for a defender. I loved the buzz of playing, the butterflies in the stomach before a game, the smell of menthol muscle rub and the banter in the change room before and after a game. It was special and bonded us together as it does with so many teams in many different sports all over the world. From the grass roots enthusiasts right up to professional players, at the end of their playing days, it's the people and the banter that is missed the most.

As the seasons continued we started losing players who were not of the right standard or personality and started attracting good solid players made of the right stuff. We progressively moved up the leagues but not at a rate that would have given a diver the bends, our ascent was typically to get promoted in second or third place, spend the following season adjusting to that level, which as a football cliché is known as 'consolidating', and then the next season going up again in a similar fashion. It was steady progress and the chairman of the club, Dick, who poured his heart and soul into the club, was ecstatic and treated us all like sons. We had gone from the fourth tier of Cardiff leagues football to the second tier in four seasons and we were all proud of what we had achieved.

The main ambition of the club was to get to the top tier and fight for promotion into the South Wales Senior League but in order to be accepted into that division the club needed its own pitch, which we didn't have. There was a big effort made by Dick to secure a venue to call our own but it didn't eventually materialize but for the moment, the focus was to consolidate in Division 1 and move on after that into the Premier. Even that was a huge step for the little Villa but one which we took to with amazing ease. The team by then was settled but for a few quality additions and we played a decent brand of football which was solid at the back and scored a few goals.

There was one particular game that always sticks out in my memory which epitomized the spirit and desire of this team. We were in a new division, playing against accomplished players who had fairly decent levels of skill compared to what we were used to. One particular team we came up against were called Porto's who modeled themselves on the Portuguese giants and played with the same flair and panache. They were a gifted and a typically arrogant bunch of players who expected to give us, these newly promoted upstarts, one almighty hammering. For some reason our team seemed over-awed by their reputation and presence as Portos eased into a 1-0 lead, the scorer nonchalantly whirling away as if it were routine and fairly academic. I gee'd the lads up by saying 'head's up, let's keep playing our game' and 'let's get our tackles in lads', obvious things but amazingly needed in the heat of battle. There is nothing better than a steady, calming influence in the heat of the fight and Dai provided us with this. I saw myself as motivating the lads, to keep telling them when they had made an important pass or tackle, keep them positive and tell them never to give in.

Midway through the first half we conceded a second goal, which felt like a crushing blow when it went in. I felt responsible for it and I was down but by no means out. It was at that point that my inner demon of determination and passionate desire came to the fore in adrenalin fueled frenzy. I was angry and hurt and absolutely could not contemplate being humiliated in this way. I heard the patronizing celebration of the Porto's players in my head like a slow motion film, like they were laughing at us. It lit the fire within me, I had to do something, I had to lead by example, I needed the ball to come my way and for me to do something with it, to give the lads hope. I looked around me and heads had dropped, we were now 2-0 down and with a mountain to climb. Half time approached and I saw Dai looking as though he was struggling for form, his energy looked low. We needed a spark of genius, a moment, a turning point, but who was going to provide it, my boys looked like beaten boxers, out on their feet.

Then that 'moment' happened that I craved, I was like a coiled spring, a man on the edge, I was shouting and cajoling my team mates for better effort, more desire, more passion and shouting never to give up. I was in my warrior mode and at times like that I had a sort of tunnel vision where I was in the zone and everything seems like it's in slow motion as my heart raced and I saw everything clearly. The moment in the match that I will never forget came just at the perfect time, just before half time. Their goalkeeper rolled the ball out to the left and their left winger picked up the ball and started off on a run to raid down our right side, my side, my territory, my domain. He skipped skillfully around the man in front of me and had designs on beating me as well. He thought wrong. I waited for the mistake to happen rather than throw myself recklessly into a tackle but when it happened I put everything into it and made it count. He just touched the ball a little too heavily in front of him and into my path but rather than creating a 50/50, he had created a 70/30 in his favour. I had no right to win that ball but I launched myself into that tackle as if my life depended on it, I wanted that ball, I was hungry for it, the fire in my belly was strong and I was not going to be denied. Then CRUNCH, I felt a stabbing pain in my shin and ankle which I felt for a brief second before realizing I had actually won the ball. By now the silky skilled winger was on the deck clutching his knees while I dug the ball from under my feet and motored up the pitch leaving him in my wake. I heard squawks of dismay from their team saying he had been fouled but I continued and the ref said 'Nothing wrong with the tackle, play on lads'. I carried on up the pitch and nudged the ball past their defender and whipped in a near perfect cross to the far post for our striker to head home. It was a beautiful moment for me and I shouted with unbridled joy as I stared round at my team mates and shouted 'C'mon, we can do this'. It was half time and we were 2-1 down but all to play for all of a sudden.

In the half time team talk Dai told us to keep going and to keep it tight but singled me out for special praise saying he wished he had eleven Liam O'Conner's out on the field and that my tackle, run and cross was the turning point in this game. It was that 'moment' that was needed, it was not beautiful or a stroke of genius but it was blood curdling desire. I was overjoyed and felt 10 feet tall as we all went out for the second half. We were now all up for the fight, we sensed blood, sensed a weakness that they may not have the stomach for a fight. We were right as we eventually equalized and late in the game scored the winner to take the game 3-2. I was physically exhausted, hoarse from shouting, battered and bruised and mentally drained and I could not have been more content. We all looked at each other in the change rooms after that match and knew that we had something really, really special and something that could not be bought. In fact I would go as far to say as something that even some top professional teams sometimes lack and that was desire. There was a spark in the eye of each and every one of us and a quiet determination that this would be our season to shine.

And so it would prove to be as after a brief six weeks out with a torn left ankle ligament I returned hungrily to a team who were so far unbeaten in the league. I have only ever picked up two injuries in football and this one knocked my confidence but after a lot of training and putting it to the test the injury healed well and I eventually got my place back in the team. My return was not all glorious though and provided a comical respite for all involved. Everyone was supportive of me as I returned to fitness and my big return was to come on as a substitute near the end of a game against Grange Quinns where we were 4-0 to the good. The game and points were safe as I warmed up, gave a high five to the man I was replacing and raced into the penalty area to defend a corner. 'Aaah, it's good to be back' I thought as I panted up towards the man I was about to mark, full of spirited enthusiasm and in danger of trying a wee bit *too* hard. As the corner was taken I went to clear it with my left foot and sliced the ball into my own net and past our hapless keeper. My first touch was an own goal and I wanted the ground to swallow me up. Everyone on the pitch was laughing, even the people watching on the sidelines and I couldn't help but join in and laughed at myself. It was one of those moments and in the end proved academic as we ran out 4-1 winners. At least I was on the score sheet.

That season for me was my most successful and proudest moments in football as we finished the season unbeaten and in first place. It was absolutely a magnificent achievement considering the caliber of teams in that Division. For any team in any league, anywhere in the world to go seven months without defeat is an accomplishment no matter what level you're playing at. We were a great group of individuals but more importantly we were a real team who fought for eachother tooth and nail when up against it. I had accomplished something that could never be taken away from me and I still have that league winner's medal. The Villa were now a Premier Division team and chairman Dick was a mightily happy man.

Chapter 30

Calum was now 18 months and getting quite a handful but he was a special little boy who I loved so much. I used to take him to Forrest Park a lot and play with him on the swings and let him climb and explore as much as he could. He was a little action man and I was proud of him. Plans were afoot though, it was time for us to have a holiday back to my adopted country, back to South Africa. I had chatted at length to Leanne about it for years but now we were in the position where we could go out and enjoy ourselves. It was the summer shutdown in MELUK where we had two weeks off and I needed to go to my spiritual home and see my family. It had been seven years since seeing my sister Pauline, who was married to Leonard, and little did I know it at the time, going through her own private hell within her relationship. Cei, my little plum, had grown up, she was 16.

Arriving in South Africa is always magical for me; there is warmth and vibrancy about the people and the land. My heart and soul starts to remember real sunshine again. When we arrived it was August, the middle of a Highveld winter but it was still beautiful to me even though the ground gets arid and dry during that time of year. Leanne had never before been anywhere remotely near South Africa so everything was a brand new experience for her as I tried to see my home through her eyes. Mum, Dad and Cei picked us up from the airport and we stayed with them in their home in Northmead. It wouldn't be long before we met up with Pauline and Leonard, Chrissy and Ryan, the two wonderful and beautiful additions to my sisters little family, Chrissy with her angelic face, such a lovely girl and still the same today and Ryan with his chubby little cheeks and pursed lips. It was wonderful to catch up again and tell stories over a beer; it felt like a really close family bond once more, something I had missed for a long time.

I had some lovely heart to hearts as well with my little Cei, my forever little sister. I was imparting my 27 year old wisdom with her and cracking jokes all the time, it was really special. Leonard was his usual laid back self and always ready for party mode which at the time for me was a welcome distraction but I didn't realize what misery it was heaping upon my sister in general. Happily the family agreed to all go down to the South Coast for a long weekend in Margate which for me was heaven. I have explained before that my heart soars when at the coast and this time was no different. We were all to go down in a convoy of three cars with Leonard, Pauline and the kids in their Mark 1 VW Golf, Mum, Dad and Cei in their bright blue VW Beetle and me, Leanne and Calum in Paulines white VW Beetle. It was a veritable VDUB Club convoy chugging down to the sunny south coast. We were all excited and set for the seven hour trek with flasks of tea and ham and tomato rolls. Our little German chariot was exactly like Herbie from 'Herbie Goes To Hollywood' apart from the racing stripes, but it did have a personality all of its own and I don't mean a loyal and free spirited one, more like a demonic wolf in sheep's clothing. The thing was possessed.

Getting down to the coast, our progress was decent and we made the habitual stop at Harrismith for food and fuel but a few hours later, having just passed Pietermaritzburg, disaster almost struck. With the last leg of the journey in sight and on a four lane stretch of tarmac I smelled burning within the little car. This wasn't unusual because Leanne was puffing away on a cigarette in the back with Calum strapped in next to her. Now

I'm not too sure what the real story was and I'll never know but Leanne started shouting at me in a blind panic 'I'm on fire, the seat between my legs is on fire!'. As quickly as I could safely manage I pulled over onto the hard shoulder just before a massive interchange where another huge road was merging in from our left so it was just as well I pulled off when I did. I could smell an unusual, rubbery, burnt hair smell and I was starting to panic thinking my little family were frying in the back.

I stopped the car, got everyone out onto the hard shoulder and noticed that there was a smoldering hole the size of a fist in the seat between where Leanne's legs would have been. Thankfully those seats aren't bolted in, well at least this one wasn't, as I pulled it out and threw it onto the earth next to the car. By this point the hole had grown to the size of a side plate at an alarming rate as the tinder dry horse hair was burning rapidly within the seat itself. I threw handfuls of earth on the stricken seat which did the job and put the fire out straightaway. When I looked inside the car I noticed a flickering flame on the battery which was situated underneath the seat. The fire was on a little rubber mat between the positive and negative terminals. I quickly put this out as well by throwing earth on it, panicking that the car may burst into flames if it got too close to the fuel lines. I eventually made sure there was no more smoldering from any other parts of the car before putting the seat back and getting Leanne and Calum into the other cars.

My theory could have gone two ways, it was either a cigarette end which was dropped onto the seat and melted right through into the horse hair which in turn set the battery mat alight or the steel springs within the seat itself, with the weight of a person on the seat above the battery, shorted out the battery terminals, causing a spark which in turn lit the horse hair. We'll never really know but either way, Leanne, Calum and I were lucky but it didn't stop us feeling really guilty about ruining the seat in Pauline's little car.

We arrived at our destination, a lovely hotel right on the beach and it was a tonic to hear the waves crashing onto the beach with the apartment window open. How beautiful it was to stand on the balcony at sunset and watch the fiery orange orb dip below the horizon whilst sipping an ice cold Castle lager. Chrissy, Ryan and Calum all got on well and were small enough to have a bath together, such a cute picture it was. Margate is the type of place where it is remote enough to feel you are away from the madding crowd yet has a small town where you can wander and shop for a few hours if the mood takes you. It's quaint and a particular favorite of many unpretentious South Africans. We had the most wonderful time playing on the beach, swimming with the kids in the sea and eating out at the local steak restaurant on warm and balmy evenings. A particularly memorable time was when we all sat around the round table in the apartment one evening and played Pictionary together while the kids were in bed. This sounds very ordinary and hardly worth mentioning but it was magic because every single one of us was laughing, and I mean laughing with tears in our eyes and aching stomachs. Leonard was particularly funny and this is how I remember him, so full of life and laughter. I always love doing things together as a family and playing games is such a wonderful way of pulling everyone in. Unfortunately in our fast paced, technology ruled lives we have lost sight of this and it is easier to become isolated due to the convenience of communication via alternative forms such as social media sites, mobile phones, Skype and the rest of it. But that holiday taught me the value of having innocent fun with family which didn't cost anything and didn't require consuming endless bottles of alchohol. It was a good lesson indeed.

That weekend went by in a glorious sun hazed blur of hot days at the beach, the smell of cocoa butter sun tan lotion and that wind-swept gritty feeling of being on the sand. Crashing, vibrant green waves, the taste of salt in the air and the smell of fresh fish completed the cocktail party to my senses. I was in heaven. Calum loved the sand and sea and so did Leanne but she did unfortunately suffer with a mild bout of prickly heat which is the most horrible itchy rash brought on by the sun. It's awful as there isn't really an effective way of dealing with it apart from laying in the bath. You scratch the itch and it flares up within a split second even worse than before to the point that you feel like ripping your own skin off. Thankfully it passed briefly and lasted no longer than a day.

So now it was time to go home and having done my best to patch up the seat, the car still smelled like the inside of a charred world war two tank. One other unfortunate idiosyncrasy was that the fuel gauge didn't work and was permanently on empty so apart from filling her up before the long journey, I didn't know how much fuel I had left at any given point. Dad did try to reassure me by saying confidently 'Well, we've got the other Beetle so when we've got a quarter of a tank left we'll fill up again'. That was sound logic so off we went on our return trip home with the excitement of the coast all behind us and the endless Orange Free State roads ahead of us.

On one of those straight roads that goes on for mile after mile, with nothing either side of you but 'mealie' fields, I discovered that this satanically possessed Beetle had not finished trying to terrify us. With Leonard and Pauline in the front of the three car convoy and myself and Leanne at the back, we were cruising happily down a very flat section of road when the engine started revving at full throttle. I took my foot off the accelerator thinking I was being a bit leaden footed but it made no difference at all, the car still wanted to go as fast as its little tires would carry it. I was feeling a pit of worry in my stomach as I didn't know what was going on but I tried to keep calm by being very silent. We were still a few miles on and bombing through the countryside getting closer and closer to Mum and Dad in front of us, with me applying the brakes constantly to keep the runaway train in check. I was getting worried that I would burn the brakes out though as this little steed just wanted to run. Leanne eventually picked up that something was wrong as she sensed that my hands clasped around the steering wheel in a death grip and a bead of sweat running down my ashen face wasn't normal. 'What's wrong' she said. 'Oh, I think Herbie has gone psycho on us' I smiled nervously. Eventually I flashed my headlamps repeatedly at Dad to stop and I started to break hard in order to bring this crazy animal to heel. With the accelerator at full throttle and me standing on the brakes there were opposite forces at play which caused a fair amount of juddering as we came to a stop and I quickly switched off the engine. Just before I did so the engine roared even loader as if in its final death throes before becoming silent. I sat in the seat still gripping the steering wheel and half expecting the engine to turn itself on and the bonnet to start opening and closing in a maniacal Stephen King kind of way. Thankfully it didn't as we sat there in silence, just the heat shimmering off the bonnet.

Dad had stopped in front of us as he got out and sauntered over. 'Alright mate, what's up' he said. 'Car is out of control Dad, it's gone bloody mental as if the accelerator is stuck on'. 'Let's 'ave a look son' he said as he rummaged in his tool kit. He flipped the engine cover up at the back and had a quick look at it. We were in the middle of no-where in the baking hot sun with no emergency pick up cover, I was beginning to feel very uneasy when Dad popped his head over the bonnet with a huge, larger than life smile and said 'That should do it'. All he had was a pair of pliers in his hand as he explained that the throttle spring is normally fully 'ON' if not pulled back by this large, chunky spring which had somehow worked itself off and luckily lay in the engine bay. A few seconds was all it took to stretch the spring back into its normal position and thereby hold the throttle into the 'OFF' position. All was well as I started the engine; the little Beetle had become calm again. Her fit of rage had subsided. We all set off in convoy again and I was mightily relieved to have such a practical and competent father. We were on our way.

Now this wasn't quite the end of our torment as the 'Spirit of Beelzebub' needed to exorcize one more prank before she was finished with us. 20 kilometers from Villiers and the first fuel stop in hours along this never ending strip of tarmac and we started chugging to a stop. There was not one ounce of power. We had run out of fuel as yet again I flashed Dad in front of me to stop. Naturally Dad's car was still fine for fuel, we had obviously consumed a lot more by the engine being on full throttle for a fair few miles. This time, with dusk approaching, Leonard volunteered to go quickly to the fuel station, fill a canister and bring it back for us which he did without any real hitch. The only issue was standing on the edge of a national road in the middle of no-where in the dark but at least we were all together. After about half an hour we were all back on our way having properly filled up our tanks once more. There was to be no pranks on me from Herbie in the holiday after that. It was the end of another adventure.

During the same holiday Leonard invited me to watch a game of rugby in Pretoria. One of his clients had a box at Loftus Versveld stadium in Pretoria, home of the Blue Bulls. It was a low key midweek Currie Cup game against Boland so the stadium was mostly empty but it was still a thrill to be there. The fact that we were in an executive box enabled us access to a bar and copious amounts of alcohol as well as curry and rice with all the delicious sauces. With legendary Springbok Joost van der Westhuizen playing it was a special treat in so many ways to see the great man playing. I loved this and was knocking back the beers with relaxed abandon but one thing did worry me and that was the scant disregard for the drink driving laws as everyone in our party of people were pretty well far gone. Leonard really did like to party and we found ourselves in a pool hall after the rugby, knocking back 'Springbok' shorts and having a whale of a time. I was having fun, don't get me wrong, but I would happily have gone straight home after watching the rugby which is what I thought we would be doing. I felt uncomfortable being out and didn't need to be in party mode on a week day even if I was on holiday.

Meanwhile, Leonard was gleefully knocking back the liquor whilst playing game after game of pool and it looked like he was only just getting started. After a short while he sensed that I wanted to leave and so eventually we did, but it was four of us in his VW Golf driving from Pretoria to Joburg on the return journey. This was completely the wrong thing to do, four very inebriated young men in a car including the driver. Unfortunately this is the norm in South African culture due to the great distances between places, no safe public transport system to speak of and a weak justice system for anyone found drink driving. The three ingredients together create an unusually high mortality rate involving youngsters on the roads but the culture is that this is seen as the luck of the draw, 'ya pays ya money, ya takes ya chance'. There is no real peer pressure that you are committing a criminal offence as such, rather that it would be a bit of a bummer if you got caught and had to pay a fine. On the way home I heard a couple of the lads chatting and laughing about how funny it was that in their 'wilder days' they would race other cars and play a game that entailed being so close to the car in front that the person in the vehicle couldn't see their headlights. I mean how ridiculously moronic is that? They thought this was macho and admirable and silently I sunk into my seat wondering what level of intellect thought this was even remotely clever. Despite the stupidity in abundance that was on show that night we all managed to make it home safely, but that was not always to be the case.

It had been a wonderful holiday packed with memories that Leanne, Calum and I would never forget but it was time to go home and get back into the swing of things again. I had enjoyed my adventure but this had ignited a little spark within my soul, my love of South Africa had not so much been rekindled because it was never lost but it brought back a yearning to be there again. I dismissed this out of hand as an option because Leanne would not leave the UK and wouldn't consider leaving her family there which I totally understood but my flame for Africa still flickered within me. I saw my future as firmly in Cardiff and indeed with MELUK, I didn't know any better and I had become part of the furniture there. I mean what else did I know, what else would I do? When I look back, all those feelings of not being able to do anything else with my life were very firmly rooted in fear. Fear is the most destructive 'F' word in the English language, the feeling that paralyzes us. 'What if I try something new and I fail?' I had a lot to learn.

Chapter 31

Now speaking of doing things different, one evening Leanne and I were going on our usual Thursday night out to the Penarth Ex-Servicemen's club for a few cheap beverages with her Mum and Dad. This had become part of our routine and despite Kirsten's habit of becoming a slurring, legless, Southern Comfort soaked heap accompanied by Angus's disdainful look, I actually looked forward to it. I didn't completely overdo it as I had work the following day but it was a lot of fun. In order for us to do this we paid a babysitter from down the road to look after Calum, that babysitter was 16 year old Bernice who loved being in the house by herself and indeed loved Calum so much that she would often buy him gifts and clothes. She was a trustworthy and lovely girl with such personality and we knew we were in safe hands.

We would always get a taxi from our house at 7pm on those Thursdays and be in Penarth fifteen minutes later, supping on a cold beer. The taxi driver on one occasion though was my cousin Simon who ended up not charging us. I hadn't seen him in years and Leanne thought we both looked very similar, she thought I'd been keeping a secret brother from her. Simon and

I chatted and eventually he mentioned that he attended a Do-Jo every week in Treganna where he practiced the martial art of Shotokan Karate. I was intrigued and wanted to know more, he was a few years older than myself as well with a little family so I thought 'Why can't I do this?' If Simon was progressing then I could too. He really sold it to me and it aligned with what I wanted to do. I really wanted to train in something that could be lasting and which I could learn from. I admired the self-discipline and quiet confidence of all martial artists I had ever met, the confident, happy exterior that masked a steely reserve underneath. I wanted to be like that too, I craved moving on to another level as I felt pretty stagnant in my life.

I chatted to Simon a few more times before I eventually plucked up the courage as a 28 year old man to go down to the St Mary's School on a cold Tuesday evening for a two hour taster session. I was so nervous but really wanted to do this. Simon, his two young sons and his daughter Bailey were all there practicing with him so I had quite a support mechanism alongside me. I was a rank novice; I knew nothing of the martial arts so it meant I became a white belt with all the other youngsters who were white belts. When I say youngsters, the youngest was about seven years old and apart from me the oldest about ten. We were arranged in the Do-Jo in rank from white belts in the far right column over to a small column of black belts on the far left and everything sequentially in between.

It was really embarrassing to say the least to be fumbling around trying to get different techniques of punching correct and doing the 'banana' walk with children of an average age of eight. I felt like a six foot beacon of incompetency at first and wondered why I was putting myself through this. I remember feeling the humiliation of being shown by a little ten year old boy where to put my trailing foot as we turned to go back up the Do-Jo. I sheepishly said 'thank you buddy' as if we were the same age, and on one level we were. At first it felt impossibly difficult to remember all this 'stuff', how to remember what angle your fist should be when making a punch, that your stance should be as low as possible and that your feet should always be shoulder width apart with your hips straight, back straight, left quadricep parallel to the floor, your head never supposed to go up and down when you walked forward. All these things, my mind was pickled, my body was exhausted and this just the first session. Could I do this twice a week for two hours each? You bet I could, I was determined to. I was still yet to learn the kata which is a series of set moves which when done as a group in synchronicity is a wonderful display of power, precision and control. I wasn't quite to that level yet.

At the end of each session my muscles burned with fatigue, my brain was aching with all the information I had taken in, I would drive home feeling spent but absolutely wonderful about it. Along with football and the running I was doing to keep fit for that, the Karate training and stretching needed to perform that discipline enabled me to become as fit as I had ever been in my life. It has to be said that although I was more than fit playing football, Karate introduced a whole new type of fitness, using different muscle groups altogether. In Karate you are required to be more explosive, precise and dynamic whereas in football you needed more stamina over a longer period with occasional bursts of explosion. A three minute sparring bout could be more exhausting than a whole 45 minutes of football, especially when you are getting your face pummeled by a lightning fast black belt. After three months of learning, faltering and practicing techniques I had mastered all my basics and my kata. It was time to be graded in order to move to the next belt, red belt.

The good thing about our class was that it was small, no more than fifteen people, and with three black belt 'Sensei's' watching over us, we had expert tuition and were taken to an excellent standard. We weren't allowed to be moved to the next level until we had absolutely thoroughly mastered what we had to learn at our respective levels. The sensei did not want to grade students just because they had been there for three months; he wanted a reputation of producing quality, no matter how long it took. If you were not made of the right stuff, you would not be graded even if it meant losing a student in the process. I absolutely loved the simple Japanese philosophy and wisdom that emanated from these sessions. Most martial arts are not about gaining the skills for beating people up and becoming a bully, they are about self discipline and self respect for oneself and others. The idea is that you learn these skills as a form of self defence to look after yourself and your family and should only ever be used as a last resort. You are always taught to walk away from trouble as the first choice but if called upon, you are able to deal with trouble quickly and efficiently. It breeds a solid, genuine and quiet confidence in yourself that is truly liberating and brings an inner peace that does not look for violence or trouble. Few people understand who have never practiced but I know and sense when I am in the presence of a martial arts student without them having to say anything. I loved the ethics of the importance of learning the basics well. We were taught that you never stopped practicing your white or red belt kata's, even if you were a third Dan black belt. The reason being that the basics you learned in the beginning formed the roots of what would become your tree of knowledge and that those roots would always need nurturing if the rest of the tree were to grow. It was so beautiful and so simple and I totally bought into it.

It was time for my grading and I don't think I had ever been so nervous in all my life and that included things such as exams in college, my driving tests, my wedding, playing in a cup final, the birth of my children and interviews for jobs. It really was a nervous time for me and as my name was called to perform my newly learned skills in front of my sensei I was almost at the point of vomiting. During the grading I was so focused that my breathing became secondary and I started hyperventilating. When you don't get oxygen to the brain you start making mistakes so my sensei told me to breathe and relax as he continued to put me through my paces. I eventually completed the half hour grueling test and was told at the end, when everyone else had all been through their own grading that I had passed. We all sat cross legged, as if in school, waiting to hear if we had passed or not. I cannot tell you how wonderful it was to hear those words that I had passed, for me it was such a monumental achievement.

The grading system in Karate goes from white, to red, to yellow, orange, green, blue, purple, three separate brown belts and then black, to which there are numerous levels again. On my first grading I went from white, directly to yellow, I was mightily proud. During the few years I practiced and lived Karate I managed to get to blue belt and was on the cusp of my purple belt grading before I had to stop, the reasons for which will become apparent later. Two of the proudest moments during my time practicing

Karate were when I was invited to perform at tournaments with the club. The first of which was in Port Talbot with a group of us from the club. At the time I was an orange belt and very nervous, not knowing what to expect from the day. The tournament I had entered meant I was going to be fighting in bouts against other Karate people from around Wales. The format being that you were put into different weight categories but that everyone who was fighting wore either a red or white belt, irrespective of your actual status. Before going onto the mat to fight you would take your normal belt off and put on the red or white belt. Astonishingly enough for my weight division I won my first few bouts against opposition with a higher grading than myself. I found myself in a semi-final against a very experienced black belt, and when I say experienced it is because his black belt looked more grey than black when he took it off, it had been washed that much. He had been wearing that black belt a long time.

I started the bout nervously and showed the guy a lot of respect but we were taught to fear no-one and to respect all. At first we were both sizing eachother up hoping that either would make the first mistake. The scoring format was such that you scored a point for a successful, controlled punch to the head or torso. Any punch to the opponent's legs or arms didn't count. A particularly well executed technique would be rewarded with two points but the aim was that the bout would continue until somebody reached six points. I opened the score against my opponent by punching him fully on the nose and mouth as he dropped his hands down from his face for that split second, 1-0 to me. Thirty seconds later, the exact same thing happened. He left himself amazingly open for what seemed an eternity as I planted another right handed punch to his nose, this time seeing it split open and for blood to start pouring from it as it started to get rather swollen. 2-0 to me. I thought I was in the ascendency until the real spirit of this experienced fighter started to take control. He very calmly opened me up as he saw me tiring and totally winded me with a punch to my solar plexus. 2-1 to me. It was as if those first two punches sparked him into life as he proceeded to pick me off and made it 3-2. Then another crushing blow to my stomach and I needed an enforced time out to recapture the breath from my body. This guy was good and experienced enough not to panic when he was trailing. He eventually beat me 6-3 on points but I was really proud of my achievement on that day. I had reached the semi-finals of a national Welsh tournament and paved the way for the black belt in our club to take the winners medal. Ray Beckham, one of our sensei's at the club, thanked me for softening his competition up for the final as he proceeded to beat the guy that knocked me out in the semi's. All four semi-finalists shook hands and hugged each other in mutual respect for what we had all just done. It takes real guts to get up and fight a stranger who has done you no harm at all. What an amazing experience that was.

I was to go one better a year later in a tournament in Fochryw in the Welsh valleys where I got to the final of a competition for all levels below brown belt. When I fought in that competition I was by now a blue belt and ended up losing in the final against a guy who I had the better of but was disqualified for using excessive force with a punch. In Karate it is all about control and accuracy. When you attempt to score a point on the face of an opponent you are not meant to launch your fist into their face with all your might, it isn't the point of the sport. You are supposed to make very firm contact, on and off in order to be awarded the point, you are meant to show control with your punch. Unfortunately I didn't as I was twice asked to sit out for a few seconds while the coaches attended to their man. Time and again I was getting the better of my opponent and twice I managed to get a firm but apparently 'too excessive' hit to his face. I was 3-2 up when I was disqualified in the final. I was absolutely gutted at not having won because I knew I was the better fighter by a mile, which everyone agreed with apart from the umpire. I was despondent but still cherished my runners up medal. In two short years I had gone from feeling very idiotic with a group of eight year old children to fighting in tournaments and doing really well. The black belts actually loved fighting me as they knew that I would always keep coming at them no matter what they threw at me, they would more often than not beat me but I was learning a lot and getting better and better.

Chapter 32

During this time I felt like I was outgrowing myself and my relationship. I was learning and moving forward, had given up smoking a long time ago in return for a healthier, physical life of Karate, running and football. Leanne and I were meandering and I had no intention of getting married even though we had a son. Unfortunately I had a wandering eye but never acted on it, unlike my time in Japan. So my relationship was less than healthy and I started to take interest in a young girl. Again I feel self conscious talking about this but my story wouldn't be my story if this part wasn't told.

The young girl in question was 17 year old Bernice; our babysitter. She lived nearby and was always popping in to see us, to see Calum mostly whether or not she was babysitting. She loved him and also enjoyed our company as well. She was a pretty girl who loved sport and being active and used to have innocent banter with me which I found really funny coming from a young girl. Initially I found Bernice's visits irritating as I wanted my own home to be our little sanctuary and didn't want a girl around my space, our family space. It was awkward though as she did enjoy babysitting with very little notice so we had a precious resource in a very selfish way. I didn't really want to upset things so mostly let her come round and visit when she wanted. Her relationship with Leanne was sisterly and they got on really well, having glasses of wine together, watching movies and generally being good, close friends.

There was no issue in the beginning, I either enjoyed her youthful, sarcastic, teenage presence or found it tiresome, depending on my mood at the time. Then unfortunately she started blossoming into quite an attractive young girl. Because of her outgoing, confident personality she was magnetic in that way but now she became physically attractive as well. My first reaction was to dismiss it and ignore her as much as I could but as she grew older she started being flirtier in a way she was unaware of. It was innocent enough, things like certain looks when I said certain things and kicking my feet if both our feet were in the same vicinity in the living room. Silly things really, but I was wize enough and perceptive enough to realize that maybe there was some sort of crush going on. I still dismissed it and thought no more about it but before I knew it I started thinking about her and missing her if she didn't come around to our place. Gone were the times where I would hope she would leave us in peace.

Without realizing it she became a wedge between Leanne and me. It was a very thin one to begin with but one which became a welcome distraction rightly or wrongly. Bernice was blissfully oblivious, or so I thought. It was by no means healthy or right but I was happy for some female attention. Leanne and my relationship, although strong was imperfect. I'm not by any means comparing Bernice to an unwanted plant life but as an analogy she was a weed that grew between a crevice in a rock. There was a crack in our relationship that was subtly exploited and one which I allowed. Had we been strong in our relationship I would not have let this go any further but I let it develop over the course of many months. Bernice did not by any means set out to cause any heartbreak, she was not a vindictive person or in the least bit calculating. She had an innocent crush which she did not really want to explore but at the same time didn't know what to do with. Above all she loved Calum and showered so many gifts upon the little man.

In the beginning I was a bystander in my own house being amused by this girl but as the months grew I started to really need to see her as if I was falling for her. It was quite unsettling and disconcerting but there was little I could do, little I wanted to do to stop it. I would look at myself in the mirror and wonder what on earth I was thinking. On one occasion I found myself slapping myself in the mirror trying to drum some sense into me. It became excruciating for me as we as a family would go out and have fun whilst Bernice would tag along 'to look after Calum' but underneath it all we seemed to need to be with eachother on some level. It was frustrating on two critical levels that I could not discuss with anyone and one was that I wanted something I could never have and the other was that I had something that I didn't want. Bernice would never openly admit it and I could not approach the subject yet there was something tangible bubbling under the surface that I couldn't control.

Leanne was utterly without a care in the world but part of me wanted her to realize what was going on in order to put a stop to it and become jealous, but put a stop to what? Become jealous of what exactly? Subconsciously I wanted something to blow. Nothing was really happening; it was all going on inside my head mostly. This raging storm within me, within my relationship drove me to despair and I was not coping at all well.

In work I was disinterested and going through the motions, trying to be out of the office as much as possible, popping home for no reason other than that I could, even though I could have been sacked by doing so. On one occasion I borrowed the company pool car to genuinely go and get some parts from Port Talbot to satisfy a shortage and on the way back picked Bernice up at college to have a chat and drop her home, all in work time. At home, apart from Calum, I just lived for the weekend or seeing Bernice. It was one of the most horrible times in my life; I had no control at all. I had genuinely fallen in love with this girl that I couldn't have and couldn't touch, daren't touch. It was as if she were a beautiful doll in a plastic box that couldn't be opened. She didn't have the emotional maturity to express anything she felt but I knew deep down there was something. By now I was utterly and completely unhappy in my relationship with Leanne,

I was fixated on Bernice. I loved the way she looked. I was smitten but I couldn't show it.

At that time I was unable to talk to anyone at all. I couldn't talk to any of my mates because they all knew and loved Leanne; I couldn't talk to family as they were so far away and couldn't understand what I was going through, well at least this is what I thought at the time. People in work were about the only people I could chat to but there's no way I could open up completely. I was stuck and had precious few outlets for emotion. It was an unimaginably hard time where I didn't even want to be in my own skin.

Fortunately I did at least have the distraction of decorating our bathroom and kitchen. Part of that process was to hire a builder who was a friend of Leanne's family in the Penarth area. Len smashed out the existing box room upstairs, our third bedroom, and repaired the walls and ceiling. This would ultimately become our new upstairs bathroom. The same happened with the hideous little downstairs bathroom, behind the kitchen, which was ripped out and destined to become an extension of our kitchen, a dining room with French windows looking out onto the back garden. The kitchen itself was completely transformed from its brown 1970's style décor to a modern, fully equipped kitchen that I completely tiled at a later date when I had more money.

The old box room became a beautiful big bathroom, with a brand new bathroom suite installed, that I was going to tile. It took me many evenings after work to finally complete that tiling but when I had finished it was a masterpiece that I was proud of and became a focal point of our home. We were no longer bathing in a freezing cold little rear bathroom but a warm, large luxuriant one upstairs with an ample corner bath and a huge walk in corner shower. I had grafted hard and had many cups of tea whilst chatting to Bernice up in that bathroom, covered in dust and grout. It was worth it because it looked stunning but Bernice was still locked behind a glass door in my heart and I was still unable to do a thing.

Around that time my cousin Jimmy was getting married to Anne and plans were put in place that they were going to be moving away from Cardiff.

Although we didn't see each other as often as we used to, I was devastated at Jimmy moving to England, Wisbech in particular, right on the east coast of England and what felt like a million miles away. Throughout my whole life Jimmy had always been my closest friend, more like a brother than a cousin and I was going to miss him badly but at least he was still with us in spirit.

Then on May 15th 1999 my world was turned upside down and unexpectedly shaken to its foundations as I learned that my brother-in-law, Leonard Putney, had been killed in a drink driving accident back in South Africa. As I was told I went into a sort of trance that didn't allow me to cry initially. I couldn't speak to anyone about it as none of my friends knew him but I thought of my poor sister, Pauline, and what she must have been going through at the time. At that point their relationship was teetering on the brink but it was still the most horrible time for her and her two little children, Chrissy and Ryan. It was a bright sunny day and I remember the feeling of deep grief within me but of feeling disconnected and isolated. I could not believe it was real, I looked at people and became annoyed at how trivial their moaning had become about the weather. Again I was in a bubble of my own emotion but at least I did break down and grieve in the quiet of my own space. Was he really gone? Nothing seemed to matter after that for a while. Whilst watching the FA Cup final a week later between Manchester United and Newcastle United, I remember looking at my friends, mostly whom were Man Utd fans, and thinking how trivial and unimportant this game of football now felt. They were dining out on a feast of yet more silverware for their beloved team and I felt disconnected from that emotion. Since I hadn't seen Leonard in two years and prior to that I hadn't seen him in at least eight, it was understandable that I should feel removed from it all. I wasn't though because we had played cars together, played football together, gone to church together, had braai's in one another's houses together, had sleep over's. His Mum was like a second Mum to me, Aunty Jill. He was gone and would never be back. The most ironic thing of all was that he was trying to turn over a new leaf in his relationship and on the night he was killed, was the only one in the car not under the influence of alchohol. Their vehicle was not at fault, they were hit by a vehicle whose occupants themselves were completely drunk.

So with a relationship that was floundering and with me reaching a plateau at MELUK I felt like I was in the wilderness. Jimmy was in a different part of Britain but at least I was still doing karate and football and keeping really fit. Calum, my little beacon of hope was the only thing that kept me with Leanne for as long as I did but even this couldn't possibly hold any longer, our relationship was like a raft taking on too much water and disintegrating in the process.

Chapter 33

That year it was the big millennium eve year, it was 1999. This was the year that Wales hosted the rugby world cup and the nation was gripped with the fever of this six week long extravaganza. It was the most atmospheric of times leading up to the tournament with Wales flags everywhere, the team doing really well and a general air of optimism around the country. The city was a buzz of electric energy and it was a pleasure to walk around seeing people wearing red everywhere. I distinctly remember this time in as much as I was elated about the rugby and it's excitement but at the same time I felt hollowness that I couldn't have Bernice for myself, she was so near and yet so far away at that time. The world cup itself was an amazing success and united the nation but alas the power of the southern hemisphere teams was to deny another northern hemisphere win. This time it was Australia who won, beating France in the final after having beaten the Springboks in a pulsating semi-final in Cardiff. I was fortunate enough to watch a pool game, Wales versus Japan in a convincing win for Wales.

Later on that year, with millennium eve approaching, everyone was talking about the parties they were going to and what they were going to be getting up to, obviously almost exclusively centered on the consumption of alchohol and the premises in which they would take part. The whole world was going crazy for this amazing milestone but Leanne and I were not planning on going out because Bernice was of an age now to also want to go out and party. She didn't particularly want to baby sit on millennium eve so we had resigned ourselves to staying in.

Even so, Leanne and I had struck up a good relationship with my cousin Simon from karate and his wife, Tonia and we would occasionally go out to the Victoria Ballroom club, the place Mum and Dad had met all those years ago. Simon was like Jimmy but older and a little wizer and of course he was my karate buddie as well. We all got on really well, Leanne was very easy company with most people and her warmth and affectionate personality was always like a magnet. By happy coincidence, Nicholas, Leanne's brother, told us that his plans had changed for New Years Eve and that he wouldn't mind babysitting if we wanted to go out. 'Too right we would, are you sure Nick?' was our response. Before we knew it, we had booked a dream ticket to the hustling, bustling, extravaganza that was….erm, The Victoria Ball Room. Since everything had been booked up weeks in advance, this was our only choice. It wasn't the boozy bright lights of downtown Cardiff city centre but it was still a place to have a beer and a bit of fun. It was Simon that had got us the tickets and we were really quite grateful for them but truth be told, it was going to be quite an amusing evening.

As we entered the club we saw a poster advertizing the evening's entertainment as 'The Magnificent Mario – Italian Cabaret Artist' followed by 'An evening of Bingo'. Leanne and I looked at each other with looks of bemused bewilderment and horror as we took in the magnificence of Mario, large and sweaty, mid-fifties, with a barrel of a frame, confidently mingling with his adoring fans. When I say adoring fans I mean the little old white haired pensioners with cataracts. He had an archetypical round, jolly face with fleshy jowls and pencil moustache as he belted out the hits of yesteryear. The older generation in the club, which was 90%

of them, couldn't get enough of him as he selected the next song on his Casio keyboard. 'Oh lord' I thought, 'let's just get a beer in as quickly as possible'. There were old ladies looking wistfully at Mario with a faraway look of nostalgia, hands clasped to their faces as he churned out 'I would do anything for love' by Meatloaf and other such classics. We were in an inescapable time warp, the club was on lock down and there was no escape. Mario and his red cumberband were having the time of their life alongside his adoring throng of fans of 60 plus. It was the sort of night where you just had to sit and go with the flow and order another Black Russian. At the end of the beautifully delivered 'Shaddupaya face' we heard the compare excitedly informing the crowd that it was the time we had all been waiting for; That moment at last. Get your special highlighter pens out because it's BINGOOOOOO....... There was an excited hush of anticipation as I broke the silence with stifled laughter amid looks of disdain from the pro Bingo ladies. I looked around me for support but my allies stared dolefully into their drinks as if they didn't know me, they had succumbed without a fight and sat with marker pens and bingo books, poised for action. They had been subliminally manipulated and were now bingo zombies. Meanwhile, at the bar I heard Mario, the Italian maestro order a beer saying 'Arrighi luv, gerrus a LAAHGAH with a dash will you sweethaaaht' in broad Cardiffian. I hastily stuffed my imaginary autograph book back into my pocket, the magnificent Mario was a mortal, just like me.

I got back to my seat and it was straight into the bingo, 'Here we go' I said to Leanne, with a look of disbelief. Every time I heard 'Two little ducks...... aaaaah tawenny tooo' followed by a very risqué 'LEGS............... ELEVEN' with accompanying wolf whistles I packed up laughing. The funniest though was little old ladies with blue rinses get excited by the call for '69' and then a naughty 'ooooohh'. I couldn't stop laughing and I thought they were going to get Mario to eject me, especially when I shouted 'HOUSE' when I didn't even have a bingo card in front of me. You should have seen the looks I got though; I thought one of the nanna's was going to chin me. It was all good fun but by the end of the night Mario was still going for gold, belting out the Tom Jones and Frank Sinatra songs. It was Millennium eve and most of my mates were at the Millennium stadium watching The Manic Street Preachers and seeing fireworks exploding all around them. Here we were, as the clock struck 12, listening to the Magnificent Mario sing 'I am the music man' by Black Lace. Yes, THAT SONG, the piano one, the 'Pee ya, pee ya, pee yan noh, pee yan noh, pee yan noh' one. This, my friends and family, was the first song I heard going into a new millennium and I have never been the same since.

However it was on one of these evenings out that I blurted out to Tonia about my feelings for Bernice and in turn she gave me the standard advice that a younger girl was not very wize at all. In time I would live to regret ever telling Tonia this. Simon and Tonia themselves had their issues, the same as Leanne and I and all was not well. For me and Leanne I had long since passed caring but she still hung on for what I suspect would be for nostalgias sake. My heart breaks for the time she saved up money for me to go on a long weekend to Liverpool with all the football boys of The Villa. It was such a lovely act of generosity, care and sincere thought. I felt I didn't really deserve it because my heart was elsewhere and I think she knew it at that stage. This time of my life was a real low point but we had our little man to consider through all of this. I knew I had to get away from the relationship but I kept thinking of Calum, my little boy. He was everything to me at that time; he was my little buddy and my little ray of sunshine. We would do so much together, go to the park, play football together and have really wonderful times. He was my north, my south, my east, my west and I loved him with all my heart. Regardless of the biological link, he was mine and I could not bear to imagine life without him under my roof. On the other hand I absolutely needed to be out of my relationship with Leanne so something had to give way. It was not going to be easy and I faced a crossroads. Stay in an unhappy relationship for the sake of Calum or leave it causing much pain and heartache for both Calum and Leanne.

During all this my feelings for Bernice grew and grew and on some telepathic level we got closer and more entwined in each other's thoughts. Whether she wanted it or not, Bernice was also falling in love but she resisted it for as long as she possibly could because she knew the magnitude of what was happening. This wasn't some teenage fling, this was ending what she thought was a sacred marriage. Incredibly, and as I write I can't believe this happened, Leanne and I would do things knowingly and half aware that the other knew what was going on. For example, Leanne would go out for an evening with the girls and I knew she would be with other guys but I genuinely wanted it to happen for her sake. I wanted her to feel wanted because she was attractive and deserved it and there were guys out there who wanted her. At the same time, Bernice would spend evenings with me having wine and watching TV as Calum slept peacefully upstairs. We would chat and enjoy each other's company and it was all totally and utterly harmless. Even so, still at this point, Bernice would never have dared intimating that she felt anything for me. Meanwhile, it took all my self control not to tell this young girl how I felt. She still didn't know on a conscious level but we both knew there was something there, it was impossible to ignore.

Then one evening we had friends over for a few drinks at our place including Bernice and her two friends. As was so often the case, during the middle of the evening we would get hungry and order a Chinese takeaway which would necessitate me walking around to Cowbridge Road to pick it up. On this occasion though Bernice's two best friends, really lovely, down-to-earth twin sisters from Whitchurch wanted to walk with me which I agreed to. On the way back from the Chinese my emotions got the better of me as I poured my heart out to them of how I felt about Bernice. They said they knew anyway and that Bernice felt the same but she was terrified of the consequences and didn't have the emotional armory to deal with such a thing.

This was a kind of breakthrough for me because as unhealthy as the situation was, it meant I had at least been able to verbalize things to somebody. Naturally they would have told Bernice so it was a matter of time before we would speak to each other openly. For Bernice there came a moment, a green light if you will, a moment she felt compelled to act upon. She just needed a reason to give herself license to get closer to me and that reason was when she was out with Leanne and the girls. Bernice noticed that Leanne was getting a lot of attention from a rather large man and that Leanne was absolutely lapping it up and not resisting at all. Bernice came sprinting back to the house, out of breath, blanched cheeks, reeking of alchohol and telling me all about the shenanigans with this young man called John. I smiled and told her not to worry in the slightest because I wanted this to be, I needed this to happen. This was my leverage, my way out.

The weeks that followed became more and more intense between Bernice and myself until the point was reached where I poured my heart out to this young girl. We were holding hands, crying and looking into eachothers eyes but she still could not really let her guard down fully. She felt it was just wrong on so many levels and in a way she was right and had a better moral compass than I. I eventually wrote her a letter for her to take away and digest in the cold, clear, sober light of day. I knew we had something between us and I just wanted to know if she felt the same way. I really just wanted her to be honest with me as to how she felt.

The reply was really mature and touching and had me elated because she told me that there was definitely an attraction there and that she loved the person I was but she was terrified. She was at the tipping point where the guilt was being outweighed by the love. I had an answer and that was all I needed in order to loosen the grip of my relationship with Leanne. If I had any lingering doubts as to whether I should end the relationship with Leanne or not, it was powerfully terminated by a very firm talk I had with Carly, Keith's sister. She told me that her father and mother had stayed together through their teenage years because of her and Keith but that she had wished both of them would have split up years earlier to fulfill their happiness. In an ironic way it put more pressure on the children that they stayed together because of them. Keith and Carly wanted their parents to be happy and in their marriage they were not. They were mature enough to realize that they could still have their parents but just in different houses, and at least happy.

This was the rubber stamp for me as I decided once and for all that Leanne and my relationship had to come to an end. Such was our closeness that we got a few bottles of wine in and a Chinese takeaway and had a real heart to heart. Only we could celebrate a break up in this way. We both agreed amicably that we should go our own way, we both told eachother that we loved one another but on another soul mate level. We were definitely soul mates, of that there is no question, but we should never have had a physical relationship together. Up to that point, she was the best, most wonderful friend I could ever have had. We cried an awful lot that evening, we hugged, we laughed and we almost celebrated our release. It was really quite weird but absolutely the right thing to do. We were still great friends but we both knew we needed the physical side of the relationship and no amount of trying was ever going to fix it. We talked about the good times through tears and the bad times through laughter but all the way through our break up we were amicable and sensible. It was so incredibly difficult but this was it, this was us breaking up after eight years and eight months together.

I would be lying now if I said I never had any regrets about my relationship with Leanne but I will say this, Leanne taught me how to live and how to laugh and I will never forget her wonderfully warm influence on me. If I have ever portrayed her in a negative way, that is more a reflection on me than her because she is a special soul. My regrets were that I should have listened to my inner voice, my heart more. In the beginning, when I had a fling with Gwen, that should have signaled the end of our relationship as it was. We should still have continued as the close friends we would always be but unfortunately we or I took the easier option of doing nothing, which ended up hurting a lot more people in the process. It was a mixed feeling of relief and happiness, sadness and loss and of breaking up a little family. Apart from Calum not understanding what was going on, I was on the way up again. It was the end of a huge chapter in my life.

Chapter 34

The Beautiful Faultline - (2000 – 2003 – Eiddew Street Continued)

It was May 2000 and Leanne and I were still trying to sort out what was going to happen with the logistics of the split up. Who was going to live where and more importantly where was Calum going to stay? I know that during the cold, sober moments Leanne would have settled back into our routine of being together but I was having none of it, I had been given my pass as such and I wanted to make this official. It was very awkward that Leanne was still staying in the house as she tried to look for a little flat to stay in and I was sensitive about not slipping back into our routine. We had already agreed that she would look for a new place whilst Calum would stay with me and keep settled in his little home, his little bedroom with all his toys. Because things were fortunately amicable between us there was a very open agreement regarding Calum, which is what we both wanted. We put Calum first when making our decisions, we were mature enough to put our own needs last.

Then one evening, my year long yearning for Bernice reached a crescendo as we walked back from an evening out chatting. For some reason I can't recall if we were simply out for a walk on a summer evening or if we had gone for a drink at the 'Vic' but the conclusion to the evening was all that really mattered in my mind. Leanne was looking after Calum back at the house whilst Bernice and I were out. You cannot imagine how much I wanted and needed to be with this girl at this point in my life. She was everything I desired and when I looked back at how dark the days were when I couldn't be open with her, now that I had permission, I didn't want to waste a moment.

Trying to get across to you, the reader, just how dark, depressing and frustrating those days were when I wanted Bernice but couldn't have her is difficult for me to describe. I thought that it was something that could never be, that she shouldn't or couldn't love me because it was wrong. The heart knew differently though and thankfully so did Bernice's. I really, really loved Bernice and was desperate for her to love me back, but that aspect I could not control, I couldn't make her love me and if I could have I would have. So you can imagine my elation when walking back through Treganna on a late spring evening in May we kissed for the first time. I was on top of the world. Never had Treganna looked so beautiful in the evening, the world was suddenly a wonderful place.

As we reached the door of 25 Eiddew Street, I was delirious and had no care for any consequences of my actions. Now up until this point Leanne was not aware that Bernice and I were together so when we both appeared at the door, drunk and full of joy she was not too impressed, even though we were 'officially' not an item any more. Admittedly I could have and should have handled this more sensitively than I did but to be honest, I didn't care. I was like a released prisoner in an all you can eat buffet. When Leanne figured out that we were together she hit the roof and told me to get out of the house, both of us in fact. She was hurting and could not believe what she was seeing. Later that evening, when I had escorted Bernice back to her house I managed to get back into my house even though the front and back doors were very firmly locked. I got in through the tiny back window on the second floor, via a pair of step ladders and into Calum's room whilst he slept. Leanne was sleeping downstairs on the couch unaware so got quite a shock in the morning when I sauntered down, sheepishly.

It was surreal that we were still under the same roof but apart, still living our separate lives but in each other's company. It wasn't healthy and it had to change, straight away. I wasn't prepared to put my life on hold for an instant longer, I had a lot of catching up to do and I wasn't going to sneak around in the process. Leanne in the interim had struck up a more than healthy relationship with John who himself had a flat on Cowbridge Road which Leanne moved into rather rapidly. It was such a strange time in my life because on one hand I had found what I had been looking for (enter Bono) but on the other I worried that Calum was unsettled and that his safe nest was being ripped apart. I did also worry that Leanne was going off the deep end headlong into another relationship that perhaps she didn't need but I quickly told myself that it was no longer my problem. For the first time I was being selfish.

The weeks and months that passed that summer were the most glorious time for me as you can well imagine. It was the pinnacle of everything I wanted and needed at that time in my life. I wanted to ensure that our relationship went at her pace because I didn't want to frighten her off and I didn't want to rush her into anything she didn't want to do.

It was around this time in the summer that a load of friends and family went out for my cousin Jimmy's stag party. My cousin Simon was also there in a crowded pub in Treganna as I told him of my new found liberation in my relationship with Bernice. I knew he was unhappy in his relationship, the same as I had been, and I told him that he owed it to himself to make himself happy. Perhaps that was the confirmation he needed or perhaps it was just one of many messages he needed to show him his way. Ultimately it became the beginning of the end of his relationship with Tonia and it was obviously a hard time for them both. Tonia suffered the worst though and she was a woman scorned. I think she accused me of fueling the fire within Simon, giving him the ammunition and courage to end it. Perhaps I was seen as the devil incarnate by telling

Simon the advice he wanted to hear. None-the-less it caused bitterness within Tonia towards me, with me being completely oblivious since I had not even see her at all during that time.

Those months were absolutely amazing but not without their issues or, should I say, my issues. Back then I was still massively insecure and had a huge jealous streak that could prove damaging. With her basic need for going out with the girls I was on pins to think that perhaps she would meet someone else, it was a real and genuine fear I had after waiting so long to be with her. She was not that sort of girl though and I needn't have feared but the insecurity was all in my head, my issue, not whether she was loyal or not. There were a couple of unfortunate occasions where I blew up and my volatile temper got the better of me which frightened the life out of Bernice. There were also awkward occasions where I was invited out by my old group of friends with me wanting to bring Bernice around but feeling the atmosphere change as we joined them. Again it was understandable because my friends had spent almost nine years talking about 'Liam and Leanne' and now here was 'Liam and the babysitter'. As genuine and open hearted as my friends were it was always going to be a strain for both Bernice and I. It's no wonder she didn't want to come to many functions with me and my old group of friends. Likewize, I wasn't keen on going to rave's or talking about the latest cell phones that were out. I was young at heart and still am, but I wasn't eighteen.

The obvious problem was that the age gap caused issues that we couldn't do much about. If Bernice started acting like the teenager she was around her peers it was difficult not to feel completely out on a limb. I mean a group of over-excited female teenagers on a night out was not exactly my idea of fun so I left Bernice to do her own thing. My wild partying days, as far as I saw it, were over. I had had my share of walking back home at 5am in the morning where as Bernice was just starting out on this big adventure. I wanted her but I didn't necessarily want to relive my youth.

When I mention this time to most people I feel sheepish and acknowledge the metaphorically raised eyebrow of how wrong it must have seemed. On a moral level it was deemed wrong by some people. Their judgment was understandable but they weren't walking in my shoes. Twelve years between two people is a lot, even when you are a lot older but at the time, I absolutely needed this and I didn't care. Did I think this was going to last forever? I wanted it to but was just happy to live for the now.

Chapter 35

During the time we were together we were dogged by a series of threatening and fairly scary phone calls to the house. At first it was a nuisance where the person on the other end would just hang up but then the caller started becoming more confident and personal with comments. I thought it was somebody bored enough to want to waste their time irritating me but when it started becoming more and more frequent it became something more than irritating but nothing to really worry about. Eventually I just took the phone off the hook but I felt this obviously wasn't the final solution.

While all this was happening Leanne had struck up quite a relationship with 'Big John' and I was happy that they were getting on well. John was ironically friends with Bernice as well so our paths crossed quite frequently. John and I got on well and he was good for Leanne, I thought. He was a little younger than her but I was hardly going to start dishing out advise about that now was I? He used to dote on little Calum and I was heartened to think that my little boy was surrounded by people who loved him. Whether he was staying with Bernice and me or Leanne and John, he was always going to be okay. Additionally it was a bonus that as couples we got on well with each other. Yes, I know it sounds totally bizarre but that is fortunately the way things worked out. There was no animosity at all, in fact there was a bit of teasing between Leanne and Bernice over the whole situation. We realized it was an abnormal situation but it could have been a whole lot worse. John was a big shaven headed man but a friendly giant and worked in a brand new cable and phone company that had just started operating in the Cardiff Bay area. Although they don't trade anymore, their name shall remain anonymous for reasons that will become apparent later on in this chapter.

Leanne and I were chatting one day whilst John and Bernice were elsewhere and she intimated to me that she still held a bit of a torch for Calum's Dad, Gareth. I was shocked but moreso amused and wondered why she was telling me this since she seemed happy with Big John. Gareth, if you remember, had his heart broken by Leanne when we got back together before Calum was born. He would have taken Leanne back in a heartbeat but Leanne wasn't sure. Ultimately it wasn't my problem so I didn't give it a second thought. However there was one occasion when Bernice and I were over at John and Leanne's flat having a few drinks and a braai when I spotted Gareth in a car over the road. It seemed as if he was spying on us because when I spotted him and our eyes met, he started his car and left. It was all a bit strange to me. I knew Leanne had been in touch with him because she told me but I wasn't sure what was said. I wondered if Gareth needed confirmation that I was well and truly off the scene and perhaps by seeing me at Leanne's flat, he figured I wasn't. Maybe he thought she was deliberately toying with him. The only reason this is relevant to my story is that at the time I thought it was linked to the phone calls. Was I right? All was to be revealed in the months that followed.

The phone calls kept on coming and were becoming more and more sinister to the point that Bernice answered the phone one evening and was immediately in tears. A gruff, disguised male voice on the other end of the phone whispered menacingly 'Tell Liam I'm going to break his legs the next time I see him'. She was appalled and understandably upset but I told her nonchalantly that whoever it was had no chance, 'have you seen the size of these tree trunks for legs?' I smiled. It felt as if I was in a fight with a ghost, blind folded and frustrated. I was angry and told her she wasn't to answer the phone any more. This was getting a bit too close to home now and it was starting to cause me concern. I was wondering who on earth would want to pursue us in this way, I didn't understand it.

A few weeks passed with phone calls virtually every night so I decided that we needed to log these calls with the police. Their action was to set up a logging system with the cable and telephone company whereby any time we received a call of that nature, we were not supposed to speak but just punch a code into the phone which was then logged. So every time a nuisance call was made, although we were unaware of the number it was being logged at the phone company so at least they knew the number themselves. They in turn were supposed to pass it to the police for further investigation.

Then one day, whilst in work, I received a phone call out of the blue from Bernice and she was in a panic stricken state of tears. She had just got home from college and had noticed a letter in the door of her house addressed to her Mum and Dad as 'Bernice's parents'. She thought nothing of it but when her next door neighbor came running in to her with the same letter in the same envelope she knew something wasn't right. The little girl, who was a close friend of Bernice, and whose name was Naiomi, had intercepted this letter as it was delivered into her house. When Bernice read the letter she started to get really scared and that's when she phoned me. The content of the letter went along the lines that I was a pedophile operating in the area and that if any responsible parents had young children that they should be on red alert for the threat that was Liam O'Conner in number 25. I raced home, heart beating and feeling very, very threatened. Who on earth was trying to ruin me in such a way; I just couldn't believe what was happening. Just when I was getting my life together and started becoming happy in my relationship, this was happening. WHY!!

Bernice and Naiomi discovered, to their horror, that every house in the street had one of these letters delivered into their letter box but fortunately they were all still sticking out and were therefore able to be retrieved. By the time I got home they had managed to collect them all and predictably there wasn't one in number 25. I was shocked and appalled and the repercussions of what this could have meant were not lost on me. It was most certainly a false accusation but strangers in the street seeing me walk around with a teenage girl would not have hesitated throwing the book at me if they had not known the full story. It felt like a knife to the gut and Bernice was inconsolable and frightened. She told me that her Dad needed to speak to me about it so I braced myself for an angry father wanting to punch my lights out. He was a lovely man though and surprisingly calm and just wanted to know exactly what was going on. I told him that I was totally innocent and he accepted it but as a parting question, like Columbo, he asked 'Do you think we should tell Bernice's Mum about this?' Now fortunately she was on holiday at the time but I felt the best thing to do was to be honest and open because I had nothing to hide. I told him that we should tell her, even though it wasn't what she would want to hear, but that at the same time she should know. I saw warmth in his eyes as I said that. He knew that I was telling the truth and that Bernice's mum needed to know whether nice or not. It was a lucky escape but we were by no means out of the firing line just yet. We had a hidden enemy, someone hiding behind a veil of secrecy, a coward who wanted to destroy me and Bernice or maybe just me. We burned all the letters apart from one which we kept as evidence for the police. Again, I went to the police station and logged this as a potential threat but knew that the police couldn't really do much.

More weeks passed and this time when the phone calls were made they seemed to know our whereabouts. Having entered the house, the phone would ring and a voice would say in a threatening tone 'enjoy your walk?' and then just hang up. It was becoming freakier and I tried as hard as I could to ignore it, to shield Bernice from it. We had so many calls like that, like when I would pop out to the shop for five minutes in the evening and when I got back, Bernice would be in tears, saying they had phoned as soon as I closed the door. They had started screaming abuse at her the moment I left. You may be thinking at this point 'why on earth didn't you just change your number?' but the fact was we would have no chance of catching the offender if we had of. Our number was the bait as such, our only real hope of reeling the phantom menace in.

And thankfully this is what eventually happened, entirely thanks to my new found friend, John. Yes, he who worked at the phone company that provided my service. I was so, so grateful for his intervention because without him I would never have got to the bottom of the mystery. We were living a 'who-dun nit' and John was integral to us solving it. John managed to go onto my phone number profile on his system and noted the calls we were logging against the phantom number. It was a recognized Cardiff code '02920' number coming from a house in the Ely area. Not only that though, there was another number which could not be traced. I was amazed that he was able to get an address but he *did* have access to all this information and could well have been sacked on the spot if any of his bosses had found out. I was still none the wiser though because I didn't know anyone who lived at that address. The plot was indeed thickening.

I had a phone number and now an address, but what was I going to do? I decided I was actually going to go to the address to see if I could recognize anyone going in and out. I was now in reconnaissance mode and gathering intelligence in order to strike back. Unfortunately I didn't end up seeing anyone going in and out of this dingy little house and left feeling like I had made no progress. The next thing for me to do was to call the number, and I did so with a fair amount of nerves. I dialed the number and eventually a man's voice picked up the receiver at the other end. 'Hello' was the answer in a very uninterested manner. 'How would you like to come over to my house and try breaking my legs then?' I said. 'Who is this?' came the reply and then there was a dead tone. He had obviously realized who he was speaking to and just hung up. I rang back the following night and said 'I'm on to you'. It was at this point that I got the police involved again and gave them all the information I had without compromising John. The police visited the house where the phone calls were coming from and established who the person was. It was the brother of somebody I knew. That same brother, not wanting any trouble, soon told the police that although the calls were coming from his house, it wasn't him making the calls.

At the same time, I still couldn't understand where the calls were coming from that seemed to know where we were at all times. There's no way that it could have been the Ely number either because there is no way they could have seen us from there, it was well over a mile away. The second number picked up by John would prove to be the one which the mystery people were calling from. The police, having interviewed the person at the Ely address, informed me that it was the brother of Simon's wife. Tonia, Simon's wife no more. However it turned out that Tonia and daughter Bailey must have gone to her brother's house as a sort of refuge and made the calls in order to gain some revenge. The second number was coming from a block of flats on the opposite side of the road from us and made by Bailey and her boyfriend. It was Bailey and co making the calls but fuelled by the bitterness of Tonia. It was them who had been terrorizing us for all this time and the police wanted to know if I wanted to press charges or not.

'Did I want to press charges' against somebody who had put Bernice and me through the mill in the way that they did? You're damn right I did, but first I needed to talk to Simon. The police had apparently been around to the family home already so the noose was tightening for Bailey and Co. I was appalled and aghast at such venomous behavior but I suppose I was the person Bailey saw as breaking up the marriage of her parents. It wasn't true but I was the convenient target, the only part of the problem that was tangible to her, I was the only person she could exact her rage on. I was a sitting target and boy did she hit us with her arrows.

I wasn't looking forward to meeting Simon, I was unsure how he would be considering all that had happened. I was nervous and so was he but blood is thicker than water and we hugged each other straight away. Simon said that what Bailey had done was despicable and unforgivable which I agreed with but told him I understood why she was hurting. Simon said that their marriage break down had nothing to do with me but that Bailey saw me as someone to pin the blame on. She *did* feel I was to blame. The police had apparently been to their house and taken a statement which had frightened the life out of her. They had also interviewed myself and Bernice and asked if we wanted to press charges. I told Simon that I wouldn't press charges because of him and that he was family but Bailey needed to understand that she could potentially have ruined my life with the accusations of pedophilia. In this day and age people are absolutely beyond sensitive on the matter, and rightly so. I didn't feel relief as there was nothing to be relieved about but I was really glad it was over, it was a horrible time. Simon and I left on good terms and I know he went on to more happiness in his life in another relationship.

There was, however, some overspill in that Naiomi's Dad viewed me with suspicion and contempt for years after that. The reason, I think, is that I offered to take Naiomi to an indoor play centre with Calum when she was a little girl. It was an innocent act of generosity on my part because she was lonely and playing in the street by herself but it was taken as part of my plan to molest this little girl, bearing in mind that this action had happened years before these accusations came to light and I had cleared it with her Mum before doing so. I imagined the poor little mite being grilled over and over in order for her to tell them I had done something indecent. Fortunately between Bernice and Naiomi's protestations of my innocence her Dad was appeased but it didn't stop months of evil stares in the street and bristling tension towards me prior to that. Thankfully it was now all over but there had been damage to mine and Bernice's relationship. Unfortunately the bond was not strong enough and our fledging relationship was unable to withstand it.

Apart from the phone calls and letters it was in fact a lovely summer with Bernice and we had the most wonderful times together which I look back very fondly on. However, with all that happened and with the age gap, our time together would be like that of a rainbow. It was beautiful and nourishing to the soul but temporary and without substance. I had my own issues which had never been addressed, the little ginger-headed outcast; the little boy within me was still there. I still carried him inside me and when I felt scared, threatened or jealous, the man was able to protect that little boy, but not in a good wholesome way. I still think that Bernice couldn't handle what she saw when I had my dark moments and this was another reason for us parting ways. Also the fact that we didn't share a lot in common caused a strain that we could not have done anything about. After some arguments and silent treatment we called time on the relationship but it left me feeling sad and alone. It was the best thing for both of us ultimately but I didn't feel that at the time, I was quite devastated and hoped that we could patch things up but we never did. The will from both sides was just not strong enough.

Chapter 36

It was approaching autumn and for the first time in ten years I was single and alone. I didn't really know what to do with myself. Should I try and go on dates? I didn't really feel like it initially but it felt odd to even think about it. How would I go about it? Where, when and with whom? I didn't really need to be in a relationship but I did miss companionship. At the same time Leanne had started dating someone I knew. She and John had also parted ways, much to the devastation of John and Leanne started dating the guy that knocked the box room into a bathroom. It was Len and apparently there had been chemistry between them from the first day. There I was feeling guilty about the break up and for wanting Bernice whilst Leanne was eyeing up the builder. I was pleased for her though but still wondered why she had to dive headlong into the next relationship after having just finished the previous one.

Len was good for Leanne though and gave her the stability she needed at that time. With Len being thirteen years her senior, he was wize enough to secure what he had and go about setting some ground rules which, in retrospect, were needed. Up until Leanne met Len, she would often just pop in on the off chance to see how I was doing, all very innocent of course but Leanne and I still had a really close friendship. Leanne is a free spirited person and if she wanted to do that she just would. Now that she had met Len though, he was having none of this 'friend' business which I entirely understood and didn't have a problem with at all. I respected it and if I were in his shoes, would have been exactly the same. I felt better for Leanne that she was with a man who would look after her and to be honest, that was a signal that we would no longer be as close as we were used to. Likewise he also took Calum under his wing which I was grateful for.

With Leanne and Len quickly settling into a flat in Treganna, it meant Calum was able to start living with his Mum again, which I felt was right for him. At least this way he didn't have to be whisked away first thing in the morning and dropped to Leanne in order that he get to school on time. I unfortunately wasn't able to drop Calum to school because I started way before 9am. As much as I would miss my little man, it was right that he was with his Mum. When Leanne and I split up it was the single most difficult thing I had ever done up until that point to look at him in the eye and tell him that Daddy wasn't going to be with Mummy any more. It was painfully hard in the saddest way and I will never forget the lost look in his eyes for as long as I live. He had a look of confusion and I could tell that it was too much for him to process, he was only three. All I could tell him was that he had two lovely homes, with a Mum in one and a Dad in the other and that he was deeply loved. Anyone, and there are millions out there, who has ever been in this situation will know how hard it is.

For Calum's sake it was important that he got into a routine which is what Leanne, Len and I all agreed on. From the beginning we all said that we would put Calum first in our decision making and that our separation wouldn't become his problem and that we leave our ego's and differences to one side and put the little man first. It meant more structure to his days and therefore his life, there would be no popping round to see how he was after work or just taking him to the park when I wanted to. It was hard but fair. It also meant that I would now be seeing Calum every other weekend which was hard to take but again I knew it was right. Deep down and on a soul level that I was yet to comprehend, I knew Calum needed to be with his Mum rather than me. When it was my turn to have Calum for the weekend I was elated on those Fridays, I just could not wait to pick him up from school. I would leave work, do a bit of shopping and then pick him up. He would see me from the entrance of the school doors and run into my arms. I would pick him up and hug him and hug him, trying to keep the tears at bay. The other mothers at the school would look on warmly at the scene, probably in acknowledgment of the situation.

The weekends would be full on, 100% Calum O'Conner time with little of it for myself. I would be exhausted in the evenings of a weekend having been nonstop with my little side kick at the park, at the movies, at the beach, at ten pin bowling and whatever else took our fancy. The worst time, and one which I grew to dread, was dropping him back off on a Sunday evening. I would be driving him to the little flat, trying to be upbeat but knowing I was going home to an empty house, a shell for two weeks. Those trips were the longest for me as I would put Calum in the front with me and listen to some music in the car while we drove. I would put my hand on his little knee and his face would look up at mine and smile, his innocent brown eyes looking like he was trying not to look sad. I would say goodbye at the front door and watch him as he carried his little plastic bag of cloths and a teddy. I can never forget how he would walk up the steps with his little jeans and jersey on and smile and wave. Those little hands I marveled at when he was born, those little hands now waving goodbye to me once more. Waving awkwardly and as if he didn't know how to be, he was happy to see his Mum yet really sad to be seeing his Dad go away again. On the journey home my eyes would be swimming in tears as I kept repeating the vision of his lovely smile in my head, his handsome little face trying to look brave. My little buddy, my little Bonner, my little man, I miss you so much.

After a while I began to enjoy my time alone in the house and started to become quite the bachelor boy that Cliff Richard so admired in himself. I became more comfortable with just my own company and although I was constantly without money, I was happy that I was getting to know me and spending time on myself. The reason I became so hard up all of a sudden was because there was no longer two incomes. I was more than happy to have the house but the extra money for groceries and entertainment that Leanne's wages covered were now missing. When I was with Bernice I squandered a lot on booze and going out without thinking of the consequences. As a result I built up a few debts which I was struggling to pay off. The credit card I had was maxed out at £2 000 and I was just paying interest each month. I had nothing to show for that expenditure either, nothing tangible that I could actually sell. My overdraft was at its limit every month and was at such a level that my wages would be paid in and by the time my bills were all paid, I was deep into my overdraft again. I was not managing my money at all well and had no budget, no direction, no goal and no discipline when it came to money. Often time I would simply miss payments and hope for the best, bury my head in the sand. I actually got into real trouble at one point when I hadn't been paying my council tax so a bailiff was sent around to confiscate property. On the first visit the bailiff came to the house and inspected everything I had and said that by the following week, if I had not made a payment I would start having goods confiscated to go towards the payment of my bill. I hastily set up an agreement whereby I would pay the arrears off a little extra each month. My furniture remained intact thankfully.

In work the belts were being tightened so I couldn't work any overtime, there was an overtime ban which meant I couldn't earn any more than I was. I was used to going out and having a good time without really feeling it when I was in a relationship. Now that I was the only one paying for the mortgage, the electricity and food bills, it doubly took its financial toll. I had stopped all the going out and partying but I couldn't eat into my debt. I got to the point where the bank could no longer help me, they said I needed to seriously reduce my overdraft and get rid of my credit card. They also removed my debit facility from my account and demoted me to having an electron card which was the most basic card available at that time and meant that all you could do with it was draw cash out of the wall. It was the sort of bank card a young teenager would be given as a novelty so my ego took quite a pummeling. I had to live leaner and sell whatever I could in order to get back on the lean path to freedom.

I decided that I had to slash my food budget in half and give up the niceties I had previously been used to. I gave myself a budget of £10 per week for entertainment which for me meant a curry and a couple of bottles of wine on the weekend. I started living off 20p thinly cut, everlasting long life white bread which must have been soaked in formaldehyde. I lived off the cheapest tins of tuna and beans that money could buy. My cupboards looked painfully uniform with all the cans the same white and blue stripes, no matter what the product. Opening my food cupboard was like opening an army ration store. I had to fight my way out inch by painful inch. For protein, turkey became my most favoured source because it was so cheap. I would by 1kg of breast fillets, cut them into small cubes, marinate them in soy sauce and grill it all for the week. I quickly had to learn how to budget, how to manage money better and to start being more careful with money. I became really disciplined and didn't spend what I didn't have, in fact I couldn't have even if I tried, because of the financial constraints put on me by the bank. I was determined to dig myself out of this financial hole I was in. Unfortunately I still had a negative association with money; my blue print was always 'lack of' and 'never enough'. I didn't think I was capable of manifesting more money, I just thought I had to spend less and that was that. This is what I did do though and it worked because after a few years I was back on track. It was one of my biggest lessons in life.

Eventually it dawned on me that I should think about getting Leanne off the mortgage. When we bought the house, despite us not being married, both of our names were on the mortgage. In the eyes of the law that house belonged to us both even though I was living in it alone and had been servicing the mortgage by myself. The solution was simple. The bank that I had the endowment policy with told me that all I had to do was stop the policy, which both people would have to sign. Upon stopping the policy we would both get a share of the money we had so far accrued. Back then there was a financial package where you had an endowment policy with a separate building society which 'guaranteed' a lump sum to pay off your house mortgage 'and more' after 25 years. At the same time you paid your lender just interest on the mortgage so you effectively never saw your mortgage reducing. It made sense in principle and was the vogue back in the early nineties and beyond. However, for the second year in succession, I had a letter from the endowment people that my profile wasn't performing and that I needed to increase my premium which was another reason for me to stop it and just cash in. By stopping that though meant you reverted back to a standard repayment mortgage which was my intent. Ultimately though, it meant the same thing, getting Leanne to sign the endowment in order to release funds.

So the first step was to get Leanne to agree to sign off her side of the endowment and for us both to get a small lump sum. Simple right? We were both good friends after all. Wrong! I was quite amazed by the response that she wasn't prepared to do so unless she was going to receive maintenance payments by me for Calum. So I was by myself, trying to dig myself out of a hole whilst Leanne and Len were living together in a flat with a double income and still asking me for more. I was incredulous and bemused to say the least. I had stood by Leanne and accepted Calum as my own for all those years and now that she was safely in a relationship with another she decided she wanted to drain every last drop that she could out of me. I still think that this was more Len's influence than Leanne because she was not that way inclined in all the years I knew her. Maybe she was still hurting from the split up and wanted a measure of pay back or even revenge, I'll never know, but it wasn't the Leanne I knew. Ultimately it caused me a problem and a break down in my relationship with both of them.

Now, unbeknownst to me at the time, in order to pay the governments prescribed maintenance the child had to be your own flesh and blood. Since Leanne and Len were adamant that I pay them something I didn't feel they were entitled to, they forced me into a corner that I had to fight my way out of. I sought professional advice which lasted no longer than fifteen minutes of a lawyer's time. He said quite bluntly and quickly that the only way I was eligible to pay was if I was the father through blood. The only way I would be able to prove I wasn't was through a blood test for me and Calum. He drafted Leanne a letter to tell her as such and to propose setting up an appointment to take the necessary blood samples. Naturally Leanne knew that this was a Cul-De-Sac for her new idea of apparently much needed passive income. This in turn created a status quo with respect to me trying to get the endowment papers signed by both of us. Unfortunately for Leanne it meant that the accrued endowment would only go into the bank account of the person who was actually paying it, me. Leanne knew this and weeks of stubborn refusal passed until I reminded Leanne and Len that we should still be thinking of Calum, not ourselves, when it came to his welfare. I told her that there was financial welfare and emotional welfare and that we should not destroy the emotional welfare that we could both provide if we focused entirely on the grabbing of financial welfare. In a separate and covert meeting and without Len's influence she decided that the right thing to do was to sign those papers.

Suddenly I had a cheque for £5 400 which I was to use as wisely as I could by wiping out my credit card debt, Burtons account and overdraft in one swooping motion like a cloth cleaning a very dirty table full of crumbs and tea stains. It was wonderfully liberating to have got back into the black once more. I had managed to learn some valuable lessons on budgeting and money management, I had eliminated quite a fair amount of debt and I was proud of myself for having grown up financially at the age of 30. I still had some work to do though before Leanne and I were parted financially, once and for all. I needed to still remove the 'Leanne Armstrong' from the bank statements that reflected our mortgage status. Although the endowment was now dead and over, we still had the house in both of our names to contend with. This proved to be even more difficult to negotiate especially as I was, by then, in another relationship, more of which later on. But for now and in order to conclude this epic tale of financial enthrallment (or perhaps not) I still had to manage a potentially ugly situation as delicately as I could.

The relationship between myself and Leanne and Len had degenerated due to the whole financial situation of me not having to pay maintenance and also with Leanne being removed from the endowment policy. I had to very gingerly speak to her about removing her from the mortgage but I did know that I would have to pay her a fair chunk of money in order to do so.

Ultimately I needed to settle with her by giving her fifty percent of the accrued equity in the house. There wasn't a huge amount of equity left considering I had lived there for seven years but it was still a sizeable amount. Eventually, after protracted negotiations, an agreement was made where she would receive a sum equivalent to be able to put a decent deposit down for their own little house. It meant I was completely free financially even if it did mean having to remortgage once more to fund it. The financial chapter was now closed.

Chapter 37

And so it was time for the season of festivities in the year 2000 and I was out to have some much needed fun after a year of financial restraint. I went out on the town with the lads from MELUK and just wanted to let my hair down, let go a bit. After a fantastic evening of typically festive bar and club hopping I found myself in the company of my colleague Bruno, 'The Buffalo' or 'Buffy' the Italian charmer. It was just he and I left after a brutal evening of drinking and we were both keen to continue our evening with some female company. After walking out of a steak house in the early hours on St Mary's street we happened upon two attractive ladies. By this stage I was ready to go home but Bruno was insistent on at least getting their phone numbers. His persistence paid off and we ended up in another club having a fantastic time, dancing as much as my exhausted body would allow. We ended up getting their numbers and said goodnight. The girl I had clicked with was called Gabrielle and a few weeks later I found myself on a date with her on a cold January evening. It was just me and her......
oh and plus her sister and her boyfriend. She had apparently brought them along to ensure I wasn't Charles Manson the second and after establishing that we could at least get along together she gave her sister the signal that

she could go home. Almost as soon as she left she became quite emotionally unstable and accused me of looking at other women in a night club which was bizarre on a first date.

Bizarrely enough, however, I was still quite keen despite this psychotic behavior and outside the club she said without any hesitation, 'I have made my mind up already Liam, please can we go straight back to your house'. I wasn't expecting to be going at such a pace but agreed to go with it. In the taxi on the way to my house she told me she had previously been an exotic dancer in Ghana which seemed appealing and weird at the same time. She also mentioned that she was a gypsy living in a caravan in Barry 'and was proud of it'. To me, that sounded like an unwarranted defensive statement, like she was laying all her cards on the table and now was the time for me to accept or back out of the 'agreement'. I wasn't sure how to take this girl; she really was quite intense and out of control. After an evening's entertainment I woke up in the morning with the sound of 'Psycho' playing in my head and her on all fours straddling me, like a wolf with its prey, staring manically into my face. It was enough for me to almost scream in terror but I barely gathered myself before saying 'uhm, fancy some breakfast then?' After a hasty morning snack I hurriedly ushered her out of the house with a look at my invisible watch and a blow of the cheeks, saying I had a game of football soon and that I really had to get going. It was the last I saw of her and officially the weirdest date I had been on. I didn't make contact, I thought it was best to put this date into the category of 'bunny boiler' and move on swiftly. Yes she was attractive but boy was she strange. Maybe she thought that I was equally weird but that will be her story.

Soon after that I stumbled upon an attractive girl on a night out with my close mates Keith, Hughie, Jon and Ray. It was in a club on Mill Lane near the Hayes, the night was just beginning and as we entered the club I locked eyes with a girl and she immediately beckoned me over as if to say 'I want you'. It was the quickest I had ever made such an acquaintance with a member of the opposite sex and we immediately hit it off. My friends stood by quite amazed and somewhat bemused because we hadn't all been out since Bernice and I had split up and now I was being whisked away barely five minutes into our evening out. It was all quite thrilling and I felt very confident and wanted. The girl in question was called Ruth and she was a lovely person. She wasn't the typical type I would go for but I decided that I needed a bit of fun and she also had such warmth to her personality which was always something I sought. I remember our third date was to go and watch 'Hannibal' near her home in Caerphilly and even though it was a great film, which I thoroughly enjoyed, I almost fainted with nausea. In one particularly graphic scene, whilst attempting to go to the toilets, I was seconds away from falling like a log down a very dark set of steps. Later that evening we went back to her house but things didn't quite go as well as we had hoped because I heard little footsteps come down the stairs and say 'Mummy, please can you come and tuck me in'. It didn't in any way put me off the relationship but it did cast my mind back to Calum which in turn made me think that what we were doing had an effect on a little innocent child. Although we were two mature adults having fun I realized that it could become more than that, which I was prepared for but with the right woman. I sensed very early on in the relationship that there may be a lack of chemistry and since my experience with Leanne; I was not prepared to go any further if it meant 'working' on that aspect of the relationship because chemistry shouldn't have to be worked on. At that stage in my life I needed it to be like wild fire or not at all, there were to be no half measures now. I had at least learned and now had the self worth to acknowledge when something wasn't right for me. Ruth was a lovely girl and I know she really wanted us to work but after the evening at her house with her nine year old daughter calling down to her made me realize that I had to be all in or not at all. Ruth deserved one hundred percent of something great, for her sake and for the sake of her little girl. That 'something great' was, unfortunately, not going to be me.

By now I was deep in a spiritual wilderness and even though I had no longing to go back to church at all, I did feel the need to be with people with more spiritual substance to them. I had outgrown the club scene and even going to pubs didn't have the same pull that it used to. I was growing up and wanted a bit more from life. All my friends were all still fully subscribed to the pub culture and I wondered now who I was if I wasn't part of that scene. With me ambling along in my career, even though I had

had a second stint in Japan, I was now quite unhappy in my role. I had certainly leveled out and saw no way of ascending to any further heights at MELUK. The will and desire to climb the corporate ladder was not there at all for me. In fact I resented the automatic mindset that dictated that my next move was into a supervisory role. At that stage of my career I had no intention of leaving though, I mean after eleven years I didn't really know anything else. I had become part of the furniture and was scared of moving on. In a way I had become too safe in my environment but was unhappy at the same time. I knew things had to change and comparing my journey through life as a hike through the wilderness, I was getting to the stage where I was reaching a cliff edge where I had to jump into the deep waters below or stay stranded at the top.

I was approaching 31, was single, fit and healthy with a house of my own and out of any financial trouble. I should have been happier than I was but something was lacking, there was a void in my life. To an extent, I still missed Bernice in lots of ways and secretly would loved for us to have got back together but when I analyzed it I knew we had parted for good and that it was the right thing for both of us. I was fundamentally unhappy and also a little lonely but of course, still had everything to live for. I was by no means in a depression but I knew I needed change. I had no idea what that change would be though.

After a phone call with Mum, who was still in SA at that stage, I decided that I needed to fast. I had heard that to gain answers to the questions you were pondering, it was important to cleanse the soul, to de-clutter the mind and to stop all the unwanted background noise. An effective method to bring the essence of the soul to the fore was by fasting which to me seemed a bit odd but I was willing to try anything. I needed to hear answers but I needed the means to hear them. I knew that the answers would come from within if only I could quiet my mind and let God back into my life. Since I had not been to church for over a decade, I wrongly assumed I was no longer in Gods favour, even though I knew he still loved me. I fasted for two days solidly, not eating a single thing and only taking in water and tea. No alchohol passed my lips during that time as I prayed for guidance and asked God to take control of my life in what had become a disorientating desert.

The answers were by no means immediate and I acknowledged the need to be patient and for things to unfold in a natural way. Shortly afterwards I received an email from my sister Pauline telling me of her pending marriage to Danny in March of that year. The year was 2001 and she said she would love me to be there if I could afford to come out for the wedding. I had no hesitation and made sure I had the money to book two weeks off in South Africa to be there. I decided I was going to surprise my Mum at the same time by suddenly making an appearance without her even knowing I was coming. I was thrilled to be going back out to my Africa once more and had no idea of what was about to happen in my life. Little did I know it at the time but this trip was to be the biggest watershed moment in my life to date. The rest of this chapter would become an exciting journey that I would not have envisioned happening in my wildest dreams.

Metaphorically speaking I could see the cliff in front of me and on a soul level I knew that there was great change coming. It was mid March when I flew out and I was picked up from the airport by Pauline and Danny. I had never met Danny but he seemed like a very large, Portuguese gentle giant. He was a big, olive skinned, athletic looking man with a shaven head and sunken eyes that made him look somewhat menacing. We both hit it off together as we loved football and his charm and charisma settled my nerves in the initial time we met. Pauline had met Danny through an internet dating forum and he was her knight in shining armour as he plucked her up from financial ruin. Pauline had lurched from one relationship crisis to another in the years that followed Leonard's death and Danny was the solid, settled if not scary looking protector that would put an end to her woes. I could see that despite Danny not being someone I would have pictured my sister with, they loved each other dearly. Following Leonard's death Pauline had really hit rock bottom financially, to the point of moving back in with Mum, Dad and Cei with Chrissy and Ryan in tow. Leonard's business had been doing poorly and there was no safety net and no house. It was a desperate time for her but it felt that she had come through it all and was now going to be well cared for. I couldn't express how happy I was for her; she had struggled by herself with me on the outside, in another country and unable to do anything for her. I was so relieved to see her happy and cared for.

When we arrived at their lovely home in suburban Farramere it was a pleasant surprise. This area was one of the most beautiful and sought after areas in Benoni and growing up as kids in Northmead, we always used to think anyone from Farramere were a lot more well to do than us. Not that Northmead was anything but an idyllic place to grow up but Farramere was perceived to be posh and out of reach for us. It was a lovely home and a lovely area and as we went through the electric gates and onto the drive I felt immediately at home. Meanwhile Mum was house-sitting for them after having been told that she needed to wait in for the cable TV repair man to arrive. It was one of those moments that I absolutely love and had such joy administering such an unexpected surprise. Pauline and Danny walked into the house first with Mum having no clue that I would be there, I hadn't told her that I was coming. As I walked in I put my Afrikaans accent on as if to be the cable TV guy and said 'Hello, I've come to fix the cable box'. Mum glanced up whilst sipping a cup of tea and I thought she was going to collapse there and then on the kitchen floor. She said 'Oooh, aaah, I can't believe it, I don't BEE-LEEEIVE it, aah hello my lovely boy'. Followed by 'somebody pinch me, am I dreaming this?' It was such an amazing homecoming, Mums reaction will forever be etched into my memory. It was too big a surprise for her to take in initially but after five minutes we were nattering away as if we had never been apart.

The wedding was to be on the weekend so there was a fair amount of running around to be done in order for the big day to commence. I was to be best man even though I didn't really know Danny but it was explained that I needn't worry about a speech. Danny was very much a loner so it was unsurprising that I was suddenly thrust into the spotlight as the second man at the wedding. It meant I would be wearing some very lovely pre-ordered cloths for the day and I was only too pleased to take my place in proceedings. Not having the pressure to make a speech meant I was able to just commence with the formalities and enjoy myself as much as I could.

There was a lovely service at the Benoni Church of Christ where I caught up with many old friends from what seemed like another lifetime. I enjoyed being in that modern church and it did bring back some lovely memories but for today it was all about Pauline and Danny. I met a few of Danny's side of the family and one or two of his friends, one of whom was a red-headed girl who briefly introduced herself to me. I was the driver of the married couple and took them for a photo shoot first at the Lakeside mall waterfront and then proceeded on to the reception venue at a function hall in Kempton Park, a beautiful setting.

I remember making small talk with lots of people, some I knew and some I didn't. The first dance commenced, which was Chicago's 'you're my Inspiration' and I looked at Pauline. She was so happy and yet vulnerable, almost childlike. I saw the hurt in her eyes that she had been through previously and almost felt it all but now she was dancing with her husband, safe in his arms and looking up at him with happiness and warmth in her eyes. I was really feeling emotional anyway but when that song played, the delicate, sensitivity of it hit me like an arrow and I just couldn't stop crying. I was supposed to be the chivalrous, unflustered best man and here I was acting like a big girl's blouse. I gathered myself before the song finished but it had really struck a chord within me, it was such a beautiful moment and one which I will never forget. I decided to pop out quickly for a bit of fresh air and whilst outside I noticed the petite red-head girl who seemed to want to talk but my mind was too preoccupied to make too much conversation. I remember saying something along the lines of what a beautiful song that first one was and she smiled gently and knowingly.

As beautiful as this girl was I didn't feel it was right to even attempt trying to chat to her, after all I would be heading back to the UK in just over a week so it hardly seemed viable to start anything. To be perfectly honest I was more intent on having a good time dancing and partying than sitting down to chat. It was a wonderful evening filled with laughter, dancing and good food washed down with the occasional beer. I danced with my little sister Cei and then also Pauline and then with all our friends in a huge circle. It was a special night but ultimately it ended early as we were all pretty worn out after a long and exhilarating day. The rest of that holiday was a bit of a blur but plenty of time was spent catching up with Mum, Dad and Cei whilst Pauline and Danny took their Honeymoon to Durban for a few days.

Pauline, however, pulled me to one side one day and said 'Remember that pretty red haired girl?' and with an arched eyebrow I returned 'Yes, what about her?' 'Well she wouldn't mind getting in touch with you, wanna swap email addresses?' 'Yep, okay, why not' I said, acting a lot cooler than I felt. From the insecure little ginger nut that I was as a little boy, I felt confident and wanted without really being arrogant and conceited. I was really quite excited at the prospect of talking to this lovely looking girl but to be honest I wasn't sure what to expect. I eventually packed up and returned home to the UK blissfully unaware that the universe had used this holiday to plant a seed in my heart that would eventually blossom into something wonderful, colourful and vibrant.

Lightning Source UK Ltd.
Milton Keynes UK
UKOW03f0703020617
302464UK00002B/217/P

9 781504 370547